Come
before Winter

Come before Winter

...AND SHARE MY HOPE

CHARLES R. SWINDOLL

MULTNOMAH · PRESS

Portland, Oregon 97266

Cover design: Michael Standlee
Photographer: G. Robert Nease
Editor: Larry R. Libby

COME BEFORE WINTER
© 1985 by Charles R. Swindoll, Inc.
Published by Multnomah Press
Portland, Oregon 97266

Printed in the United States of America

Library of Congress Cataloging in Publication Data

Swindoll, Charles R.
  Come before winter—and share my hope.

  1. Meditations. I. Title.
BV4832.2.S884   1985   242   85-11590
ISBN 0-88070-110-2 (hdbk.)
ISBN 0-88070-234-6 (pbk.)

88   89   90   91   92   93   —   10   9   8   7   6   5   4

CONTENTS

Mid-Winter's Blast

WHEN PERSEVERANCE STEADIES OUR COURSE

131

Winter's End

THE PROMISE RETURNS
227

Acknowledgments

A book with this much feeling and in touch with so much of life could not possibly have emerged from a single source. The ideas and words are my own, but the artistry, the photography, the design, and the format, woven through this volume like an elegant piece of tapestry, are the combined effort of many. All are to be commended for their commitment to excellence.

—Larry Libby and Tom Womack worked in harmony with me, offering splendid and useful suggestions for putting truth into action.

—Michael Standlee, my gifted and creative artist, gave the book its cover, its color, its vivid pictures, ultimately its warmth . . . even in deepest winter.

—Helen Peters, my faithful secretary, stayed with the typing of the text and offered invaluable comments at just the right moments.

—Finally, my colleague and friend, John Van Diest, publisher of Multnomah Press, is to be commended for his tireless effort and flawless integrity. For ten consecutive years he has believed in me, encouraged me, and committed himself to publishing my material in a manner that is rarely found in professional ranks. Much of the credit for the beauty of this book goes to the man at the top who said yes when others would have said no.

INTRODUCTION

ise counsel came to my ears many years ago. Almost three decades, now. Because it was spoken by a mentor I held in highest esteem, the words remain fresh in the creases of my brain to this day.

"If you wish to communicate the truth of Scripture, it is essential that you identify with the subject."

Which means? If I want to teach Corinthians, I should join the church in ancient Corinth! Or if I want to understand the pressure of standing before the philosophers and politicians on Mars Hill, I need to walk through the Athenian marketplace—stand in the midst of the Areopagus—feel the sting from their stoic stares. My mentor was right: Personal identification and effective communication are inseparable.

All this brings me to "come before winter." It is dungeon talk. The words are not original with me. They emerge from a classic chamber of horrors hidden deeply beneath the streets of century-one Rome. Isolated in that grim and grimy hole, surrounded by stone blocks black with age, was a lonely prisoner whose days were numbered. His name was Paul. His friend was Timothy—the one to whom those three words were addressed. As I drop into his dungeon and identify with the old man, a chill makes me shiver.

I am afraid.

I feel terribly alone.

The rattle of heavy chains only increases my anguish. No gleams of sunlight penetrate the damp and gloom of my Mamertine misery. My needs are several, all of them intense.

I need my cloak. I must have left it at the abode of Carpus in Troas. You'll have no trouble spotting it, Timothy. It's an old thing, but it's been on my back through many a bitter winter. It's been wet with the brine of the Great Sea, white with the snows of the rugged peaks of Pamphylia, gritty and brown from the dust of the Egnatian Way, and crimson with my own blood from that awful stoning at Lystra. The cloak is stained and torn, Timothy, but winter's coming and I need the warmth it will bring.

I also need the books. You remember them. The ones I read under candlelight as we rode out the rough waters of the Aegean and endured the rigors of Macedonia together . . . those scrolls that fed my mind with fresh bursts of hope and stimulating ideas. Bring along those books, my friend.

I especially need the parchments! Those are my most treasured possessions, Timothy. How I need the comfort of King David's psalms, the fortitude from the prophets' pens, the insights and perception from Solomon's proverbs. Yes, the

*parchments. Surely they will help keep my heart warm and my hopes high in this
desolate place.*

*But Timothy, I need you. How desperately I need you! Make every effort to
come . . . come before winter. Come before November's winds strip the leaves from
the trees and send them whirling across the fields and swirling through the busy
streets above me. Come, before the snow begins to fall and covers flat carts and
frozen ponds with its icy blanket. Come, my friend . . . the time of my departure
has arrived. Soon the blade will drop and time for me will be no more. I cannot
bear the thought of midwinter without the warmth of your companionship . . .
those eyes of understanding, those words only you can bring to get me through this
barren and bitter season. Make every effort to come before winter.*

As I said earlier, it's dungeon talk. A desperate reaching out for
reasons to go on. If Paul did not see Timothy before winter, he would
never see him again.

Do you identify with those feelings? Do you understand dungeon
talk? If so, welcome to my world. We understand each other. You and I
will connect in the pages that lie before you. *Come Before Winter* is for
people like you and me. People who occasionally find themselves in depressing places of confinement or restraint, with no sense of purpose or
direction. I call such experiences the winter of our lives.

Candidly, I like all the seasons. I attempted to say that when I wrote
Growing Strong in the Seasons of Life. I like spring with its refreshing buds,
its fragrant blossoms, its splashing streams of new hope. I like summer—its warm, gentle breezes that make palm trees sway . . . its sultry
afternoons, its long days, its lingering, nostalgic sunsets. I like autumn
with its crisp, morning dawns, its inimitable kaleidoscope of colors,
smells, and sounds. And winter? Yes, even winter. As I understand it better, I'm learning to like it more! With its clear, cold nights . . . its stars
like platinum-headed nails driven into the vault of heaven . . . its lacy
icicles, its stunning landscapes of white on white. But . . .

But there is something strangely solitary about winter. Altogether
unlike the other three seasons, winter pleads for companionship. Its
naked trees seem terribly forlorn and barren. Its harsh blizzards that
push even the strongest of fowl south drive us inside our own world. No
other season in life's annual cycle better represents reality as we attempt
to live out what we claim to believe. Just as a calendar cannot skip those
bone-chilling months, we cannot escape the barren days! Prisoners in
our own dungeons of discouragement, loneliness, and spiritual impo-
tence, we struggle to keep our equilibrium . . . to make sense out of such
apparent insanity. It seems as though God has forever sealed shut the
storm windows and drawn the drapes on hope and happiness.

That may be the way it seems, but this volume has been written to
announce that is not the way it is! As you will soon discover, these pages
fall into three sections, each of which offers words of reassurance that

we are not alone during those wintry days. I have dedicated the first section to preparation—those before-winter days when warmth begins to fade, when the winds of adversity whip at our coattails, when doubt—like the morning frost—blights our faith, when storm clouds hover and apprehension mounts. There's hope as we prepare for such times, since our God comes before winter, offering needed comfort.

This leads, of course, into midwinter's blast, when perseverance steadies our course. Though days are bleak and time seems to stand deathly still as the darkness thickens, He stays near. And as we reach out across the damp, inky cell, we find God's hand reaching back and becoming our only source of companionship. Thankfully, our panic subsides. How essential is His hand in ours!

And then, at long last, winter's end. The promise returns . . . new hope, reshaped values, deeper commitment. A patch of blue sky breaks through my dungeon window. The snow has begun to melt. Finally, in grace, God's other hand pulls back winter's drape. The sun! That long-awaited source of light shines again.

To all my fellow-strugglers who find today's dungeon dark, damp, and distressing, I offer these words of understanding. I invite you to identify with the subject on each page. When you do you will discover that the One who came before winter, who steadied your steps when all else failed, is still your Companion and Friend.

Before Winter

PERIOD OF PREPARATION

Before Winter

uring our sojourn in New England, my family and I were introduced to four distinct seasons of the year. Having never before witnessed the breathtaking beauty of autumn in Vermont or New Hampshire, we spent many an hour oohing and aahing our way through blazing forests and over hillsides strewn with fragrant wild flowers. As the queen was forced to confess upon seeing Solomon's kingdom, "the half had not been told us."

Nor were we prepared for the frigid months of winter that were sure to follow.

Nature pulls a surprise attack on all New England novices! It is a brief period of unseasonably warm, mild weather very late in autumn or early winter . . . called "Indian summer." Newcomers to the area get the false impression that there will hardly be much of a winter, so they continue their sightseeing and relaxation with little regard for the deep freeze that inevitably arrives.

Seasoned souls of that area are not so foolish. Wisely, they use that brief interlude to prepare for winter's bitter blast. Storm windows and doors are fixed in place as well as a dozen or more other chores that make a statement to the oncoming clouds and early snow flurries: "Welcome . . . I'm ready for ya!"

Early on I learned a valuable lesson from native New Englanders, a lesson with obvious spiritual overtones: The winter can be endured with much greater success if you prepare for its arrival.

This section is all about that.

An ancient Israeli monarch once referred to the importance of preparing one's horse for the day of battle, and a prophet named Ezekiel intensified and personalized the command by issuing the directive, "Be prepared . . . prepare yourself!"

Let's do that. Since we know that winter's chill is sure to come, bringing its relentless blizzards and ruthless winds, let's not be fooled by today's lazy haze. Get those storm windows up . . . snow tires in place . . . shovels and scrapers, coats and boots, hats and gloves . . . and don't forget the toboggan and the sled. We're talkin' a whole new attitude this year.

"C'mon winter . . . I'm ready for ya!"

THINK WITH DISCERNMENT

here is a Persian proverb that sounds more like a tongue twister than sound advice. My high school speech teacher had us memorize it for obvious reasons:

He who knows not, and knows not that he knows not is a fool; shun him.

He who knows not, and knows that he knows not, is a child; teach him.

He who knows, and knows not that he knows, is asleep; wake him.

He who knows, and knows that he knows, is wise; follow him.

All four "types" can be found on every campus, in any business, among all neighborhoods, within each church. They don't wear badges, nor do they introduce themselves accordingly. You'll never have someone walk up, shake your hand, and say, "Hi, I'm Donald. I'm a fool." Chances are good that the last thing he will want you to discover is the deep-down truth that "he knows not that he knows not."

Then how in the world are we to know whom to shun, to teach, to awaken, or to follow? *Discernment* is the answer. Skill and accuracy in reading character. The ability to detect and identify the real truth. To see beneath the surface and correctly "size up" the situation. To read between the lines of the visible.

Is it a valuable trait? Answer for yourself. When God told Solomon to make a wish—any wish—and it would be granted, the king responded:

". . . give Thy servant an understanding heart to judge Thy people to discern between good and evil" (1 Kings 3:9).

And who doesn't know about the wisdom of Solomon to this very day? Paul informs us that discernment is one characteristic that accompanies genuine spirituality (1 Corinthians 2:14-16). Hebrews 5:14 calls it a mark of maturity. Discernment, you see, gives one a proper frame of reference, a definite line separating good and evil. It acts as an umpire in life and blows the whistle on the spurious. It's as particular as a pathologist peering into a microscope. Discernment picks and chooses its dates with great care. It doesn't fall for fakes

... or flirt with phonies
... or dance with deceivers
... or kiss counterfeits goodnight.

Come to think of it, discernment would rather relax alone at night with the Good Book than mess around with the gullible gang. You see, it's from that Book that discernment learns to distinguish the fools from the children . . . and the sleeping from the wise.

Before you start in on the old bromide, "But that doesn't sound very loving!" better take another look at John's counsel. You remember John. He's the guy known for his tender love for Jesus. He wrote:

> Beloved, do not put faith in every spirit, but prove (test) the spirits to discover whether they proceed from God . . . (1 John 4:1 Amplified Bible).

In today's talk: "Stop believing everything you hear. Quit being so easily convinced. Be selective. Think. Discern!" Undiscerning love spawns and invites more heresy than any of us are ready to believe. One of the tactics of survival when facing "the flaming missiles of the evil one" (Ephesians 6:16) is to make certain we have cinched up the belt of *truth* rather tightly around ourselves. And what helps us do battle with the enemy also strengthens us in relationships with friends.

A Christian without discernment is like a submarine in a harbor plowing full speed ahead without radar or periscope. Or a loaded 747 trying to land in dense fog without instruments or radio. Lots of noise, a great deal of power, good intentions . . . until. I don't have another Persian proverb to describe the outcome, but who needs it? It happens day in, day out . . . with disastrous regularity.

Do I hear you say you want it, but don't know where to go to find it?

- ◆ Go to your *knees*. James 1:5 promises wisdom to those who ask for it.
- ◆ Go to the *Word*. Psalm 119:98-100 offers insight beyond our fondest dreams.
- ◆ Go to the *wise*. Discernment is better caught than taught. Those who have the disease are often highly contagious.

This offer is good throughout life and comes with a satisfaction-guaranteed clause. All may apply, even those who think they know it all, and know not that they know nothing.

COME ASIDE

Study the hard words Jesus had to say about discernment in Luke 12:54-57. Is there anything in these verses you've needed to hear?

Then look over 1 Corinthians 2:12-16 and think about this passage as you thank God for making His wisdom available to us.

It's about time

'm a sucker for time-management books.

Some people can't say no to a salesman at the door. Others have the hardest time passing up a free puppy . . . or driving by a garage sale without stopping. Still others find it almost impossible to withstand the urge to gamble. Not me. My weakness is books on the investment of my time. Books that tell me how to replace being busy with being effective. Books that caution me to think things through before before plunging into them. I often recall what Bernard Baruch once said:

> Whatever failures I have known, whatever errors I have committed, whatever follies I have witnessed in private and public life, have been the consequences of action without thought.

The antidote to that problem is described best by Paul in his letter to the Ephesians:

> Look carefully then how you walk! Live purposefully and worthily and accurately, not as the unwise and witless, but as wise—sensible, intelligent people; Making the very most of the time—buying up each opportunity—because the days are evil.

> Therefore do not be vague and thoughtless and foolish, but understanding and firmly grasping what the will of the Lord is (5:15-17 Amplified Bible).

Verses like those always grab my attention. Some alarm down inside my system goes off whenever I sense a waste of energy in what I'm doing—when there is some leak in my time dike I have failed to plug. Without wanting to be neurotic about it, I get a little nervous when I think I am *not* living "purposefully," when I am failing to "buy up each opportunity," as Scripture so clearly commands. The verse that appears just before the passage I quoted shoves a long, pointed index finger into the chest of its reader as it shouts:

"Awake, O sleeper. . . ."

Today, we'd say it like this: "Hey, wake up. Get with it, man!" The easiest thing in the world is to drift through life in a vague, thoughtless manner. God says there's a better way. He tells us to take time by the throat, give it a good shake, and declare: "That's it! I'm gonna manage you—no longer will you manage me!"

That's a major secret to living above our circumstances rather than under them. Let me mention a few specifics. Some people are always running late. Yes, always. *Punctuality* is simply a time-management matter. Some folks feverishly work right up to the deadline on every assignment or project they undertake. The job usually gets done . . . but the hassle, anxiety, and last-minute panic steal the fun out of the whole thing. *Starting early* and *pacing oneself* are time-management techniques. And some seem forever in a hurry, pushing and driving, occasionally *running* here and there. Again, another evidence of *poor planning.* Time management allows room for ease and humor, much-needed oil to soothe the friction created by motion.

Which brings us back to the counsel in Ephesians 5. Living purposefully, worthily, accurately . . . being sensible, intelligent, and wise in the rationing of our time.

In a book I just finished, *The Time Trap* (I told you I was a sucker for such volumes), I came upon a list of the most popular time wasters. They helped pinpoint some specific areas of frustration I must continually watch.

- ♦ attempting too much at once
- ♦ unrealistic time estimates
- ♦ procrastinating
- ♦ lack of specific priorities
- ♦ failure to listen well
- ♦ doing it myself—failure to delegate
- ♦ unable to say no
- ♦ perfectionism—focusing on needless details
- ♦ lack of organization
- ♦ failure to write it down
- ♦ reluctance to get started
- ♦ absence of self-appointed deadlines
- ♦ doing first things first

Who hasn't heard the true story of Charles Schwab and Ivy Lee? Schwab was president of Bethlehem Steel. Lee, a consultant, was given the usual challenge: "Show me a way to get more things done with my time." Schwab agreed to pay him "anything within reason" if Lee's suggestion worked. Lee later handed the executive a sheet of paper with the plan:

> Write down the most important tasks you have to do tomorrow. Number them in order of importance. When you arrive in the morning begin at once on No. 1 and stay on it until it is completed. Recheck your priorities, then begin with No. 2 . . . then No. 3. Make this a habit every working day. Pass it on to those under you. Try it as long as you like, then send me your check for what you think it's worth.

That one idea turned Bethlehem Steel Corporation into the biggest independent steel producer in the world within five years.

How much did Schwab pay his consultant? Several weeks after receiving the note, he sent Lee a check for $25,000, admitting it was the most profitable lesson he had ever learned.

Try it for yourself. If it works, great. But don't send me any money for the idea. I'd just blow it on another time-management book . . . which I don't have time to read.

COME ASIDE

To rev up your mental motors for the daily task of setting priorities, take an unhurried look at 2 Peter 1:3-11.

Now go ahead and make a priority list of the most important tasks you want to accomplish in the next twenty-four hours.

MEGACHANGES

 hey're called inverted-L curves. They illustrate how incredibly accelerated our times really are. Consider three specific examples.

Figure A represents the growing number of people on earth from several thousand years ago to the present. Are you sitting down? Hold on tight. Not until 1850 did the number reach one billion. By 1930 the world population had doubled. In a brief thirty more years (1960) it shot up to three billion. Since then we've already arrived at five. Demographers project by the end of the century . . . seven billion.

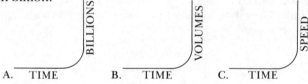

A.   TIME   B.   TIME   C.   TIME

Figure B represents the number of books published in the world each year. Virtually none until A.D. 1500. Only 35,000 by 1900. Today? Still sitting down? Would you believe over 400,000 volumes per year? And that number is rapidly increasing.

Figure C represents the maximum speed of human travel, another mind-jarring fact we seldom consider. Until 1800, top speed was 20 miles per hour on horseback. The train came along and it jumped to 100 miles per hour. In 1952 the passenger jet whisked us through the sky at 300+ miles per hour. By 1979 that speed had doubled. To be accurate, I should also add that the manned space flight (1961) was clocked at 16,000 miles per hour!

Anyone with a few hours to spare at a local library could extend the list. More inverted-L curves could be used to illustrate the increase in scientific data in medicine, physics, chemistry, astronomy, biology, the computer industry, the number of people becoming literate, and on and on. Such massive winds of change can seem frightening to thinking people. But when we add the *Christian* perspective, it can get downright exciting. How will we respond to such challenges brought about by these mega-changes? Extraordinary times will require of us extraordinary wisdom, vision, boldness, flexibility, dedication, willingness to adapt, and a renewed commitment to biblical principles that never change.

But anybody who thinks we can operate the same traditional ways we did a hundred years ago (would you believe twenty-five?) is not only shortsighted, he is blind. The church of the 1980s and 1990s must get beyond the 1950s. The secret, of course, is adapting to our times without altering God's truth.

In his top-selling book, *Megatrends*, John Naisbitt suggests ten major trends now occurring that have a direct bearing on life and business today. These require "megashifts" on our part if we hope to cope. In times like these, complexities grow by quantum leaps and it becomes ever more difficult for folks to make sense out of life's riddles.

No transformation is more explosive than the first "megatrend" that Naisbitt suggests. It began in the mid or late 1950s: From an *industrial* society to an *information* society. Communication satellites have transformed earth into "a global village" (Marshall McLuhan's words). Today's sophisticated technology knows no bounds. Now more than sixty percent of us work in "information occupations." Farmers, who as recently as the turn of the century constituted more than one-third of the total labor force, now represent a mere three percent . . . and steadily on the decrease. In fact, today more people are employed full time in our universities than in agriculture. And only thirteen percent of our entire labor force is engaged in manufacturing operations today.

Less than a hundred years ago the Sunday sermon was the chief occasion of community instruction . . . the *only* time for formal instruction of *any* kind. The Bible was the nucleus of shaping minds and determining decisions. What a difference today! The barrage of information that now competes for parishioners' attention is incredible. Living on the vertical stem of the inverted-L, we are the target of a deadly accurate dense-pack of information: an endless number and variety of books, media persuasion, and secular propaganda with its appealing influences flying at us at the speed of light.

Our thinking is changing.

Truth is now up for grabs.

This is illustrated by the public opinion shift in one brief generation on such subjects as long-term marriage, child-rearing, homosexuality, abortion, authority, integrity, capital punishment, individual fulfillment . . . and . . . and . . . and . . .

Want some survival advice? Get a megagrip on the changeless, timeless truths of the Bible. God's Word. Otherwise you'll be blown away as you accelerate around the curve of an inverted-L.

COME ASIDE

Read about more coming "megachanges" for this world—promised by the Lord Himself—in Isaiah 24 and 25. Ask God today to use these passages to stretch your thinking and anchor your faith.

AFTER THE AVALANCHE

ob could write about wounds. His words were more than patronizing platitudes and armchair proverbs. He'd been there and back again. He could describe intense inner suffering in the first person because of his own sea of pain.

Step into the time tunnel with me and let's travel together back to Uz (not like the wizard of ——, but like the land of ——). Wherever it was, Uz had a citizen who had the respect of everyone, since he was blameless, upright, God-fearing, and clean-living. He had ten children, fields of livestock, an abundance of land, a houseful of servants, and a substantial stack of cash. No one would deny that the man called Job was "the greatest of the men of the East." He had earned that title through years of hard work and honest dealings with others. His very name was a synonym for integrity and godliness.

Then, without announcement, adversity thundered upon him like an avalanche of great, jagged rocks. He lost his livestock, crops, land, servants, and—if you can believe it—all ten children. Soon thereafter he lost his health, his last human hope of earning a living. I plead with you to stop reading, lay this book in your lap, close your eyes for sixty seconds, and identify with that good man—crushed beneath the weight of adversity.

The book that bears his name records an entry he made into his journal soon after the rocks stopped falling and the dust began to settle. With a quivering hand, the man from Uz wrote:

> Naked I came from my mother's womb,
> And naked I shall return there.
> The LORD gave and the LORD has taken away.
> Blessed be the name of the LORD (Job 1:21).

Following this incredible statement, God adds:

> Through all this Job did not sin nor did he blame God (1:22).

Right about now, I'm shaking my head. How could anyone handle such a series of grief-laden ordeals so calmly? Think of the aftermath: bankruptcy, pain, ten fresh graves . . . the loneliness of those empty rooms. Yet we read that he worshiped God, he did not sin, nor did he blame his Maker.

Well, why didn't he? How could he ward off the bitterness or ignore thoughts of suicide? At the risk of oversimplifying the situation, I suggest three basic answers:

First, *Job claimed God's loving sovereignty*. He sincerely believed that the Lord who gave had every right to take away (Job 1:21). Stated in his own words:

> Shall we indeed accept good from God and not accept adversity? (Job 2:10).

He looked *up*, claiming his Lord's right to rule over his life. Who is the fool that says God has no right to add sand to our clay or marks to our vessel or fire to His workmanship? Who dares lift his clay fist heavenward and question the Potter's plan? Not Job! To him, God's sovereignty was laced with His love.

Second, *he counted on the promise of resurrection*. Do you remember his immortal words:

> I know that my Redeemer lives,
> And at the last . . . I shall see God (Job 19:25-26).

He looked *ahead*, counting on his Lord's promise to make all things bright and beautiful in the life beyond. He knew that at *that* time, all pain, death, sorrow, tears, and adversity would be removed. Knowing that "hope does not disappoint" (Romans 5:5), he endured today by envisioning tomorrow.

Third, *he confessed his own lack of understanding*. What a relief this brings! Job didn't feel obligated to explain the "whys" of his situation. Listen to his admission of this fact:

> I know that Thou canst do all things,
> And that no purpose of Thine can be thwarted. . . .
> Therefore I have declared that which I did not
>   understand,
> Things too wonderful [too deep] for me, which I did not
>   know. . . .
> "I will ask Thee, and do Thou instruct me"
>   (Job 42:2-4).

He looked *within*, confessing his inability to put it all together. Resting his case with the righteous Judge, Job did not feel compelled to answer all the questions or unravel all the burning riddles. God would judge. The Judge would be right.

Could it be that you are beginning to feel the nick of falling rocks? Maybe the avalanche has already fallen . . . maybe not. Adversity may seem 10,000 miles away . . . as remote as the land of Uz. That's the way Job felt just a few minutes before the landslide.

Review these thoughts as you turn out the lights tonight, my friend, just in case. Consider Job's method for picking up the pieces.

Cloudless days are fine, but remember: Some pottery gets pretty fragile setting in the sun day after day after day.

COME ASIDE

Beginning at Job 38:1, read as much as you have time for of this stormy message from the Lord to Job (it continues through chapter 41). What is God communicating here to you?

CLOSING THE DOOR TO LUST

amson was a he-man with a she-weakness. In spite of the fact that he was born of godly parents, set apart from his birth to be a Nazarite, and elevated to the enviable position of judge in Israel, he never conquered his tendency toward lust. On the contrary, it conquered him. Several things that illustrate his lustful bent may be observed from the record of his life in the book of Judges.

1. The first recorded words from his mouth were: *I saw a woman* (14:2).
2. He was attracted to the opposite sex strictly on the basis of outward appearance: *Get her for me, for she looks good to me* (14:3).
3. He judged Israel for twenty years, then went right back to his old habit of chasing women—a harlot in Gaza, and finally Delilah (15:20-16:4).
4. He became so preoccupied with his lustful desires, he didn't even know the Lord had departed from him (16:20).

The results of Samson's illicit affairs are familiar to all of us. The strong man of Dan was taken captive and became a slave in the enemy's camp, his eyes were gouged out of his head, and he was appointed to be the grinder in a Philistine prison. Lust, the jailer, binds and blinds and grinds. The swarthy pride of Israel, who once held the highest office in the land, was now the bald-headed clown of Philistia, a pathetic hollow shell of humanity. His eyes would never wander again. His life, once filled with promise and dignity, was now a portrait of hopeless, helpless despair. Chalk up another victim for lust. The perfumed memories of erotic pleasure in Timnah, Gaza, and the infamous Valley of Sorek were now overwhelmed by the putrid stench of a Philistine dungeon.

Without realizing it, Solomon wrote another epitaph—this one for Samson's tombstone:

> The wicked man is doomed by his own sins; they are ropes that catch and hold him. He shall die because he will not listen to the truth; he has let himself be led away into incredible folly (Proverbs 5:22-23 TLB).

The same words could well be chiseled in the marble over many other tombs. I think, for example, of the silver-throated orator of Rome, Mark

Antony. In his early manhood, he was so consumed with lust that his tutor once shouted in disgust:

> O Marcus! O colossal child . . . able to conquer the world but unable to resist a temptation!

I think of the gentleman I met several years ago—a fine itinerant Bible teacher. He said he had been keeping a confidential list of men who were once outstanding expositors of the Scripture, capable and respected men of God . . . who have shipwrecked their faith on the shoals of moral defilement. During the previous week, he said, he had entered the name of *number forty-two* in his book. This sad, sordid statistic, he claims, caused him to be extra cautious and discreet in his own life. Perhaps, by now, he has added a couple dozen more.

A chill ran down my spine when he told that story. No one is immune. You're not. I'm not. Lust is no respecter of persons. Whether by savage assault or subtle suggestion, the minds of a wide range of people are vulnerable to its attack. Sharp professional men and women, homemakers, students, carpenters, artists, musicians, pilots, bankers, senators, plumbers, promoters, and preachers as well. Its alluring voice can infiltrate the most intelligent mind and cause its victim to believe its lies and respond to its appeal. And beware—it never gives up . . . it never runs out of ideas. Bolt your front door and it'll rattle at the bedroom window, crawl into the living room through the TV screen, or wink at you out of a magazine in the den.

How do you handle such an aggressive intruder? Try this: When lust suggests a rendezvous, send Jesus Christ as your representative.

Have him inform your unwanted suitor that you want nothing to do with illicit desire . . . *nothing*. Have your Lord remind lust that since you and Christ have been united together, you are no longer a slave to sin. His death and resurrection freed you from sin's stranglehold and gave you a new Master. And before giving lust a firm shove away from your life, have Christ inform this intruder that the permanent peace and pleasure you are enjoying in your new home with Christ are so much greater than lust's temporary excitement that you don't need it around any longer to keep you happy.

> For sin's power over us was broken when we became Christians and were baptized to become a part of Jesus Christ; through his death the power of your sinful nature was shattered. Your old sin-loving nature was buried with him by baptism when he died, and when God the Father, with glorious power, brought him back to life again, you were given his wonderful new life to enjoy (Romans 6:3-4 TLB).

But lust is persistent. If it's knocked on your door once, it'll knock again. And again. You are safe just so long as you draw upon your Savior's strength. Try to handle it yourself and you'll lose—every time. This is why we are warned again and again in the New Testament to *flee* sexual temptations. Remember, lust is committed to wage *war* against your soul—in a life-and-death struggle—in hand-to-hand combat. Don't stand before this mortal enemy and argue or fight in your own strength—run for cover. Cry out for reinforcement. Call in an air strike. If you get yourself into a situation that leaves you defenseless and weak, if your door is left even slightly ajar, you may be sure that this ancient enemy will kick it open with six-guns blazing. So don't leave it open. Don't give lust a foothold . . . or even a toehold.

Joseph was a dedicated, well-disciplined believer, but he was smart enough to realize he couldn't tease lust without being whipped. (Read Genesis 39.) When it came time for a hasty exit, the son of Jacob preferred to leave his jacket behind rather than hesitate and leave his hide. But not Samson. Fool that he was, he thought he could cuddle lust, inhale its heady perfume, and enjoy its warm embrace without the slightest chance of getting caught. What appeared to be a harmless, soft, attractive dove of secret love turned into a reeking nightmarish vulture.

Lust is one flame you dare not fan. You'll get burned if you do.

Samson would sign this warning in my place if he could, for he, being dead, yet speaks.

COME ASIDE

Search through 1 Thessalonians 4:1-12 and find at least three guidelines for how to close your door to lust. Write them down on a card and keep it available.

SUPERSTITION

he great plague stretched across the Old Country like a thick, drab blanket. It came as a thief in the night . . . unannounced, treacherous, silent. Before it left, 25 million people on the Isles and in Europe had died. The mortality rate was astounding. In May of 1664, a few isolated cases were reported and quietly ignored. Exactly one year later, 590 died that month. By June it was 6,137; July, over 17,000; August, over 31,000. Panic struck. More than two-thirds of the remaining population fled from their homes to escape death.

It was called *Black Death* for two reasons:

First of all, the body of the victim became dark, black splotches covering the skin.

Second, the blackness of ignorance surrounded its cause. Because of this, no cure was known.

Someone came up with the foolish idea that polluted air brought on the plague. So people began to carry flower petals in their pockets, superstitiously thinking the fragrance would ward off the disease. Groups of victims, if they were able to walk, were taken outside the hospitals. Holding hands, they walked in circles around rose gardens, breathing in deeply the aroma of the blooming plants. In some cases, the patient couldn't get out of bed, so the attending physicians filled their pockets with bright-colored petals from English posy plants. While visiting the patient they walked around the bed, sprinkling the posy petals on and around the victim.

As death came closer, another superstitious act was employed with sincerity. Many felt if the lungs could be freed from pollution, life could be sustained. So ashes were placed in a spoon and brought up near the nose, causing a hefty sneeze or two. But neither flowers nor sneezes retarded the raging death rate. Not until the real cause was discovered—the bite of fleas from diseased rats—was the plague brought in check.

The awful experience gave birth to a little song which innocent children still sing at play. It was first heard from the lips of a soiled old man pushing a cart in London, picking up bodies along an alley:

> Ring around the roses,
> A pocket full of posies;
> Ashes, ashes, we all fall down.

Conceived in the mind by ignorance, superstition cultivates insecurity and sends a legion of structural cracks through our character. It feeds on exaggerated, self-made lies which grow so thick that the boughs hide common sense—and worse, God.

You find superstition in sports. Some basketball players testify they simply cannot play the game unless they go through their strange warm-up ritual. The manager of one professional baseball team doesn't dare step on a white baseline. Several pro football running backs have superstitious "dances" that follow their touchdowns—and you'd better not try to stop them! Several years ago, an Olympic runner admitted he has to rub the medal that hangs around his neck or he can't get properly "psyched up." The news media reported that one of America's Olympic skiers sticks a four-leaf clover in her jacket pocket before she hits the slopes.

Superstition enslaves many an entertainer. You wouldn't believe the mental contortions they go through before their performances. Students are superstitious about getting good grades. The elderly are superstitious about their safety at home. Mothers are superstitious about their babies at night. Men are superstitious about their success in sales or the future of their careers. Multiplied millions are superstitious about their astrological forecast.

The worst? Superstition regarding the Lord God. The Reformers were among the first to see it and call a spade a spade. They wrote of it, preached against it, publicly exposed it—and were martyred because of it. Religious superstition is ruthless.

Before you write this off as applying to anyone but yourself, take a long, hard look at your own life. The goal of superstition is *bondage*. Remember that. If *anything* in your Christianity has you in bondage, it is probable that superstition is the breeding ground. You see, our Savior came to give us the truth and set us free. Superstition, although prompted by sincerity, brings the plague of slavery. Sincerity doesn't liberate; Christ does.

You may be sincere. As sincere as a pocketful of petals or a spoonful of ashes or a song in the alley. But what good is a song if it's sung to a corpse?

COME ASIDE

Look at John 5:1-18 to see how Jesus deals with people's superstitions. In the same way, what would you like Him to do in your life? Commit 1 John 5:21 to memory.

WHO CARES?

ho really cared? His was a routine admission to busy Bellevue Hospital. A charity case, one among hundreds. A bum from the Bowery with a slashed throat. *The Bowery* . . . last stop before the morgue. Synonym of filth, loneliness, cheap booze, drugs, and disease.

The details of what had happened in the predawn of that chilly winter's morning were fuzzy. The nurse probably shrugged it off. She had seen thousands and she was sure to see thousands more. Would it have made any difference if she and those who treated him had known who he was? Probably so.

His recent past was the antithesis of his earlier years. The Bowery became the dead-end street of an incredible life. But all that was over. A twenty-five-cent-a-night flophouse had rooms you hear about, but never want to see . . . full of stinking humanity too miserable to describe. He was one among many. Like all the rest, he now lived only to drink. His health was gone and he was starving. On that icy January morning before the sun had crept over New York's skyline, a shell of a man who looked twice his age staggered to the wash basin and fell. The basin toppled and shattered.

He was found lying in a heap, naked and bleeding from a deep gash in his throat. His forehead was badly bruised and he was semiconscious. A doctor was called, no one special—remember, this was the Bowery. He used black sewing thread somebody found to suture the wound. That would do. All the while the bum begged for a drink. A buddy shared the bottom of a rum bottle to calm his nerves.

He was dumped in a paddy wagon and dropped off at Bellevue Hospital, where he would languish, unable to eat for three days . . . and die. Still unknown.

A friend seeking him was directed to the local morgue. There, among dozens of other colorless, nameless corpses with tags on their toes, he was identified. When they scraped together his belongings, they found a ragged, dirty coat with thirty-eight cents in one pocket and a scrap of paper in the other. All his earthly goods. Enough coins for another night in the Bowery and five words, "Dear friends and gentle hearts." Almost like the words of a song, someone thought. But who cared?

Why in the world would a forgotten drunk carry around a line of lyrics? Maybe he still believed he had it in him. Maybe that derelict with the body of a bum still had the heart of a genius. For once upon a time, long before his tragic death at age thirty-eight, he had written the songs that literally made the whole world sing, like:

"Camptown Races"
"Oh! Susanna!"
"Beautiful Dreamer"
"Jeanie with the Light Brown Hair"
"Old Folks at Home"
"My Old Kentucky Home"

and two hundred more that have become deeply rooted in our rich American heritage. Thanks to Stephen Foster, whom nobody knew. And for whom nobody cared.

Makes me think of a few lines out of an old poem preachers once quoted:

> And many a man with life out of tune,
>   And battered and scarred with sin,
> Is auctioned cheap to the thoughtless crowd
>   Much like the old violin.
>
> A "mess of pottage," a glass of wine;
>   A game—and he travels on.
> He's "going" once, and "going" twice,
>   He's "going" and almost "gone."

Almost. *Almost* gone. Until someone cares. And steps in. And stoops down. And, in love, rebuilds a life, restores a soul, rekindles a flame that sin snuffed out, and renews a song that once was there. As Fanny Crosby put it:

> Touched by a loving heart,
>   Wakened by kindness
> Chords that were broken,
>   Will vibrate once more.

Deep within many a forgotten life is a scrap of hope, a lonely melody trying hard to return. Some are in prison. Some in hospitals. Some in nursing homes. And some silently slip into church on Sunday morning, terribly confused and afraid. Do you care? Enough "to show hospitality to strangers," as Hebrews 13:2 puts it? It also says that in doing so, we occasionally "entertain angels without knowing it."

Angels that don't look anything like angels. Some might look like bums from the Bowery, but they may have a song dying in their hearts because nobody knows and nobody cares.

COME ASIDE

Jesus cares. Spend enough time in any of the following brief passages to engrave Christlike compassion more deeply in your understanding: Matthew 18:10-14, Mark 8:1-8, Luke 7:11-15, and John 19:25-27.

When you next encounter someone who is lost or hungry or hurting—how can you be ready to help? Be specific as well as realistic.

OFFERINGS

our response to the heading of today's reading is probably: "Oh, oh—another money plea!" or "Here we go again . . . some Christian ministry trying to get into my wallet," or "Can't we go more than a month without being reminded to give?" I hate to disappoint you, but you're wrong. Being wrong this time, however, disappoints no one!

I'm not going to talk about what you should do *when* the plate is passed. Rather, I want to talk about what you might do *before* and *after* that time. Twice every Sunday we spend five to eight minutes of very prime time doing *zero*. If you're the average, tired churchgoer, young or old, you could check one or more of the following "offering pastimes." Be honest now.

- [ ] writing notes . . . receiving replies
- [ ] checking to see who's missing in the choir
- [ ] getting better acquainted, chattering with your friend
- [ ] listening for the organist's mistakes
- [ ] observing the architecture, counting the bricks
- [ ] planning next week's activities
- [ ] drawing pictures . . . daydreaming . . . dozing
- [ ] looking around, watching ushers, checking the time
- [ ] inking out letters on the bulletin
- [ ] questioning why that fella in the new suit didn't drop something in the plate

Zero. A complete waste of time. Here we are, right in the midst of a carefully-planned worship service, drifting and dreaming away a few precious moments that could otherwise make the difference between a ho-hum and a hallelujah experience.

Ecclesiastes 3:7 refers to *a time to be silent*. The offering provides you with just such a time—to be silent. To cease from talking. To think, to reflect, to meditate, to slow your motor down and be still. If I may take the phrase in Ephesians 5:16, *making the most of your time*, to include the silent moments during the offering, let me offer some practical suggestions. Six come to my mind:

1. Take a pencil along with the bulletin stub and write down a list of the things for which you are most grateful. Ponder each . . . and thank your Heavenly Father for them one by one. Tape that list in a conspicuous place at home and look at it daily for a week.

2. Turn to the scripture that will be used in the sermon. Read it over slowly. Think only about that passage throughout the offering time. Ask God to speak to you as though you were all alone in the worship service.

3. Pick out two or three people whom you know (perhaps some sitting with or near you) and pray specifically for them. Ask God to encourage them and lift their spirits that day. You might even follow that up by greeting them after the service and expressing interest in their lives. Tell them that God prompted you to pray for them.

4. Find the hymn the organist is playing if it is familiar to you. Read the words over slowly. Allow yourself to picture the scene in the hymn and become thrilled with the message it communicates.

5. Close your eyes. Refuse every outside thought that knocks for entrance. Think back over the week that's passed. Praise God for His assistance. Confess to Him the dirt you've swept under your life's rug. Thank Him for your role in life, your job, your loved ones, your church, your spiritual gifts, your salvation, your trials, your destiny, your health, the Scriptures.

6. May I dare add another? Pray for the one who will bring the message. Ask God to give him liberty, clarity, boldness, sensitivity, insight on his feet, freedom from distractions and petty worries. It's amazing how much more the message means to you when you've had a part in its delivery.

Hebrews 13:15 gives timely counsel along these lines: "... let us continually offer up a sacrifice of praise to God, that is, the fruit of lips that give thanks to His name."

That's a switch, isn't it? The traditional offering time becomes a "sacrifice of praise" time . . . a time when God, personally, receives your offering of gratitude . . . a time when He picks the "fruit of your lips." What is *most* remarkable is how the juice from that fruit heals the ache in your left hip pocket.

COME ASIDE

To turn next Sunday morning's offering time into a sacrifice of praise, try a "dry run" now, using Jude 24-25 to fill your mind.

BIGNESS

t was a cold, blustery January night in 1973. Senator John Stennis, the venerable hawkish Democrat from Mississippi, drove from Capitol Hill to his northwest Washington home. Although old (71), he was still the powerful chairman of the Senate Armed Services Committee. At precisely 7:40 P.M. Stennis parked his car and started toward his house fifty feet away.

Out of the darkness jumped two young robbers—little more than kids, really. One nervously waved a .22 caliber pistol as the other relieved the senator of his wallet, a gold wristwatch, his Phi Beta Kappa Key, and a quarter in change. Stennis didn't fight, but he did argue with the punks and began "hollering and carrying on" (the attackers later reported), which unnerved them. The mixture of the shouting, the meager take in the robbery, and panic intensified the irritation and fear. "Now we're going to shoot you anyway," one told Stennis.

He did, firing twice. The first tore through the senator's stomach, rupturing the pancreas, severely damaging his intestinal tract. The second lodged in his left thigh. The assailants fled into the cold, black night as Stennis stumbled to his house. For six-and-a-half hours surgeons at Walter Reed Medical Center labored feverishly to repair the damage and save his life.

At 9:15 that same night another politician was driving home from the Senate . . . a man on the opposite end of the political spectrum, a Republican "dove" who had clashed often and sharply with Stennis. His name? Senator Mark Hatfield. The tragedy was reported over Hatfield's car radio that wintry night. Disregarding the strong differences in their convictions and pulled by a deep admiration for the elderly statesman plus a compassion for his plight, Hatfield later admitted:

"I had no skills to offer. But I knew there was something I must do— and that was to go to that hospital and be nearby where I could be helpful, if possible, to the family."

There was untold confusion at the hospital as fellow senators, colleagues, and curious friends and reporters overwhelmed the hospital's telephone operators. Understaffed and disorganized, the hospital crew tried their best but were unable to handle the calls and answer the questions.

Hatfield quickly scoped out the situation, spotted an unattended switchboard, sat down, and voluntarily went to work. Much later—after recovering—Stennis related what he heard happened next: "He told the girls, 'I know how to work one of these; let me help you out.' He continued taking calls until daylight." An exceedingly significant detail is that he never gave anyone his name because someone would surely suspect some political connection, some ulterior motive. Hatfield finally stood up around daylight, stretched, put on his overcoat, and quietly introduced himself to the other operators. "My name is Hatfield . . . happy to help out on behalf of a man I deeply respect," he said as he walked away.

The press couldn't handle that story when it leaked out. It boggled their minds! No way did it make sense for a liberal Republican to give a conservative Democrat the time of day, not to mention several long hours of personal assistance in some anonymous, menial task. I mean, that kind of character went out with the horse and buggy and silent movies and saying "ma'am" and "sir" to teachers. *Or did it?*

Politics and personal preferences and opinions on things like military involvement may vary among members of the Body . . . but there is a bond deep within that binds us to one another. It is the glue of authentic love, expressing itself in compassion, fairness, willingness to support, and (when possible) coming to the aid of another. Personally. Without strings attached. Committed to the protection and dignity of human life . . . regardless of how somebody votes.

And what does it take? Bigness. Being free of grudges, pettiness, vengeance, and prejudice. Seeing another in need—regardless of differences of opinion—and reaching out in solid Christian maturity. Just because you care.

That's bigness. It's living above labels . . . it's seeing beyond hurts . . . it's caring unconditionally, helping unassumingly.

And therefore it's rare. As rare as a hawk and a dove in the same nest on a cold winter's night.

COME ASIDE

Search through Luke 23 to find all the individuals whose separate contact with Jesus is described. Which ones failed to demonstrate "bigness"? Which ones did demonstrate it, and how?

YOUR TESTIMONY

ne time-honored and effective method of evangelism is the giving of your personal testimony. The skeptic may deny your doctrine or attack your church but he cannot honestly ignore the fact that your life has been changed. He may stop his ears to the presentations of a preacher and the pleadings of an evangelist, but he is somehow attracted to the human-interest story of how you—John Q. Public—found peace within.

Believe me, the steps that led to your conversion and the subsequent ramifications are far more appealing and appropriate to the lost than a pulpit exposition of John 3 or Romans 5. If you have not discovered the value of telling others how God rearranged your life, you've missed a vital link in the chain of His blessing.

On six separate occasions between Paul's third missionary journey and his trip to Rome, he stood before different audiences and presented Christ to them (Acts 22-26). Six times he stood alone. Six times he addressed unbelievers, many of them hostile and rude. Do you know the method Paul used each time? *His personal testimony.*

Each time he spoke, he simply shared how his own life had been changed by the invasion of Christ and the indwelling of His power. Not once did he argue or debate with them. Not once did he preach a sermon. Why? Because one of the most convincing, unanswerable arguments on earth regarding Christianity is one's personal experience with the Lord Jesus Christ. No persuasive technique will ever take the place of your personal testimony. I challenge you to give serious consideration to thinking through and then presenting the way God saved you—along with the exciting results of His presence in your life.

Now I'm not talking about the common, garden variety, churchy "braggamony." We have all yawned and groaned as others rambled and preached their way through a so-called testimony—which was about as fresh, appealing, and tasty as warm, month-old lettuce.

That kind of testimony never attracted anyone!

I'd like to help you carry out the project of preparing your testimony that it might become an effective, powerful missile launched regularly from your lips into the ears of the unsaved. Consider these five suggestions:

1. *You want to be listened to, so be interesting.* No one, no matter how gracious, enjoys being bored. It's a contradiction to talk about how exciting Christ really is in an uninteresting way. Work on your wording, your flow of thought, your key terms. Remember, the person isn't saved, so

guard against religious clichés and hard-to-understand terminology.

2. *You want to be understood, so be logical.* I suggest that you think of your salvation in three phases . . . and construct your testimony accordingly: (a) before you were born again—the loneliness, lack of peace, absence of love, unrest and fears; (b) the decision that revolutionized your life, and (c) the change, the difference He has made since you received Christ.

3. *You want the moment of your new birth to be clear, so be specific.* Be extremely careful here. Don't be at all vague regarding how you became a Christian. Speak of Christ, not the church. Refer to the decision you made, the moment of time when you received the Lord. Be simple and direct. Emphasize faith more than feeling.

4. *You want your testimony to be used, so be practical.* Be human and honest as you talk. Don't promise, "All your problems will end if you will become a Christian," for that isn't true. Try to think as an unbeliever thinks as you are speaking. Refuse to pick theological lint. Restrain yourself from plucking the wings off religious flies. Theoretical stuff doesn't attract his attention as much as practical reality.

5. *You want your testimony to produce results, so be warm and genuine.* A smile breaks down more barriers than the hammer blows of cold, hard facts. Be friendly and sincere. Let your enthusiasm flow freely. It's hard to convince another person of the sheer joy and excitement of knowing Christ if you're wearing a jail-warden face. Above all, be positive and courteous.

Give thought to this, my friend. Ask God to open your lips and honor your words . . . but be careful! Once your missile hits the target you'll become totally dissatisfied with your former life as an earth-bound, secret-service saint.

COME ASIDE

Review the amazing account of one man's encounter with Jesus in Luke 8:26-39. Try to sense how this man must have felt after the Lord freed him.

Next, think of three specific and important changes Christ has accomplished in your born-again life (these can be a part of your spoken testimony to unbelievers).

Finally, if you know your testimony needs some written work and planning, schedule a time for it now—and write it on your calendar.

STAY IN CIRCULATION

uring the reign of Oliver Cromwell, the British government began to run low on silver for coins. Lord Cromwell sent his men on an investigation of the local cathedral to see if they could find any precious metal there. After investigating, they reported:

The only silver we could find is the statues of the saints standing in the corners.

To which the radical soldier and statesman of England replied:

Good! We'll melt down the saints and put them into circulation!

Not bad theology for a proper, strait-laced Lord Protector of the Isles! In a just a few words Cromwell's command states the essence . . . the kernel . . . the practical goal of authentic Christianity. Not rows of silver saints, highly polished, frequently dusted, crammed into the corners of elegant cathedrals. Not plaster people cloaked in thin layers of untarnished silver and topped with a metallic halo. But *real* persons. Melted saints circulating through the mainstream of humanity. Bringing worth and value down where life transpires in the raw. Without the faint aura of stained glass, the electric modulation of the organ, and the familiar comforts of padded pews and dimmed lights. Out where bottom-line theology is top-shelf priority. You know the places:

- on campuses where students scrape through the varnish of shallow answers
- in the shop where unbelieving employees test the mettle of everyday Christianity
- at home with a houseful of kids, where "R and R" means Run and Rassle
- in the concrete battlegrounds of sales competition, seasonal conventions, and sexual temptations, where hard-core assaults are made on internal character
- on the hospital bed, where reality never takes a nap
- in the office, where diligence and honesty are forever on the scaffold
- on the team, where patience and self-control are x-rayed under pressure

It's easy to kid ourselves. So easy. The Christian must guard against self-deception. We can begin to consider ourselves martyrs because we are in church twice on Sunday—really sacrificing by investing a few hours on the "day of rest." Listen, my friend, being among the saints is no sacrifice . . . it's a brief, choice privilege. The cost factor occurs on Monday or Tuesday . . . and during the rest of the week. That's when we're "melted down and put into circulation." That's when they go for the jugular. And it is remarkable how that monotonous work-week test discolors many a silver saint. "Sunday religion" may seem sufficient, but it isn't. Deception can easily result in a surprise ending.

> Shed a tear for Jimmy Brown
>   Poor Jimmy is no more
> For what he thought was H_2O
>   Was H_2SO_4.

It's the acid grind that takes the toll, isn't it? Maybe that explains why the venerable prophet of God touched a nerve with his probing query:

> If racing with mere men—these men of Anathoth—has wearied you, how will you race against horses . . . ? If you stumble and fall on open ground, what will you do in Jordan's jungles? (Jeremiah 12:5 TLB).

Doing battle in the steaming jungle calls for shock troops in super shape. No rhinestone cowboys can cut it among the swamps and insects of the gross world system. Sunday-go-to-meetin' silver saints in shining armor are simply out of circulation if that's the limit to their faith. Waging wilderness warfare calls for sweat . . . energy . . . keen strategy . . . determination . . . a good supply of ammunition . . . willingness to fight . . . refusal to surrender, even with the elephants tromping on your air-hose.

And *that* is why we must be melted! It's all part of being "in circulation." Those who successfully wage war with silent heroism under relentless secular pressure—ah, *they* are the saints who know what it means to be melted.

You can opt for an easier path. Sure. You can keep your own record and come out smelling like a rose. Your game plan might look something like this:

Dressed up and drove to church.	Check
Walked three blocks in the rain.	Check
Got a seat and sat quietly.	Check
Sang each verse, smiled appropriately.	Check

Gave $5 . . . listened to sermon.   Check
Closed my Bible, prayed, looked pious.   Check
Shook hands . . . walked out . . . quickly forgot.   Check

Still a saint? Uh-huh . . . a silver one, in fact. Polished to a high-gloss sheen. Icily regular, cool and casual, consistently present . . . and safely out of circulation. Another touch-me-not whatnot . . .
Until the Lord calls for an investigation of the local cathedral.

COME ASIDE

Read how the church's first saints were put into circulation (and notice the results) in Acts 8:1-4 and 11:19-21. Are you as committed to the gospel's advance as these early Christians were?

Talk with God about it today.

An "Affair"

he *Myth of the Greener Grass* is a book for our times.

My friend, J. Allan Petersen, wrote it after investing almost four decades of his life ministering to hundreds of marriages and families around the world. Therefore, he ought to know the scoop regarding extramarital involvements, especially among professing Christians. The sad fact is no longer surprising—infidelity has invaded our ranks. The Body bears more ugly scars than ever in its history, and instead of hiding those scars from the public eye, we now speak of them without much embarrassment. The tone is sophisticated. The head is unbowed . . . the heart is unbroken . . . the terms are mellow. It's an "affair," remember. No longer adultery. Everybody stays calm and cool. They take a deep breath, smile, and look accepting, tolerant, and if possible, affirming.

Petersen admits:

> A call for fidelity is like a solitary voice crying in today's sexual wilderness. What was once labeled adultery and carried a stigma of guilt and embarrassment now is an affair—a nice-sounding, almost inviting word wrapped in mystery, fascination, and excitement. A relationship, not sin. What was once behind the scenes—a secret closely guarded—is now in the headlines, a TV theme, a bestseller, as common as the cold. Marriages are "open"; divorces are "creative."

The cesspool has now overflowed. It has contaminated our magazine racks, bookshelves, billboards, the live theatre, the movies, and the most powerful medium any culture has ever known, television. From daytime soaps to the nighttime interviews, not to mention primetime sitcoms and Emmy-award winning dramas, somebody else's mate is invariably getting in or out of bed with someone other than their partner.

The shrapnel of such bombardments ultimately gets embedded in our minds, brainwashing us into believing that adultery is actually "healthy" (the exact term used by Dr. Albert Ellis, a prominent sexologist), rejuvenating to marriage, and certainly understandable. Cheating is no longer a shameful act, it has come to be expected now that it's been glamorized.

It's now *fidelity*, not infidelity, that needs defending in our sex-saturated society. People who choose to stay faithful appear somewhere between mid-Victorian and square. They're about as up to date as a kerosene lamp or a wringer washer.

I read some time ago of a wife who went to lunch with eleven other women who were taking a French course together, since their children were all in school. One rather bold type asked, "How many of you have been faithful throughout your marriage?" Only one lady raised her hand. That evening one of the women related the incident to her husband. When she admitted she was not the one who raised her hand, her husband looked crestfallen.

"But I've been faithful to you," she quickly assured him.

"Then why didn't you raise your hand?"

"I was ashamed."

That's like being ashamed of good health during an epidemic . . . or being ashamed of escaping unscathed from an earthquake. But apparently when it comes to having an "affair," peer pressure shifts the shame away from the guilty.

Not everyone is so convinced. Robert J. Levin, articles editor of *Redbook* magazine, and Alexander Lowen vote "No" to such thinking. In an article they co-authored, they mentioned three ways in which infidelity destroys the future of any marriage.

First, *infidelity causes pain to the other*. A marriage exists when a man and a woman are bound together, not by law, but by love, and are openly pledged to accept responsibility for each other, fortified by the feeling of total commitment that extends from the present into the future. Virtually all such marriages begin with faith—which is to say that a man and a woman entrust themselves to each other . . . it is together that they will seek fulfillment.

The first breaking of that faith, the basic infidelity, precedes any act of extramarital intercourse. It happens when one partner decides to turn away from his mate in search of intimacy or fulfillment—and keeps the decision a secret. This is the beginning of betrayal.

Also, the sexually unfaithful husband or wife must devote time and money, as well as physical and emotional energy, to the secret "lover." Whatever is given, in effect, must be taken from one's mate. The betrayed partner is actually paying for the cheater's pleasure.

Second, *infidelity masks the real problem*. To whatever extent infidelity temporarily eases the superficial symptoms of discontent in a husband or wife—such as feeling unattractive or unappreciated—it camouflages the real malady and permits it to grow worse. Distressed by the thought of a separation or divorce, the unfaithful mate *pretends* to be faithful while searching for satisfaction outside the marriage.

All the risks notwithstanding, honest confrontation has it all over secret deception.

Third, *infidelity is destructive of the self*. The unfaithful partner who pretends that by keeping the "affair" a secret he protects his or her mate and safeguards the marriage practices the deepest deception of all:

self-deceit. Since the use of deceit transforms the person against whom it is used into an adversary, a self-deceived person is obviously his own worst enemy.

When we feel we must lie to someone who trusts us and whom we love, we are trapped in what psychologists call a "double bind." Whatever we do, we lose. This is what an unfaithful husband, for example, faces when he returns home to a wife he genuinely loves. He wants to restore his sense of closeness with her, but he knows he cannot tell her what he has done. So he lies. Lying becomes a habit.

The lies are often unconscious and unspoken and therefore not marked by pain. This is the ultimate act of self-deception. Instead of resolving conflict, it perpetuates it; the deluded person *lives* a lie. He is sick and does not feel the fever.

I seriously doubt that a long list of biblical verses would be necessary to convince anyone that infidelity displeases God. When He says, "Let marriage be held in honor among all, and let the marriage bed be undefiled; for fornicators and adulterers God will judge" (Hebrews 13:4), He means it. Finding intimacy outside your marriage with someone other than your mate *isn't* okay. It's sinful. It doesn't simplify life, it complicates.

Deceiving yourself isn't healthy, it's sick. It doesn't prove you're independent and strong . . . it's a declaration that you've got deep needs.

Sleeping with someone other than your mate isn't acceptable and adventurous, it's destructive and dangerous.

And it isn't an "affair"; it's adultery.

The grass may indeed look greener on the other side of the fence. But it's poison. A loving God put the fence there for a reason.

COME ASIDE

If the temptation to infidelity has been touching you, and you now realize it is because of deep needs in your life, use Psalm 143 to help you enter God's presence and present these needs to Him.

A TOUCH OF CLASS

t's gone on long enough. The pigsty in the landscape has to go. If we expect the tourist traffic to increase and the visitors to return to Lake Evangelicalism, we're gonna have to do something about the ugly ducklings. Some changes are long overdue.

Somebody should've tarred 'n feathered the very first stingy board member or strung up the whole squint-eyed, tight-fisted committee way back when. Whoever they were, they did us no favor. They—and the long line of those who follow in their train—are the ones who erroneously confuse excellence with extravagance. Somehow, by means of pious-sounding put-downs they succeed in convincing God's people that God's work shouldn't look too nice . . . that quality is carnality . . . that taste is waste . . . that something well done is overdone . . . that elegance calls for apology, and a touch of class belongs only to the secular.

"If it's spiritual," they say, "it shouldn't be too attractive or very expensive."

They got their way. Just look around. For years we've lived with this reputation. There are some wonderful exceptions on this big lake, I'm glad to say, but not *nearly* enough. By and large, if the theology of a ministry is conservative, so is its architecture. And its furniture. And its appointments. And its equipment. And its salaries. And its honorariums. Even its style smacks of leftovers, afterthoughts, hand-me-downs, and secondhand stuff.

Do you question that? Check with a missionary who recently opened a grab bag of clothing from the States. That's one of the reasons missionaries need a great sense of humor, by the way. It helps keep them from crying when they shake out the garments the traditional-thinking evangelical church sends their way. I know, I've been there when they wear those things for their annual costume party. It's hilarious.

No, it's downright tragic. Late one night, thousands of miles from America, after all the fun 'n games were over (when the kids were down and our privacy was secure), a handful of God's choicest saints on foreign soil told me a few of their secrets. One couple said that they had recently received a box of clothing at least twenty years out of date, soiled, with missing buttons and broken zippers. But the ultimate story was told by the family who said their home church once mailed them a box that included a container of used tea bags. No, it wasn't meant to be a joke.

Being financially responsible is one thing. Being ridiculously frugal is quite another. Why have we embraced the idea that elegance and class

51

have no place on the spectrum of spirituality? Since when is it more spiritual to play a beat-up old upright than a fine baby grand? What makes us less comfortable working and worshiping in lovely surroundings than in plain ones? Who ever said that humility and beauty cannot co-exist?

I'm honest, I've searched the Scriptures to find statements that support such an extreme emphasis on cutting every economic corner. The only place I find support for that (you're not going to like this) is in the *personal* realm . . . not in the realm of God's work. God's Word encourages us to be prudent individuals, but generous (dare I say *extravagant?*) with Him. Time and again in the pages of God's Book the saints are exhorted to be magnanimous, liberal, openhanded . . . to such an extreme that some today would find themselves almost ill at ease surrounded by such opulent loveliness.

Yes, even the ancient places of worship were stunningly beautiful. The tabernacle was a veritable golden tent that had within it fabulous works of art: sewing, tapestry, woodworking, and craftsmanship. Mouths must have dropped open. Check it out for yourself—Exodus 25-40.

And the temple that Solomon had built? One of the famed wonders of the world! First Kings, chapter 6, will blow your mind. Artistic frames for the windows. Beams and timbers—in fact, "the whole house"—overlaid with gold. Stones quarried to such a precise size they slipped into place on site. In fact, while the temple was being built, no sound of a hammer or ax or any other iron tool was heard in the place (1 Kings 6:7). Wall beams were dovetailed and "inserted" together, and each piece of furniture was a choice carving, a dazzling and unduplicated work of original art.

Why not? God's reputation was at stake. God's name was on display.

Centuries later, Paul spoke of having to learn how to abound . . . and there is no awkward embarrassment in his tone or any attempt to justify himself. Why should there be? It wasn't until much later that the scene changed . . . that Christians picked up the fallacious idea that it's admirable to look puritanical and uncreatively plain. After all, you don't have to do so much explaining. And you can forget justifying yourself if you collected most of your stuff from either a garage sale or the bargain basement. It's easier that way. You *look* more spiritual whether you are or not. Being outstanding arouses suspicion, being average doesn't. As Elbert Hubbard once said, "To mediocrity, genius is unforgivable."

Remember now, I said there are some wonderful exceptions . . . but they seem so rare. At times I guess I get a little impatient about there being so few graceful and elegant swans to beautify the landscape and make the lake more appealing. If there were, I think we'd find ourselves with more visitors and tourists than we'd know what to do with.

COME ASIDE

Look at the past (in Psalm 48) and at the future (in Revelation 21:10-27) to see how "class" is part of God's design for His dwelling place.

And what about the present? How can you be a partner with the Lord in a pursuit of excellence and a commitment to beauty?

Make it clear!

One of the toughest assignments in life is to communicate clearly what happened during a time when emotions are high. People who "fall in love" can hardly describe it. Those who endure a calamity or experience a sudden loss often convey the information in a confused manner. The same is true in car accidents.

The following is a series of actual quotes taken from insurance or accident forms. They are the actual words of people who tried to summarize their encounters with trouble.

- ♦ "Coming home, I drove into the wrong house and collided with a tree I don't have."
- ♦ "The other car collided with mine without giving warning of its intentions."
- ♦ "I thought my window was down, but I found it was up when I put my hand through it."
- ♦ "I collided with a stationary truck coming the other way."
- ♦ "A truck backed through my windshield into my wife's face."
- ♦ "A pedestrian hit me and went under my car."
- ♦ "The guy was all over the road; I had to swerve a number of times before I hit him."
- ♦ "I pulled away from the side of the road, glanced at my mother-in-law, and headed over the embankment."
- ♦ "In my attempt to kill a fly, I drove into a telephone pole."
- ♦ "I had been shopping for plants all day and was on my way home. As I reached an intersection, a hedge sprang up obscuring my vision. I did not see the other car."
- ♦ "I had been driving for forty years when I fell asleep at the wheel and had an accident."
- ♦ "I was on the way to the doctor's with rear end trouble when my universal joint gave way, causing me to have an accident."
- ♦ "To avoid hitting the bumper of the car in front, I struck the pedestrian."
- ♦ "As I approached the intersection, a stop sign suddenly appeared in a place where no stop sign had ever appeared before. I was unable to stop in time to avoid the accident."
- ♦ "My car was legally parked as it backed into the other vehicle."
- ♦ "An invisible car came out of nowhere, struck my vehicle, and vanished."

- "I told the police that I was not injured, but removing my hat, I found I had a skull fracture."
- "The pedestrian had no idea which direction to go, so I ran over him."
- "I was sure the old fellow would never make it to the other side of the road when I struck him."
- "I saw the slow-moving, sad-faced old gentleman as he bounced off the hood of my car."
- "The indirect cause of this accident was a little guy in a small car with a big mouth."
- "I was thrown from my car as it left the road. I was later found in a ditch by some stray cows."
- "The telephone pole was approaching fast. I attempted to swerve out of its path when it struck my front end."
- "I was unable to stop in time and my car crashed into the other vehicle. The driver and passenger then left immediately for a vacation with injuries."

Aren't those unbelievable!

And yet, one amazing fact is that each report was made by some sincere, serious individual who tried his or her best to be clear and concise. Emotions have a way of smearing the lens of logical thinking and precise communication.

It happens to us as Christians when we express our faith—how we were born from above and became new creatures in Christ. As non-Christians strain to follow our words, I wonder how many of them must wonder what the religious gobblydegook is all about. We think we're clear, but we're not . . . as we toss around terms familiar only to the "in" group, in phrases foreign to those in the world system (and then blame *them* for not being interested!).

Our secret language calls for a decoding process they aren't equipped to handle. How much better to talk in a plain, concrete, believable manner so the Spirit of God has the ammunition needed to complete the task!

What is it Peter advises? "Be ready at all times to answer anyone who asks you to explain the hope you have" (1 Peter 3:15 GNB).

Take that assignment from God. Be ready! See if you can write out in one, nontechnical, cliché-free paragraph about the hope within you. Your salvation experience. Or—how any person can know God in a meaningful and intimate way.

Jesus took on this challenge when He spoke with a Jewish judge named Nicodemus. And if you remember, even though our Lord was painfully simple and the rabbi was awfully bright, the man still struggled as he tried to track Christ's words. Believe me—combating confusion is quite an assignment, especially when the emotions of the heart cloud the expressions of the mouth.

It's not just that many have never heard. It's that they *have* heard . . . and have been blown away by our verbiage.

Our job? Make it clear!

COME ASIDE

Before writing out that personal evangelistic paragraph, examine Paul's words to the men of Athens in Acts 17:22-31 to see how concise and precise his speaking was at this crucial time.

FALLIBILITY

ver since I was knee-high to a gnat, I have been taught and have believed in the infallibility of Scripture. Among the upper echelons of doctrinal truths, this one ranks alongside the Godhead, the deity of Christ, and salvation by grace. We may fuss around with a few of the events in God's eschatological calendar or leave breathing room for differing opinions regarding angels and local church government. But when the subject turns to infallibility, the inerrancy of Holy Writ, I'm convinced there's no wobble room. Can't be. Take away that absolute and you've opened an unpluggable hole in your theological dike. Given enough time and pressure, it wouldn't be long before everything around you would get soggy and slippery. Make no mistake about it, the infallibility of Scripture is a watershed issue.

But wait . . . let's stop right there when it comes to infallibility. Before I make my point, allow me to quote Webster's definition:

> "Incapable of error . . . not liable to mislead, deceive, or disappoint."

While that is certainly true of Scripture, it is *not* true of people. When it comes to humanity, fallibility is the order of the day. Meaning what? Just this: There is not one soul on this earth who is incapable of error, who is free from fault, who is unable to make mistakes, who is absolutely and equivocally reliable. Can't be. Depravity mixed with limited knowledge and tendencies to misunderstand, misread, misquote, and misjudge should keep all of us free from two very common mistakes: first, deification of certain individuals (including ourselves); and second, disillusionment when we discover fault and mistakes in others.

Just as biblical infallibility assures us that each page is incapable of error or deception, fallibility reminds us that each person is capable of both. The implications are equally clear. When it comes to the Bible, keep trusting. When it comes to people, be discerning.

This includes *all* people. A chapter isn't long enough to complete a list, so I'll be painfully general and mention one group. I choose this group only because it's the one we tend not to question: those professionals whom we trust with our bodies, minds, and souls—namely, physicians, psychologists, and pastors. What influence these men and women possess! What good they do! How necessary they are! Most of us, if asked to name ten people we admire and appreciate the most, would include two or three from this category. How gracious of God to give us such splendid individuals to help us through this vale of tears! Yet each one has something in common with everyone else—*fallibility*. Those whom we most admire remind us of that from time to time; nevertheless, everything in us cries out to resist such reminders. Of the three, I believe it is the minister whom people tend most to pedestalize.

It is certainly an unscriptural practice. The Berean believers are commended for listening to Paul, then ". . . examining the Scriptures daily, to see whether these things were so" (Acts 17:11). Apollos and Paul are referred to merely as "servants through whom you believed" (1 Corinthians 3:6) and later given a rather insignificant place:

> So then neither the one who plants nor the one who waters is anything, but God who causes the growth (1 Corinthians 3:7).

It's easy to forget all that, especially in a day when we *hunger* for spiritual leaders whom we can respect and follow. And then—glory!—we come across some whose lives are admirable, whose leadership seems to be blessed of God, and whose instruction is biblical, wise, and dynamic. Everything's great until one such individual teaches something that is different from another minister who is equally admired. That never fails to leave groupies in a confused tailspin.

This is a good time to consider the sage counsel of Bernard Ramm:

> How do we settle the truth when two people of equal piety and devotion have different opinions? Does the Holy Spirit tell one person the Rapture is pre-tribulation, and another that it is post-tribulation? The very fact that spiritually minded interpreters come to different conclusions about these matters distresses many people's minds. They have presumed that if a man is yielded to the Holy Spirit, his interpretations must be correct.

> But certain things must be kept in mind. First, the Holy Spirit gives *nobody* infallible interpretations. Second, piety is a help to interpretation, but it is not a substitute for knowledge or study or intelligence. Third, all of us are still in the human body and subject to its limitations and frailties . . . we make mistakes of interpretation in Scripture as well as errors in judgment in the affairs of life.

> It is the present temptation of at least American evangelicalism to substitute a class of devout Bible teachers for the Catholic Pope. To such people the *meaning* of Scripture is that which their favorite Bible teacher teaches. But the

Protestant principle must always be this: *The truest interpretations are those with the best justification.*

I could just as easily have used an illustration regarding a physician's diagnosis or a therapist's counsel. The issue is identical, and it brings us back to where we started. If I could change a term and put it in the language of a famous historical document: All men are created fallible. Yes, all. If you remember that, you'll have fewer surprises and disappointments, greater wisdom, and a whole lot better perspective in life. Rather than slumping into cynicism because your hero showed feet of clay, you'll maintain a healthy and intelligent objectivity. You'll be able to show respect without worshiping. And when you really need to know the truth, you'll turn to the Scriptures with firsthand confidence.

If you're looking for infallibility, look no further than God's Word.

COME ASIDE

Thank God for the infallibility of His Word as you review Psalm 119:89-96.

TEENAGE TURBULENCE

hile I was away for a couple weeks of vacation, one of the books I read was by David Elkind. You may remember that name from his first work, *The Hurried Child,* a superb statement of concern regarding our tendency to rush our children to grow up fast rather than allowing them time simply to be children. As you might expect, his second volume, following on the heels of his first, addresses the subsequent social issue—the staggering number of teenagers who lack the adult guidance and support they need to make a healthy transition into adulthood. His choice of title is appropriate—*All Grown Up and No Place to Go.*

Dr. Elkind states:

> We are losing too many teenagers today. We are producing too many young people who may never be productive and responsible citizens, much less lead happy and rewarding lives. When fifty percent of our youth are at one or another time abusing alcohol or drugs, then something is seriously wrong with our society.

With intelligence, boldness, and clarity, he goes to the heart of the issue and addresses the breakdown of parental security and stability. Awash in the tide of social change and absorbed in their own voyage, seeking self-fulfillment and personal discovery, parents are often so overwhelmed that they have only minimal energy to invest in their teenager's struggles. And when you add the fact that today's parents are caught in the crossfire of social philosophies, moral standards, and conflicting value systems, even committed and well-meaning parents (especially those who desire to lead with fairness and tolerance) often lack the decisiveness teens need and expect.

Again, I quote:

> Caught between two value systems, parents become ambivalent, and teenagers perceive their ambivalence as license. Failing to act, we force our teenagers to do so, before they are ready. Because we are reluctant to take a firm stand, we deny teenagers the benefit of our parental concern and we impel them into premature adulthood. We say, honestly, "I don't know," but teen-agers hear, "They don't care."

As a father who has reared two teenagers and is currently neck deep in the lives of two more, I am naturally interested in any reliable and insightful counsel to help make this journey as wise yet pleasant as possible. While I may not applaud everything Elkind suggests, I do find his words provocative. His ideas become tasty food for thought.

While chewing on and digesting them yesterday, I was struck with an interesting analogy between today's teenagers and adolescent Christians. By that I mean a believer who is somewhere between childhood and adulthood. It's impossible to measure this individual by years—some Christians are in their teens two years after conversion, others aren't there until they've been in God's family for twenty years or more. But it seems that all who press on to maturity must endure such a turbulent passage.

It's tough enough to cope with the changes and handle the peer pressure and make more right decisions than wrong ones during those impressionable years . . . but could it be that the thing that complicates matters most is the ambivalence of those who are supposed to be the models? Perhaps the lack of stability, integrity, and decisiveness within the ranks of leadership causes many a Christian in the turbulent teen years to misread the signals and conclude, "They don't care."

I am just about convinced that it is the teenaged believer, struggling to reach a measure of spiritual equilibrium, who becomes the most disillusioned when one of his or her "spiritual parents" defects or lives hypocritically. No wonder Jesus assaulted the Pharisees! And that explains His eloquent warning about hanging a millstone around the neck of adults who cause those who are growing to stumble. I always wondered why He spoke those words with such severity. The reason is obvious. Stumbling, disillusioned believers in the fragile teen years easily lose their way en route to adulthood.

Maybe that's why there are so many in the "Family" who find themselves all grown up with no place to go.

COME ASIDE

Growing young Christians are watching you!

So how much stability, integrity, and decisiveness are you demonstrating?

Look over the apostle Paul's intense words in 2 Corinthians 11 and 12. Then, when you're able, pray with a longing heart that your own character will match the depth and strength of Paul's, by the grace of God.

THE SMALL STUFF

on't sweat the small stuff."

You've heard it. You've said it. You meant well, of course. Your motive was pure and your tone was right. In front of you was a duke's mixture of frustration, guilt, perfectionism, and low self-esteem all wrapped up in skin. Humanity at wit's end. Maybe it was your daughter or son . . . perhaps a friend, your mate, a pupil, a colleague, a parent.

Somebody said that to me the other day. It helped . . . momentarily. I needed reality's nudge. Being casual on the outside but a fairly thorough and disciplined soul within, I sometimes need to be reminded that few people will even notice the thing I'm camping on. Or care, for that matter. So? So sweating the small stuff can occasionally be a drag.

But there's another side to that coin. Greatness and the attention to detail, in my opinion, are welded together. A great piece of music is like that—carefully arranged orchestration carrying out a majestic melody with the whole sound of harmony. Haunting chords, rhythm, and lyrics. The choral group that performs is also committed to the fine line. Not much room for "Don't sweat the small stuff" philosophy.

A great piece of writing is equally a masterpiece of detail. Phrases are turned. Words are chosen, shaped, sometimes chiseled so as to dovetail into the precise meaning or description the author requires. And behind such exactness, such literary beauty? Sweat. Trust me, a lot of sweat. Because great writing, like great music, comprises not only sweeping, broad-brush scenes but also small stuff, which takes time . . . so very much time.

Great artwork is the same. Look at the masters. Observe the choice of colors, the texture, the shading. Study the lines on that ton of white marble to which Michelangelo once put his hands. Those fluid lines in David's form don't just happen to flow. It's no accident that you're surprised to find the stonework cold to the touch. Something *that* real is supposed to have warm blood in it. Why? Because the Italian genius labored long hours over the small stuff. Something inside his head could settle for nothing less.

A solid biblical basis for such an emphasis on quality is not hard to find. Consider the superb manner in which the tabernacle was designed and constructed. Next, the temple built under Solomon . . . with its "windows with artistic frames," elaborate beams, winding stairways, gold-covered cherubim, and "stone prepared at the quarry" so that "neither hammer nor axe nor any iron tool [would be] heard in the house while it was being built" (1 Kings 6:4-8, 28).

The name of God was exalted as people witnessed such detailed beauty. It still is.

What is true of grand music, great writing, priceless art, and quality construction is also true of the way some still practice medicine or law, do their architectural drawings, teach their students, type their letters, preach their sermons, play their instruments, cook meals, fix cars, coach teams, sell insurance, run a business, a home, a school, a restaurant, or a ministry. It makes them stand out in bold relief . . . clearly a cut above the average. It's not for the money or for the glory or for the fame it may bring. It's simply a matter of deep-seated personal pride and commitment. Nothing less satisfies. It all boils down to fine, rare, quality craftsmanship. Or as the *Wall Street Journal* recently called it, *Workmanship.*

Your true
value to
society
comes when
someone says,
"Let me see
your work."
Your glib
tongue may
open a door
or two and your
artful use of
the right fork
may win
an approving nod.
But the real
test of
your worth
can be measured
by the care
you give
to the job
in front of you:
A budget to plan;
A solo to play;
A report to draft;
A leaky sink that
needs fixing.
Next time you write

a memo, make
sure you get all
the facts straight.
Pay attention to
those details.
Sweat the
small stuff.

COME ASIDE

Decide now to do something special in the next twenty-four hours—something no one may ever notice except you and your Creator—in which you can demonstrate high-quality workmanship.

While you're deciding what to do, read with reverence the first chapter of Genesis—and think about *workmanship*.

THE LEGAL SWAMP

aw never fails to turn me off.

Don't get me wrong. It's not that I don't think we need it . . . it's just that it leaves me cold. It frowns and demands. It requires and warns and threatens. With a grim glare, it dares us to forget its rules or even *think* about disobeying its regulations.

I know, I know. It protects us. It gives us a recourse when we've been assaulted or abused. It's the ultimate big stick we can wave in the face of an adversary. "I'll sue!" has therefore become our favorite national slogan, which fits perfectly into our me-ism society.

"I've got my rights."
"I've got it coming to me."
"I don't have to take that from you."

Those are the overused words of our overkill generation. Parents are now being sued by their children. Teachers are being sued by their pupils. Coaches are being sued by their players. States are being sued by homosexual lovers. Spouses are being sued by their partners, and it isn't limited to unbelievers. Christians are now neck deep in the legal swamp. Christian neighbors sue each other. Christian faculty members are now filing suit against the administrations of Christian schools. Churches not only sue one another, congregations now sue their pastors—and vice versa. Parishioners who have complaints about the counseling they received from their ministers are turning to the courts to voice their anger and to seek a financial settlement.

Yes, you read that correctly. Brothers and sisters in the family of God are actually pressing charges and demanding their rights . . . sometimes to the exclusion of any attempt to reconcile face to face. You'd think 1 Corinthians 6:1-8 is either written in hieroglyphics or is no longer considered part of the biblical text. I couldn't help smiling when I recently came across a cartoon in a popular religious magazine. A vocalist is standing beside a piano. With a microphone in hand and his accompanist ready to begin, he precedes his solo with these words:

"I'd like to share a song with you that the Lord gave me a year ago . . . and even though He did give it to me, any reproduction of this song in any form without my written consent will constitute infringement of the copyright law which grants me the right to sue your pants off . . . praise God. . . ."

Don't think I'm naive enough to believe we Christians don't need law or that we never have reason to complain . . . or that I'm blinded to the fact that there are rip-off con men—wolves in sheep's clothing—who prey on and exploit flocks. We must be discerning, alert, ever mindful that human depravity must be held in check, and on occasion it must be exposed. But the way we go about it, the spirit with which we handle our conflicts, the attitudes we exhibit while working through the process of reconciliation is crucial . . . *that* is where our Christianity is often hung out to dry.

What's worse is that we choose to press the issue from a strictly legal standpoint. Even if we win the case, we don't walk away humble and grateful. We walk away proud—and even bitter. Why? Because we "got what we had coming to us . . . we got what we deserved."

It occurred to me recently (thanks to an insightful message I heard from my friend, Ray Stedman) that when people receive what they deserve, they are robbed of the joy of gratitude. Instead of being humbly thankful, they are either resentful that they didn't get more (or they didn't get it sooner) *or* they are arrogant because they got their way. And have you noticed? Joy is absent. From start to finish the process is a grim, bitter, analytical battle of wills. And even when it ends—the offense is still there. Unsmiling, untouching, and unyielding, each side walks away. There may be momentary mirth as the "spoils of victory" are divided, but while the head swells, the heart hardens.

Do you know what process God prefers? Have you considered lately what He says about the right way to resolve our disputes? Do you want to know His plan for healing offenses? Allow me:

> Does any one of you, when he has a case against his neighbor, dare to go to the law before the unrighteous, and not before the saints? . . . If then you have law courts dealing with matters of this life, do you appoint them as judges who are of no account in the church? I say this to your shame. Is it so, that there is not among you one wise man who will be able to decide between his brethren, but brother goes to law with brother, and that before unbelievers? Actually, then, it is already a defeat for you, that you have lawsuits with one another. Why not rather be wronged? Why not rather be defrauded? On the contrary, you yourselves wrong and defraud, and that your brethren (1 Corinthians 6:1, 4-8).

> And as for those who try to make your life a misery, bless them. Don't curse, bless. Share the happiness of those who are happy, and the sorrow of those who are sad. Live in harmony with each other. Don't become snobbish but take a real

> interest in ordinary people. Don't become set in your own opinions. Don't pay back a bad turn by a bad turn, to anyone. See that your public behaviour is beyond criticism. As far as your responsibility goes, live at peace with everyone. Never take vengeance into your own hands, my dear friends (Romans 12:14-19a Phillips).

> Let there be no more bitter resentment or anger, no more shouting or slander, and let there be no bad feeling of any kind among you. Be kind to each other, be compassionate. Be as ready to forgive others as God for Christ's sake has forgiven you (Ephesians 4:31-32 Phillips).

What a radical approach, but what a superior plan! Now it won't come naturally nor can it be implemented with a stubborn will and a proud spirit. Unselfishness must prevail on both sides . . . a willingness to listen, to negotiate, to yield, to confess, to forgive, to submit, to release, to forget, then to go on. Really, to allow the other person to have something he or she does not deserve. Tough, huh?

But, you see, that's what brings about the joy of gratitude . . . receiving what we *don't* deserve. When that happens, humility replaces pride. A thankful spirit cancels out arrogance. Mercy flies in the face of resentment. Rights are much less important in light of a healed relationship. Why? Simply because somebody received what wasn't deserved.

It's called grace.

COME ASIDE

Meditate—with a fresh willingness to obey—on 1 John 3:16-18.

Remembering names

emembering is a skill. Sure, there are those who have been blessed with a good memory . . . such as:

Napoleon—who knew thousands of his soldiers by name . . . or

James A. Farley—who claimed he knew 50,000 people by their first name . . . or

Charles Schwab—who knew the names of all 8,000 of his employees at Homestead Mill . . . or

Charles W. Eliot—who, during his forty years as president of Harvard, earned the reputation of knowing all the students by name *each year* . . . or

Harry Lorayne—who used to amaze his audiences by being introduced to hundreds of people, one after another, then giving the name of any person who stood up and requested it.

But these, remember, are exceptions—phenomenal exceptions. As I first stated, however, remembering is a skill, like speaking in public, singing, reading, thinking, or swimming. We improve at a skill by hard work, direct effort applied with a good deal of concentration, mixed with proper know-how. It would be safe to say that people with remarkable memories developed them because of a driving need or desire.

One of the most glaring weaknesses we often confess is in the realm of remembering names. We excuse it by saying: "I'm not good at remembering names!" or "Your face is familiar, but what was that name?" I suppose that's better than: "Your breath is familiar, but not your name."

But I'm afraid we have begun to believe something that isn't true as we make our excuses. The fact is . . . you *can* remember names! Except for a very few, rare cases, anybody can remember anybody.

The secret lies in that very brief period of time we stand face to face with another person—in fact, the most important person in your life at that moment. You see, that momentary encounter has been directed by God. He has arranged two lives so that they cross at His prescribed time—so you can be sure that the meeting is significant. So is the name! *How* you fit the name with the face—and cement both together in your memory bank—is of crucial importance.

But before I go into that, I must again emphasize the proper mental attitude we should have to begin with. Remind yourself at each introduction and handshake:

This person is important (because he or she is!).
God has arranged our meeting (because He has!).

Okay . . . there you stand, getting introduced. Zero in first on one major thing—*the name*, nothing else for a few seconds. Ignore all distractions and peripheral activity. Listen for one thing, *the name*. That is your goal, after all. Now then, I'll pass on a simple little process that works for me. It is not original with me, but I have found that it is successful when I concentrate. Three steps are involved in the process of cementing a name and the face into my mind:

1. *Impression*. Allow the name to make an impression—a dent—on your mind. Do this by being sure you have heard the name correctly. Repeat it. If necessary, spell it to the person, asking if that is the correct spelling. As you shake hands and talk for a few moments, picture the name in your mind. Secure the exact pronunciation.

2. *Association*. Here's where the fun comes. Think of an association you can link with the name. Visualize the name and think of something that sounds like it or rhymes with it. The crazier the better! Mr. Steinhaus ("stone house"). Frank Baer ("he's a big and hairy fella"). The Haughtons (they seem "haughty"). John Lincoln ("he is tall like President Lincoln"). Marlene Moody ("she is sad-looking . . . moody"). Ed Neuenschwander ("how can I forget a name like that?").

3. *Repetition*. As you talk together, use the person's name frequently in the conversation. You might introduce the individual to others in the group, and again distinctly repeat the name.

This is no guarantee . . . in fact, it may even backfire on you at times. But more often than not it will enable you to grab the other person's handle at that moment of panic when the two of you meet *again*.

Maybe you're thinking, "A name isn't that important . . . what I'm interested in is his soul." Listen—one of the keys that unlocks a person's soul is his realization that you are interested enough in him to call him *by name*! Furthermore, the Bible is filled with thousands of people who had names . . . and those names often had associated meanings: *Simon*—later *Peter* . . . *Jacob* —later *Israel* . . . *Saul*—later *Paul*. And what about the angel's firm command, "You shall call His name Jesus . . ." (Savior).

When the eternal books are open, earthly names will be read (Revelation 20:15; 21:27). When we are ushered into heaven, new names will be given to each one (Revelation 2:17).

If the Lord thinks enough of our names to write every one of them in His record, is it asking too much to learn a few as we travel here below? Of course this means that we must consider the other person important enough to remember. If you struggle with *that* you have a problem far more serious than a faulty memory!

COME ASIDE

Read Matthew 18:1-5, weighing carefully verse 5. How could these words from Jesus help you follow the three steps of *impression, association,* and *repetition* in remembering people's names?

Starting Over

nstant replays have become old hat. We now expect them in all televised sports. Whether it's a tennis pro's impressive backhand or an NBA center's slam dunk or a heavyweight boxer's smashing jab, we never have to worry about missing it the first time around. It'll be back again and again and probably *again*.

It occurred to me recently that I'd enjoy (for lack of a better title) *delayed* replays of some of the more significant times in my life. But these would be different from fixed frames on film. In "delayed replays" I'm fantasizing the possibility of going back and being given another chance to relive a particular experience that could have been handled differently. More wisely. With greater tact. In better taste. You know, all those "if-I-had-that-to-do-over-again" thoughts. What a second chance that would be!

Just think of all the things we'd refrain from saying that we blurted out the first time around. And consider the different attitudes we would have toward unexpected interruptions, unplanned babies, unrealistic expectations, unimportant details. I really think we would take a lot more things a lot less seriously, don't you?

Fun times form great memories . . . so let's hear it for fewer frowns and more smiles. Laughter lingers. It soaks into the walls of a home, coming back to encourage us many years later.

Bob Benson captures all this so well in his piece, "Laughter In the Walls."

> I pass a lot of houses on my way home—
> some pretty,
> some expensive,
> some inviting—
> but my heart always skips a beat
> when I turn down the road
> and see my house nestled against the hill.
> I guess I'm especially proud
> of the house and the way it looks because
> I drew the plans myself.
> It started out large enough for us—
> I even had a study—
> two teenaged boys now reside in there.
> And it had a guest room—
> my girl and nine dolls are permanent guests.

It had a small room Peg
had hoped would be her sewing room—
two boys swinging on the dutch door
have claimed this room as their own.
So it really doesn't look right now
as if I'm much of an architect.
But it will get larger again—
one by one they will go away
to work,
to college,
to service,
to their own houses,
and then there will be room—
for just the two of us.
But it won't be empty—
every corner
every room
every nick
in the coffee table
will be crowded with memories.
Memories of picnics,
parties, Christmases,
bedside vigils, summers,
fires, winters, going barefoot,
leaving for vacation, cats,
conversations, black eyes,
graduations, first dates,
ball games, arguments,
washing dishes, bicycles,
dogs, boat rides,
getting home from vacation,
meals, rabbits, and
a thousand other things
that fill the lives
of those who would raise five.
And Peg and I will sit
quietly by the fire
and listen to the
laughter in the walls.

Yes, if we had the benefit of "delayed replays," we would gain a lot of
perspective on life we often miss the first time around.

But unfortunately, second times around don't happen. We cannot re-
rear our children. I cannot re-pastor my first church. Initial impressions

cannot be remade. Cutting remarks cannot be re-said. Scars can't be completely removed. Tear stains on the delicate fabric of our emotions are, more often than not, permanent. Memories are fixed, not flexible.

"You mean God won't forgive?"

You know better than that.

"And people can't overlook my failures?"

Come on, now. That's not the issue at all. Most people I know are amazingly understanding. Our biggest task is forgiving *ourselves*.

The main message is clear: Think before you speak. Pause before you act.

Another chance? No chance. It's absolutely impossible to go back and start over. Today is tomorrow's yesterday . . . and "delayed replays" will never occur. Today is memory in the making, a deposit in the bank of time. Let's make it a good one!

In the now-or-later battle for priorities, it's clear where the secret lies. Let's take care of the biggies now—today. It's amazing how the incidentals will fade away when we focus fully on the essentials. And that's impossible unless we put the important ahead of the urgent.

Tell me, what will be yesterday's replays in the tomorrows of your life? The answer is not that complicated. They will be the things your "walls" are absorbing today.

COME ASIDE

Fix your thoughts for a while on the handful of priorities presented in 1 Peter 4:7-11. How well are you doing?

here are two extreme tests that disturb our balance in life. Each has its own set of problems. On one side is *adversity*. Solomon realized this when he wrote:

If you faint in the day of adversity, your strength is small   (Proverbs 24:10 MLB).

The *Good News Bible* paraphrases that verse:

If you are weak in a crisis, you are weak indeed.

Adversity is a good test of our resiliency, our ability to cope, to stand back up, to recover from misfortune. Adversity is a painful pedagogue.

On the other side is *prosperity*. In all honesty, it's a tougher test than adversity. The Scottish essayist and historian, Thomas Carlyle, agreed when he said:

Adversity is hard on a man, but for one man who can stand prosperity, there are a hundred that will stand adversity.

Precious few are those who can live in the lap of luxury . . . who can keep their moral, spiritual, and financial equilibrium . . . while balancing on the elevated tightrope of success. It's ironic that most of us can handle a sudden demotion much better than a sizable promotion.

Why?

Well, it really isn't too difficult to explain. When adversity strikes, life becomes rather simple. Our need is to survive. To make it through the night. But when prosperity occurs, life gets complicated. Our needs become numerous and often extremely complex. Invariably, our integrity is put to the test. And there is about one in a hundred who can dance to the tune of success without paying the piper named Compromise.

Now, before we get too carried away, let's understand that being successful isn't necessarily wrong. Being promoted, being elevated to a place of prominence can come from God Himself.

For not from the east, nor from the west, nor from the desert comes exaltation; but God is the Judge; He puts down one, and exalts another (Psalm 75:6-7).

Asaph, the guy who wrote those words, was correct. It is the sovereign right to demote as well as to promote . . . and we seldom know why He chooses whom.

Any biblical proof that some have been snatched from obscurity and exalted to prosperity without losing their integrity? Any examples of prosperous people who kept their balance while walking on the wire? Sure, several of them.

♦ *Joseph* was launched from a pit and a prison to the role of Egypt's prime minister (Genesis 41:42-43).
♦ *Daniel* was lifted from a lowly peon in a boot camp at Babylon to a national commander in charge of one-third of the kingdom (Daniel 6:1-2).
♦ *Amos* was promoted from a fig-picker in Tekoa, nothing more than an ancient sharecropper, to the prophet of God at Bethel, the royal residence of the king (Amos 7:14-15).
♦ *Job* was a rancher in Uz when God prospered him and granted him financial independence (Job 1:1-5).

And not one of the four lost his integrity in the process.

But the classic example is David, according to the last three verses of Psalm 78:

> He also chose David His servant, and took him from the sheepfolds; from the care of the ewes with suckling lambs He brought him, to shepherd Jacob His people, and Israel His inheritance. So he shepherded them according to the integrity of his heart, and guided them with his skillful hands.

As Jehovah scanned the Judean landscape in search of Saul's successor, He found a youth in his mid-teens who possessed a unique combination: the humility of a servant, the heart of a shepherd, and the hands of skill.

And by his thirtieth birthday, Jesse's youngest held the premier office in his nation. King. At his fingertips was a vast treasury, unlimited privileges, and enormous power.

And how did he handle such prosperity? Read that final verse again. He shepherded the nation "according to integrity." He was Carlyle's "one in a hundred."

Are you?

If so, when you give your word, you do it. Exactly as you said you would. Because integrity means you are verbally trustworthy.

Furthermore, when bills come due, you pay them. Because integrity means you are financially dependable. Also, when you're tempted to mess around with an illicit sexual affair, you resist. Because integrity means you are morally pure. You don't fudge because you're able to cover your tracks. Neither do you fake it because you're now a big shot. Being successful doesn't give anybody the right to call wrong right. Or the okay to say something's okay if it isn't okay.

Adversity or prosperity, both are tough tests on our balance. To stay balanced through prosperity—ah, that demands *integrity*. The swift wind of compromise is a lot more devastating than the sudden jolt of misfortune.

That's why walking on a wire is harder than standing up in a storm. Height has a strange way of disturbing our balance.

COME ASIDE

Read Deuteronomy 8 to uncover rich lessons about dealing with both adversity and prosperity.

Then, considering how life is going for you these days, decide which important truth in this passage you need most to remember now.

THE GIANT THAT SLEW DAVID

uring my days in New England, I heard of a teacher who quizzed a group of college-bound high school juniors and seniors on the Bible. The quiz preceded a *Bible as Literature* course he planned to teach at the Newton (Massachusetts) High School, generally considered one of the better public high schools in the nation. Among the most astounding findings he got in his replies from the students were:

Sodom and Gomorrah were lovers.
Jezebel was Ahab's donkey.
The four horsemen appeared on the Acropolis.
The New Testament gospels were written by Matthew, Mark, *Luther*, and John.
Eve was created from an apple.
Jesus was baptized by Moses.

Seriously! The answer that took the cake was given by a fellow who was in the top five percent of the graduating class, academically.

The question: *What was Golgotha?*

The answer: *Golgotha was the name of the giant who slew the apostle David.*

If it were not so pathetic, it would be hilarious. Isn't it amazing how pitifully illiterate John Q. Public is of the written Word of God? In a land filled with churches and chapels, temples and tabernacles, there is only an insignificant handful of fairly well-informed students of the Book of books. We have the Scriptures in hardback, paperback, cloth, and leather . . . versions and paraphrases too numerous to count . . . red-letter editions along with various sizes of print on the page . . . Bibles as big as a library dictionary and small as one frame of microfilm . . . yet the years roll by as one generation after another passes on its biblical illiteracy.

Our nation's technical knowledge and scientific expertise overshadow our grasp of Bible basics to an appalling degree. We are moving toward an era similar to the Dark Ages . . . when copies of the Scriptures were chained to the pulpit in the secret language of the clergy . . . when the public was kept stone ignorant of the life-changing teachings of the truth. But I see one great difference. In those days biblical ignorance was *forced* . . . in our day it is *voluntary*. Therein lies the saddest fact of all.

Upon whom do we rest the blame? Who deserves to have the finger of accusation pointed at him? Some would say the *seminaries* of America. Indeed, part of the problem does rest there. A few years ago a national periodical included an article that would verify this fact. It was entitled "The Startling Beliefs of Our Future Ministers," and it included the results of a survey taken among several major denominational seminaries. Some of the questions were answered like this:

Do you believe in a physical resurrection?	No—54%
Do you believe in the virgin birth of Christ?	No—56%
Do you believe in a literal heaven and hell?	No—71%
Do you believe in the deity of Christ?	No—89%
Do you believe that man is separated from God by birth (doctrine of depravity)?	Not concerned—98%
Do you believe in the second coming of Jesus Christ?	No—99%

If that survey indicates the heartbeat of the seminary scene, the pulse is dangerously weak. Thank God not all the seminaries were represented in this survey!

Others blame the *pulpits* of our land. That's possible, for a mist in the pulpit will invariably cause a fog in the pew. Far too many preachers are specializing in longhorn sermons—a point here and a point there with a lot of bull in between. During his days as associate professor of theology at New Orleans Seminary, Dr. Clark Pinnock illustrated this truth in a theological journal.

> The distinctive mark of theology in our day is its dreadful ambiguity. The chaos of American theology can be traced back to its roots in the rejection of biblical infallibility. . . . Preaching is not the act of unfolding our personal convictions. It is the duty of informing men of all that God has spoken. To move off from the pages of Scripture is to enter into the wastelands of our own subjectivity. . . . The Bible is a divinely provided map of the spiritual order. It contains the directions and markings to guide a person into reconciliation with God. The accuracy of a map is an important condition of its effectiveness. A distorted map can lead to shipwreck. . . .

Still others would blame this satanic, pressurized system we call the *world*—society—with its persuasive pleadings and so-called academic arguments against what is termed "a fanatical, foolish belief in the Bible." To embrace its truths, we have been told, is tantamount to committing intellectual suicide. The morticians promoting this lie have nothing to offer in its place beyond the grave, I might add, except a cold hole in the ground.

But in the final analysis, ignorance is a personal choice—*your choice.* If something is going to plug the dike, it will take *your* finger to stop the leak . . . and I mean fast.

COME ASIDE

See in Hosea 4:6 the tragic result when the leaders among God's people ignore His Word. Be warned!

IDOLS

t was the apostle John's final warning to his readers:

Little children, guard yourselves from idols (1 John 5:21).

"Watch out," says John. "Be on guard against anything that might occupy the place in your heart that should be reserved for God."

John never qualified that warning. The aged apostle deliberately refrained from classifying the idols or giving us a comprehensive list to follow. It's an unconditional command. *Any* idol, regardless of its beauty or usefulness or original purpose, is to be set aside so that Christ might reign supreme, without a single competitor.

I don't have many temptations to worship evil things. It's the *good* things that plague me. It isn't as difficult for me to reject something that is innately bad or wrong as it is to keep those good and wholesome things off the throne. That, I believe, is where the battle line begins.

Do you remember the experience of the Israelites in Numbers 21? They were hot and irritable as they wandered across the wilderness. They began to gripe about the lack of food and water. They complained again about the manna. So God sent snakes among them—"fiery serpents"—that bit many people and brought death into the camp. Realizing their sin, they begged Moses to ask God to remove the serpents. God told Moses to make a bronze serpent, hold it high up on a long pole . . . and whoever would look upon that bronze serpent would be healed. It was a miraculous, glorious provision—and it worked. In fact, Jesus mentioned it in John 3:14-15 as an example of what He would accomplish when He died on a cross. The bronze serpent had been blessed of God and was, therefore, an effective means of deliverance.

But do you know what happened to that metallic snake? If you don't, you're in for a big surprise. In 2 Kings 18:4 we read:

> He [King Hezekiah] removed the high places and broke down the sacred pillars and cut down the Asherah [idol altars]. He also broke in pieces the bronze serpent that Moses had made, for until those days the sons of Israel burned incense to it; and it was called Nehushtan.

This occurred about the sixth century B.C. The original event with the snakes took place much earlier—around 1450 B.C. For about *eight centuries* they had hung on to that bronze serpent. Can you believe that! They dragged it here and carried it there, preserved it, protected it, and polished it. Finally, they made an idol of it and even gave it a name: *Nehushtan*. That word simply means "a piece of bronze." And that's all it was. But they turned it into an object of worship. Something that had once been useful and effective had degenerated over the years into an idol.

It happens today. You can make an idol out of anything or anyone in life. A church building can become an idol to us, when all the while it is simply a place to meet and worship our Lord—nothing more. Your child can become your idol . . . in subtle ways you can so adore that little one that your whole life revolves around the child. Your mate or date can be given first place in your life and literally idolized. Your work can easily become your God . . . as can some pursuit in life. A house, a lawn, an antique, a car, a letter in sports, an education, a trip abroad, an achievement, and even that goal of "retirement" can so grip your heart that it becomes your Nehushtan.

Don't miss my point. There's nothing necessarily wrong with any of these good things. To possess them—any or all of them—is not sinful. But it is sinful when they *possess us!* Therein lies the difference. It's that sort of thing that turns a golden dream into a hollow chunk of bronze.

Honestly now . . . can you testify to the fact that you've destroyed the idols? Can you really say you are free from bronze anchors? That Christ reigns without a rival? Or would you have to admit to a personal shrine in your inner temple where you privately burn incense?

"Where your treasure is," says the Lord, "your heart is," and "out of the abundance of your heart, your mouth speaks." What does that actually mean? What you invest your time and treasure in, what you talk about, what you keep returning to in your mind reveals what's really on your heart. It's just that simple.

Your Lord and Savior wants to occupy first place. Matthew 6:33 says that when He *has* it, everything else will be added to you. How long has it been since you've enlisted your Lord's help in a private, personal temple-cleansing session? It's so easy to get attached to idols—good things, inappropriately adored. But when you have Jesus in the center of the room, everything else only junks up the decor.

"He is also head of the body, the church," wrote Paul, "and He is the beginning, the first-born from the dead; so that He Himself might come to have first place in everything" (Colossians 1:18).

Did you get that? First place in everything.

Everything.

COME ASIDE

Waste no time in asking God to help you realize and remove any idols that are usurping His place in your heart. Use Genesis 35:1-4 as an example to guide you through the cleansing process.

Then spend time in worship, meditating on Psalm 29.

OF PARROTS AND EAGLES

e are running shy of eagles and we're running over with parrots.

Content to sit safely on our evangelical perches and re-peat in rapid-fire falsetto our religious words, we are fast becoming overpopulated with bright-colored birds hav-ing soft bellies, big beaks, and little heads. What would help to balance things out would be a lot more keen-eyed, wide-winged creatures will-ing to soar out and up, exploring the illimitable ranges of the kingdom of God . . . willing to return with a brief report on their findings before they leave the nest again for another fascinating adventure.

Parrot people are much different than eagle thinkers. They like to stay in the same cage, pick over the same pan full of seeds, and listen to the same words over and over again until they can say them with ease. They like company, too. Lots of attention, a scratch here, a snuggle there, and they'll stay for years right on the same perch. You and I can't remember the last time we saw one fly. Parrots like the predictable, the secure, the strokes they get from their mutual admiration society.

Not eagles. There's not a predictable pinion in their wings! They think. They *love* to think. They are driven with this inner surge to search, to discover, to learn. And that means they're courageous, tough-minded, willing to ask the hard questions as they bypass the routine in vigorous pursuit of the truth. The whole truth. "The deep things of God"—fresh from the Himalayan heights, where the thin air makes thoughts pure and clear—rather than the tired, worn distillations of man. And unlike the intellectually impoverished parrot, eagles take risks getting their food because they hate anything that comes from a small dish of picked-over seeds . . . it's boring, dull, repetitious, and dry.

Although rare, eagles are not completely extinct in the historic skies of the church. Thomas Aquinas was one, as were Augustine and Bunyan, Wycliffe and Huss. So were G. K. Chesterton, C. S. Lewis, Robert Dick Wilson, J. Gresham Machen, W. R. Nicoll, and A. W. Tozer.

Many of the reformers qualify, as do John Newton, George Whitefield, and a long line of nonconformists—original thinkers whose lives were interwoven through the treasured tapestry of the seven-teenth, eighteenth, and nineteenth centuries.

And in our day? We could name some . . . but they are increasingly more rare as the "Entertain me" philosophy of the public outshouts those who plead, "Make me think!"

Too harsh? You decide. Who are the eagles today who offer fresh-from-the-mountain insights about world missions, biblical doctrines, evangelism, Christian education, apologetics, and the disciplines of the faith? Who are those who forge out creative ways of communicating the truths of Scripture . . . so that it's more than a hodge-podge of borrowed thoughts, rehearsals of the obvious which tend to paralyze the critical faculties of active minds?

Eagles are independent thinkers.

It's not that they abandon the orthodox faith or question the authority of God's inerrant Word . . . it's simply that they are weary of being told, "Stay on the perch and repeat after me." Eagles have built-in perspective, a sensitivity that leaves room for fresh input that hasn't been glazed by overuse.

I find myself agreeing with Philip Yancey, who admits:

> Reading religious books sometimes reminds me of traveling through a mile-long tunnel. Inside the tunnel, headlights provide the crucial illumination; without them I would drift dangerously toward the tunnel walls. But as I near the tunnel exit, a bright spot of light appears, which soon engulfs my headlights and makes them useless. When I emerge from the tunnel, a "check headlights" sign reminds me that I still have them on. In comparison to the light of day, they are so faint that I have lost awareness of them.
>
> Christian books are normally written from a perspective outside the tunnel. The author's viewpoint is already so flooded with light that he forgets the blank darkness inside the tunnel where many of his readers are journeying. To someone in the middle of the mile-long tunnel, descriptions of blinding light can seem unreal.
>
> When I pick up many Christian books, I get the same sensation as when I read the last page of a novel first. I know where it's going before I start. We desperately need authors with the skill to portray evolving viewpoints and points of progression along the spiritual journey as accurately and sensitively as they show the light outside the tunnel.

Yancey is saying we need "eagle writers" who come to their task with the abandonment of that keen-minded Jew from Tarsus. If you need an illustration, read Romans. Like a careful midwife, Paul assists in the birth of doctrine, allowing it to breathe and scream, stretch and grow, as God the Creator designed it to do. And he isn't afraid to say it for the first time, using a whole new vocabulary and style that is as original as it is accurate. There's not as much as a parrot feather on one page of that one-of-a-kind letter.

So then, which will it be? If you like being a parrot, stay put. But if you're an eagle at heart, what are you doing on that perch? Do you have any idea how greatly you're needed to soar and explore? Do you realize how out of place you are inside that cage? Even though others may not tell you, eagles look pretty silly stuck on a perch picking over a tasteless pile of dried seeds.

I've never heard anybody ask, "Eagle want a cracker?"

COME ASIDE

Dive into "the deep things of God" in Romans 6:1-14. Pore over it more carefully than you ever have before.

What possible difference in the rest of your life should these truths make—and what will you do to make it happen?

BEING WANTED

er voice was weak and fearful as she spoke to me over the phone. It was almost midnight and she kept apologizing . . . but she was so lonely and wanted someone to listen. I never got her name nor her address nor enough hints about her location to follow up our conversation. Her desperate story broke my heart. I actually wept after she said, "Goodbye—thanks for listening."

My anonymous friend wasn't wanted by her mother and dad when she was born. They placed her in a foster home and walked out of her life, leaving no clues of their whereabouts and no promise of their return. She went from home to home longing for the day when they would come back and want her and love her and accept her. *They never did*. Years passed. She became a teenage rebel—she lashed out at the world and then at herself by attempting suicide. Misery stalked her steps as she waited in vain for the return of her parents. Their absence became unbearable.

Suddenly she decided she would go and find *them*. She did! Through an incredible chain of events and so-called coincidences, she walked back into their lives one evening . . . but soon discovered she still wasn't wanted.

Her parents allowed her to stay for a while, but the relationship was forced and awkward. One morning they told her they had plans to start a new life. They were going to adopt a baby boy—and "start all over." Deep within her heart she longed to be included in that new beginning . . . but she was hesitant to push herself on them.

Reluctantly, she squeezed out the words: "I don't want to be in your way—perhaps it would be best if I were not around. Maybe I'd better leave."

To which her dad replied, "Okay, I'll help you pack." He hurriedly stuffed a few clothes into a backpack, rolled up a sleeping bag, attached it to the pack, then folded up a $10 bill and put it in her pocket. He then shook her hand, smiled, and waved goodbye.

Since that dark moment in her life, she's lived in the hills, walked the streets, slept in alleys, eaten out of garbage cans, and hunted unsuccessfully for work. Wanting neither pity nor a handout, she hung up the phone because she was cold in that phone booth and needed to find shelter before the police picked her up. I shall never forget her voice.

Somewhere at this very moment in this vast, impersonal, dangerous megalopolis called L.A. there is a girl who is confused, totally disillusioned about life . . . and terribly in need of *being wanted*.

If hers was the only story it would be tragic enough, but similar situations can be multiplied by the hundreds here in California alone. Chances are very good, in fact, that there are those in your church fellowship who feel unwanted, forgotten, unloved (and unlovely!)—and are more lonely than words can express. I wish to speak on their behalf and in their defense for a few brief moments.

Strange though it may seem, these are often the ones most difficult to love. Why? Because they *feel* unwanted, they are convinced that their lives are wasted, useless, and a bother. They wrestle with inferiority, thoughts of suicide, a twisted self-image, and a loss of self-respect. This results in all sorts of unattractive and unappealing responses. Since they entertain such a repulsive self-image, it is only natural that they *act* repulsively. This unpleasant lifestyle isolates them even more, of course, "confirming" their gutter-level opinion of themselves. What a sad, sad cycle!

Instead of loving these people, we usually label them.

Instead of caring, we criticize.

Instead of getting next to them, we react, we resent, we run.

Instead of "kissing the frog," we develop ways of poisoning it—or at best, ignoring it completely.

Consider a few suggestions which will help build needed bridges:

- ♦ Be positive rather than negative. When tempted to scowl, stop and think—"This person must really be hurting. I refuse to turn against him! Lord, how can I express Your love?"
- ♦ Be gracious rather than irritated. Remember that those surface characteristics are probably a cheap cover-up. To respond in grace and kindness will often unmask the "real person" down inside.
- ♦ Be creative rather than traditional. Look for new ways of reaching out and encouraging that person. Fight the old urge to reject and criticize. Go out of your way to show that you *really* care.
- ♦ Be available rather than distant. Open your heart *and your home*! Bridges aren't built with just a handshake at church or a smile as you get into your car after the service. Loving the unlovely takes time and effort. Availability is not optional, it's essential.

Scriptural justification for this? Yes, indeed. In fact, the entire New Testament is filled with such directives. Of course, it's easy to miss them when we are blinded by the most common disease known to man . . . selfishness.

COME ASIDE

Thoroughly consider all the instructions above, and use the well-known but much-ignored words in Matthew 25:34-40 to help you make your plans.

APPREHENSION

he scene is familiar: a hospital lobby with all the trimmings . . . soft sofas and folded newspapers . . . matching carpets and drapes illumined by eerie lighting . . . a uniformed lady at the desk weary from answering the same questions . . . strange smells . . . ash trays half full of half-finished smokes . . . and people.

Everywhere there are *people*. A steady stream pours in and out, the faces marked by hurry and worry. Surrounding me are small clusters of coffee-sipping groups talking quietly or looking into space, blinking often, lost in a world of their own anguish. Some sit alone, restlessly studying the same page of a paperback for ten minutes. A surgeon in faded green garb suddenly appears, bearing news to the waiting. Frowns cut in. Lips tighten. Heads shake. Tears flow. Everyone stares—momentarily identifying with the strangers. Soon it's quiet again, increased apprehension mounts . . . and life goes on.

If I were a bug on the wall of this sterile establishment, I'd remember other places I'd clung to in my insect excursions—other scenes of apprehension:

- ♦ in the classroom, observing the new teacher on her first attempt with junior high schoolers
- ♦ in the cramped study of the final-year med student as he crams the night before his orals
- ♦ in the airport as a dad waves goodbye to his son leaving for overseas duty
- ♦ in the nursery as an exhausted mother sits through the night beside a baby with a raging fever
- ♦ in the car traveling cross-country, moving a family to an unfamiliar neighborhood with unknown streets and untried challenges
- ♦ or in the store of a businessman, squeezed in the inflation vise, wondering how he'll make payroll on the first

Apprehension. It's as American as a Chevy V-8 or TV dinners. And it's strange. Apprehension is a notch or two above worry, but it feels like its twin. It isn't strong enough to be fear, but neither is it mild enough to be funny. It's in the category of a "mixed emotion."

In some ways, apprehension leaves you crippled, immobile. It's an undefined uneasiness—a feeling of uncertainty, misgiving, and unrest. What frustration is to yesterday, apprehension is to tomorrow.

Paul had it when he set his face toward the heavy horizon over Jerusalem. His admission is found in Acts 20:22:

"And now, behold, bound in spirit, I am on my way to Jerusalem, not knowing what will happen to me there."

A lot of emotion was packed into those twenty-one words. How did he feel? *Bound in spirit.* Why was he uneasy? *Not knowing what will happen to me.* That's apprehension. It's no sin, nor is it reason for embarrassment. It is, rather, proof positive that you're human. Unfortunately, it tends to smother your pleasant dreams by placing a pillow over your faith. Apprehension will strap a short leash on your vision and teach you to roll over and play dead when scary statistics and pessimistic reports snap their fingers.

Paul absolutely refused to run when apprehension whistled at him. Openly acknowledging its presence, he nevertheless stood his ground with the ringing words of Acts 20:24:

"But I do not consider my life of any account as dear to myself, in order that I may finish my course, and the ministry which I received from the Lord Jesus."

Apprehension is impressive until determination pulls rank on it and forces it to salute. This is especially true when determination has been commissioned by the King of kings.

COME ASIDE

We see Paul's determination expressed again in the familiar words of Philippians 3:7-15. Meditate on this passage, and be willing to ask God to show you anything you need for overcoming apprehension in your life.

CHEATING

entlemen:
Enclosed you will find a check for $150. I cheated on my income tax return last year and have not been able to sleep ever since. If I still have trouble sleeping I will send you the rest.
Sincerely,

This note was actually received by the I.R.S. some time ago. We chuckle because the sender was willing to be honest *up to a point* . . . just far enough to help relieve his guilty conscience . . . just far enough to help his sleep to return . . . but not far enough to make a clean break.

Philip Bailey, the nineteenth-century poet, once made this stabbing statement:

> The first and worst of all frauds is to cheat oneself. All sin is easy after that.

To cheat one's self. Really, that lies at the heart of *every* human act of deception. The traveling businessman who pads his account or misrepresents his production is cheating himself, not his company. The student who takes his exam in a dishonest fashion cheats himself, not his school. The wife who carries on an illicit affair with a secret lover isn't cheating on her husband but on herself. The salesman who violates the rights and confidence of others by withholding information or exaggerating beyond the truth is cheating himself, not the buyer. The writer who lifts the writings of another and inserts them into his own manuscript without giving professional credit cheats himself, not his reader.

Bailey suggests that such frauds tear so large a hole into our moral fiber that "all sin is easy after that." Bailey speaks the truth. Once we have opened the door to Bluebeard's secret chamber and begin to feel comfortable amidst the torture of a murdered conscience, we can easily handle anything our old nature comes up with.

Ask Adolf Eichmann. Once he learned to tolerate the starvation scenes of central Poland, the gas chambers of Dachau and Auschwitz were easy to handle. When you can starve a few Jews to death without feeling, it's no big thing to slaughter them by the millions.

Ask Spiro Agnew. Once he learned to live with himself as a mayor who compromised with close, rich friends of big business, the office of vice president didn't slow him down. Cheating on a small-time basis didn't stop when he got promoted . . . it accelerated.

The guy who has his hand in the petty cash today will be the crook in the books tomorrow. This is true, of course, unless he counteracts his dishonest bent.

God gives us the key in Ephesians 4:20-25 that unlocks the secret of overcoming our bent to cheat. After telling us the importance of laying aside the old self (which is corrupted with the "lusts of deceit"), He says we are to put on the new self—to let the renewed spirit of our minds take charge! And what is step one in that process? The twenty-fifth verse spells it out. The Living Bible says:

> Stop lying . . . tell the truth . . . !

Stop lying to yourself, first, then to others, second. Honestly admit that cheating is self-deception, that the biggest loss is suffered by *you*, not others. Refuse to rationalize or excuse or defend your cheating another day. And never forget that a person who hangs around Christians and looks the part of a dedicated saint can be a cheater right down to the core.

Judas is the classic example. He stole from his buddies even though they trusted him with the money (John 12:6). He was the one who bargained with Jesus' enemies and betrayed Him with a deceptive kiss. But the saddest fact of all is this—Judas cheated *himself*, not the Savior nor the disciples. The old English couplet is true:

> Still as of old, man by himself is priced; for thirty pieces,
> Judas sold himself, not Christ.

Having a problem sleeping because you are uneasy about your dishonesty? Wonderful! You ought to be glad you can't sleep. It's the cheater who *sleeps* who's really got a problem worth losing sleep over!

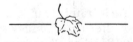

COME ASIDE

Learn everything you can from the example of Zacchaeus (in Luke 19:1-10) on how a man short on integrity finds it through Christ.

In what ways might God want you to follow this man's example?

KEEPING CONFIDENCES

an you keep a secret?

Can you? Be honest, now. When privileged information passes through one of the gates of your senses, does it remain within the walls of your mind . . . or is it only a matter of time before a leak occurs? When the grapevine requests your attention from time to time, do you refuse to help it climb higher, or do you encourage its rapid growth, fertilizing it by your wagging, unguarded tongue? When someone says, "Now this is confidential," do you respect their trust or ignore it . . . either instantly or ultimately?

The longer I live the more I realize the scarcity of people who can be fully trusted with confidential information. The longer I live the more I value those rare souls who fall into that category! As a matter of fact, if I were asked to list the essential characteristics that should be found in any member of a church staff or officer on a church board . . . the ability to maintain confidences would rank very near the top. No leader deserves the respect of the people if he or she cannot restrain information that is shared in private.

Our minds might be compared to a cemetery, filled with graves that refuse to be opened. The information, no matter how juicy or dry, must rest in peace in its coffin, sealed in silence beneath the epitaph "Shared in confidence—Kept in confidence."

A portion of the Hippocratic Oath, so familiar to the physician, comes to my mind:

> And whatsoever I shall see or hear in the course of my profession . . . if it be what should not be published abroad, I will never divulge, holding such things to be holy secrets.

You and I wouldn't give a plugged nickel for a doctor who ran off at the mouth. The same applies to a minister or an attorney or a counselor or a judge or a teacher or a secretary . . . or a close, trusted friend for that matter. No business ever grows and remains strong unless those in leadership are people of confidence. No school maintains public respect without an administration and faculty committed to the mutual guarding of one another's worlds. When leaks occur it is often a sign of character weakness and action is usually taken to discover the person who has allowed his mental coffin to be exhumed and examined.

Information is powerful. The person who receives it and dispenses it bit by bit often does so that others might be impressed because he or she is "in the know." Few things are more satisfying to the old ego than having others stare wide-eyed, drop open the jaw, and say, "My, I didn't know that!" or "Why, that's hard to believe!" or "How in the world did you find that out?"

Solomon writes strong and wise words concerning this subject in Proverbs. Listen to his counsel:

> Wise men store up knowledge,
> But with the mouth of the foolish, ruin is at hand (10:14).

> When there are many words, transgression is unavoidable,
> But he who restrains his lips is wise (10:19).

> He who goes about as a talebearer reveals secrets,
> But he who is trustworthy conceals a matter (11:13).

> The one who guards his mouth preserves his life;
> The one who opens wide his lips comes to ruin (13:3).

> He who goes about as a slanderer reveals secrets,
> Therefore do not associate with a gossip (20:19).

> Like a bad tooth and an unsteady foot
> Is confidence in a faithless man in time of trouble (25:19).

> Like a city that is broken into and without walls
> Is a man who has no control over his spirit (25:28).

From now on, let's establish four practical ground rules:

1. Whatever you're told in confidence, *do not repeat*.
2. Whenever you're tempted to talk, *do not yield*.
3. Whenever you're discussing people, *do not gossip*.
4. However you're prone to disagree, *do not slander*.

Honestly now, can you keep a secret? Prove it.

COME ASIDE

Discuss with the Lord those four practical ground rules, and be willing to commit yourself to following them.

Make Psalm 19:14 and Psalm 141:3 your prayer.

ULTIMATE REJECTION

 few years ago, on Valentine's day, a couple was enjoying a romantic drive along a wooded section near Belle Chasse, Louisiana. Something white, shimmering in the trees, caught their eyes. Their investigation led them to a dead teenager hanging from a limb, a white bedsheet knotted tightly around his neck. A farewell note, laced with despair, was near the trunk of the tree. It was addressed simply to "Mom and Dad."

> I never did develop into a real person and I cannot tolerate the false and empty existence I have created. . . . What frustrated me most in the last year was that I had built no ties to family or friends. There was nothing of lasting worth and value. I led a detached existence. . . . I am a bomb of frustration and should never marry or have children. It is safest to defuse the bomb harmlessly now . . . simply cremate me as John Doe.

Authorities circulated the youth's description and fingerprints to police across the country. He was later buried—unidentified and unclaimed.

Grim and gripping though they are, such scenes and words are not that unusual. Time once was when a minister dealt with self-inflicted deaths only once every six to eight years . . . now it's every six to eight *months*, and sometimes more than that. Our nervous age seems on trial for its life and the fuse on the powder keg is becoming shorter by the day!

Here are the facts—all of which can be documented. By the time you read them, the epidemic will be even more acute:

- Once every minute someone in the United States attempts suicide.
- Every day, seventy Americans take their own life . . . that's nearly three each hour—every day.
- In this country, there are twenty-four percent more deaths by suicide than by murder.
- In Los Angeles County, California, more people kill themselves than die in traffic accidents.
- Suicide is the number nine cause of adult death in the United States. For Americans between fifteen and thirty years of age, it is the number three cause of death . . . it is

the number two cause among teenagers.

♦ The suicide rate for Americans under thirty years of age has increased three hundred percent in the past decade.

♦ Until recently, women attempted suicide three times as often as men (but men succeeded three times more often).

♦ The latest statistics show a drastic increase in successful attempts by women—especially young black women.

♦ Four of five people who commit suicide have tried it previously. Unsuccessful attempters usually try again.

♦ Contrary to popular opinion, people who threaten suicide often mean it. The old myth "those who talk don't jump" is dangerously false. Threats should be taken seriously.

Suicide, the ultimate rejection of one's self, plays no favorites and knows no limit. In my files and memory are unforgettable cases that span the extremes: a successful banker, a disillusioned divorcee, a runaway, the son of a missionary, a mother of three, a wealthy cartoonist, a professional musician, several collegians, a Marine, a retired grandfather, a medical doctor, a middle-aged playboy, a brilliant accountant, a growing number of teens who were in junior and senior high schools. These individuals struggled with feelings of loneliness, worthlessness, insecurity, a lack of hope, intense perfectionism, alienation from meaningful relationships, and a tragic sense of feeling unloved and unlovely.

In all of this darkness there is one beacon of light. People considering suicide usually *want to be rescued.* They leave clues that read, "Help me!" They drop hints, consciously or unconsciously, that announce their intentions.

Sensitive, concerned observers ought to be alert to the signals. Here are a few : (1) talk about suicide; (2) a sudden change in personality; (3) deep depression; (4) physical symptoms—sleeplessness, loss of appetite, decreased sexual drive, drastic weight loss, repeated exhaustion; (5) actual attempts; and (6) crisis situations—death of a loved one, failure at school, loss of a job, marital or home problems, and a lengthy or terminal illness.

These, of course, are not "sure signs," but anyone that seems unusually suspicious warrants your time and offer of help. Occasionally, all that is needed is someone to step in and be a friend . . . a listening ear . . . a support to lean on . . . a shelter in the time of storm. That's Romans 15:1 in action. That's *genuine* Body life!

We who are strong ought to bear the weaknesses of those without strength.

Certainly you should contact your physician or ask advice from your local suicide prevention hot-line if you become reasonably concerned. A close friend, a professional counselor, a church officer, or a pastor might also be of valuable assistance. Don't hesitate to seek advice.

The need is urgent . . . and always great. During the time it took you to read this, seven people in America attempted to end their lives.

COME ASIDE

As you consider this need, look again to Jesus, in Matthew 12:15-21.

NVY

hakespeare called it "the green sickness." Bacon admitted "it has no holidays." Horace declared that "tyrants never invented a greater torment." Barrie said it "is the most corroding of the vices." Sheridan referred to it in his play *The Critic* when he wrote, "There is not a passion so strongly rooted in the human heart as this." Philip Bailey, the eloquent English poet of yesteryear, vividly described it as "a coal [that] comes hissing hot from hell."

And speaking of hell, no one has done a better job of portraying envy than Dante. In his *Purgatory*, you may recall, the envious sit like blind beggars by a wall. Their eyelids are sewed shut. The symbolism is apt, showing the reader that it is one of the blindest sins—partly because it is unreasonable, partly because the envious person is sewed up in himself. Swollen with poisonous thoughts. In a dark, constricting world of almost unendurable self-imposed anguish.

What exactly *is* envy? How does it differ from its twin, jealousy? Envy (the more sophisticated of the two) is a painful and resentful awareness of an advantage enjoyed by another . . . accompanied by a strong desire to possess the *same* advantage. Envy wants to have what someone else possesses. Jealousy wants to possess what it already has. Jealousy is coarse and cruel. Envy is sneaky and subtle. Jealousy clutches and smothers. Envy is forever reaching, longing, squinting, thinking (and saying) sinister insinuations.

When you stop and think about it, envy is the worse of the two. God declares several times that He is a "jealous God" . . . but not once does He admit envy.

Envy finds acceptable ways of expressing its resentment. One favorite method is the "but" approach. When I talk of someone I envy, I may say, "He is an excellent salesman, *but* he really isn't very sincere." Or "Yeah, she has a brilliant mind, *but* what a dull teacher!" Or "The man is an outstanding surgeon, *but* he doesn't mind charging an arm and a leg."

Another favorite avenue of expression envy enjoys to travel is the "reversal" approach. Someone does a good job and I cast a shadow over it by questioning the motive. An individual gives a truly generous gift, and we mutter, "He's obviously trying to make an impression." A Christian couple buys a new car and a few pieces of nice furniture. Watch out! There will be somebody who will squeeze out an envious comment like, "Well, they probably don't tithe. We'd have a lot more money to spend if we didn't tithe."

One wag wrote this doggerel:

> I hate the guys
> Who minimize and criticize
> The other guys
> Whose enterprise
> Has made them rise
> Above the guys who criticize.

The "unfavorable comparison" approach is equally cynical. The baritone does a commendable job on Sunday as an envious pew-sitter thinks, "Compared with Robert Hale, he's a dud." Or "If you think my neighbor has a nice lawn, you ought to take a drive out to Palos Verdes. Those places will make the Franklins' grass look like it has the mange!"

It's a curious fact that envy is a tension often found among professionals, the gifted, and the highly competent. You know, doctors, singers, artists, lawyers, business men and women, authors, entertainers, preachers, educators, athletes, politicians, and all public figures. Strange, isn't it, that such capable folks find it nearly impossible to applaud others in their own field who excel a shade or two more than they? Envy's fangs may be hidden, but take care when the creature coils . . . no matter how cultured and dignified it may appear.

Envy in Scripture? Look at the facts. It sold Joseph into slavery, drove David into exile, threw Daniel in the den, and put Christ on trial. (If you question that, better check Matthew 27:18.) Paul tells us that it's one of the prevailing traits of depravity (Romans 1:29), and a team member that plays in the same backfield with profanity, suspicion, and conceit (1 Timothy 6:4).

The answer? *Contentment.* Feeling comfortable and secure with where you are and who you are. Not having to "be better" or "go further" or "own more" or "prove to the world" or "reach the top" or . . .

Having some big struggles with envy? Eating your heart out because somebody's a step or two ahead of you in the race and gaining momentum? *Relax.* You are *you*—not them! And you are responsible to do the best you can with what you've got for as long as you're able.

Remember, the race isn't over. And even when it is, a lot of things you got hot and bothered about during your lifetime won't even show up in eternity. I don't care how many trophies or awards or dollars or degrees may be earned or won on earth, you can't take 'em with you. So it isn't worth the sweat. Death always cures "the green sickness."

COME ASIDE

Think about the ingredients for contentment implied in the famous Hebrew blessing in Numbers 6:24-26. How would you turn this passage into a prayer for yourself? Do that now.

ENCOUNTER ON THE DAMASCUS HIGHWAY

arious methods are employed to communicate the good news of Christ to the lost. Some of the approaches appear to be successful and effective on the surface, but underneath they leave much to be desired.

Take the *Redskin Approach*, for example. The philosophy behind this method is: *The more scalps, the better*. The major emphasis is numerical—telling the absolute maximum number of people every day about salvation, regardless. This approach is *decision centered* and little (if any) effort is directed toward follow-up or discipleship. Redskins aren't difficult to identify. They can usually be overheard counting (out loud) the scalps in their belts or seen shooting their flaming arrows into every wagon train they spot during the day or night.

The *Harvard Approach* is quite different. The thinking behind this method is: *Let's all discuss the world's religions*. Since it's *reason centered*, it attracts both genuine and pseudo-intellectuals. The modus operandi is invariably a vague discussion that shifts from Bahai to Buddhism . . . from the pros and cons of no prayer in public schools to the rapid growth of the Rajneeshies in the 80s. This approach is educational and occasionally quite stimulating, but it suffers from one mild drawback— no one ever gets saved! Specifics regarding salvation by grace through faith are frowned upon. The direct discussion of forgiveness of sins through Christ's blood at the cross and His miraculous resurrection is about as welcome in a sophisticated rap session on religion as a life-sized bust of Martin Luther would be in the Vatican.

Perhaps the most popular is the *Mute Approach*, which promotes: *I'm just a silent witness for God*. The best you can say about this method is that no one ever gets offended. That's for sure! The saint who settles for this *self-centered* approach could be tagged a Clairol Christian. No one knows for sure but God. Somewhere down the line this person has begun to swallow one of Satan's tastiest tidbits: "All God expects of you is a good, silent life. Others will ask you about Christ if they are interested in hearing." You know, I can count on one hand (and have fingers left over) the number of people in my entire life who have suddenly come up and asked me about Jesus Christ. While no one can discount the value of a godly life, that *alone* never brought anyone into the family of God. "Faith," please remember, "comes from hearing . . ." (Romans 10:17a).

I submit to you the *Philip Approach*. This *Christ-centered* method is set forth in a series of seven principles drawn from Acts 8:26-40. That grand and gifted gentleman was engaged in a city-wide crusade at Samaria. God was using him mightily (8:5-8). Suddenly the Lord spoke to Philip and instructed him to leave the city and spend some time in Gaza, a desert area (v. 26). Faithful Philip "arose and went . . ." (v. 27). He was *available* (Principle 1).

He then encountered a distinguished statesman from Ethiopia enroute back home via his chariot (v. 28). Of all things, he was reading Isaiah! The next verse tells us that the Spirit of God prompted Philip to go and get acquainted with the traveler. Philip was *led by the Spirit* (Principle 2). In today's terminology, he felt a keen and definite assurance that God would have him strike up a conversation and later, quite probably, share with that person the magnetic claims of Christ. In other words, he sensed that God was clearly opening the door.

As you'd expect, Philip cooperated. *Obedience* (Principle 3) is essential.

He then heard the man reading aloud (v. 30) and calmly asked, "Do you understand what you are reading?" What an excellent start! *A proper opening* (Principle 4) is essential. Philip didn't barge in and start preaching, nor did he crank out a canned, broken-record series of statements. He simply asked a logical, yet leading question. The statesman instantly invited the stranger to come and sit by him and assist him in his quest for understanding (vv. 31-34).

This remarkable response was met with great *tact* (Principle 5) on Philip's part. Even though he had his foot in the door, he remained gracious, courteous, a good listener, and yet sensitive to the time he might speak of salvation.

When that moment came, he "opened his mouth" (v. 35) and became *specific* (Principle 6) concerning faith in the Lord Jesus Christ. No reluctance. No vague dialogue about religion . . . he spoke only of the Savior, the main issue.

The last few verses describe the brief but memorable *follow-up* (Principle 7) Philip employed in this case.

As you rub shoulders with hungry, thirsty humanity and sense their inner ache for help and hope, keep these principles in mind. Let's become more alert to those empty chariot sidecars God wants us to occupy. You may even begin to feel comfortable in them before long. You know what? There isn't any place I'd rather be when Christ returns than riding shotgun in a twentieth-century chariot.

COME ASIDE

Turn to Acts 8:26-40 and examine for yourself Philip's manner and method in evangelism, referring to the principles outlined above.

Then pray. Which, if any, of these principles needs more of your attention?

Getting Involved

itty Genovese was brutally attacked as she returned to her apartment late one night. She screamed and shrieked as she fought for her life . . . yelling until she was hoarse . . . for thirty minutes . . . as she was beaten and abused. Thirty-eight people watched the half-hour episode from their windows with rapt fascination. Not one so much as walked over to the telephone and called the police. Kitty died that night as thirty-eight witnesses stared in silence.

Andrew Mormille's experience was similar. Riding on a subway, the seventeen-year-old youth was quietly minding his own business when he was stabbed repeatedly in the stomach by attackers. Eleven riders watched the stabbing, but none came to assist the young man. Even after the thugs had fled and the train had pulled out of the station, as he lay in a pool of his own blood, not one of the eleven came to his side.

Less dramatic, but equally shocking, was the ordeal of Eleanor Bradley. While shopping on Fifth Avenue in busy Manhattan, this lady tripped and broke her leg. Dazed, anguished, and in shock, she called out for help. Not for two minutes. Not for twenty minutes. But for *forty* minutes, as shoppers and business executives, students and merchants walked around her and stepped over her, completely ignoring her cries. After literally hundreds had passed by, a cab driver finally pulled over, hauled her into his taxi, and took her to a local hospital.

I heard of an experiment a small band of seminary students carried out on fellow members of their class some time ago. I know it is true because I later spoke with one of the men involved. The class was given an assignment on Luke 10:30-37, the familiar account of the Good Samaritan. The assignment was due the next day. Most of the men in that class traveled along the same pathway leading to the classroom the next morning. One of the seminarians in the experiment wore old, torn clothing, disguised himself as though he and been beaten and bruised, and placed himself along the path, clearly in view of all the young students making their way back to class. With their assignments neatly written, carefully documented, and tucked under their arms, not one seminarian so much as paused to come to his assistance or wipe the catsup off his neck and chest.

Intellectually, the assignment on love and caring was completed. But personally? Well, you decide.

What's happening? Why the passivity? How can we explain the gross lack of involvement? John Darley and Bibb Latane wrote an insightful article in *Psychology Today* a number of years ago, entitled "When Will

People Help in a Crisis?" They pointed out that a bystander will not intervene in an emergency unless he (1) notices that something is happening, (2) decides that this is an emergency, and (3) takes personal responsibility for doing something.

That's worth thinking over. Initially we must be alert enough to notice something is happening. The event has to penetrate beneath the fog of our private world—you know, our self-centered thoughts and activity and preoccupation. Somehow we have to sense the distress signals of others. But even then we probably won't intervene unless we consciously decide that an emergency is, in fact, occurring. And that means we're ultimately willing to guess wrong . . . or be embarrassed . . . or even get hurt ourselves. Because involvement boldly believes "This is my responsibility. I really care. Even if nobody else will help, I must!" Risky? You better believe it! On occasion it can be downright embarrassing.

I had a restaurant owner tell me that he once took a first-aid course because he had no knowledge of what to do when people choked on food. He said that he learned many helpful techniques, but the one lasting lesson he'd never forget was this: *Forget your pride!* When you determine you're going to assist someone in distress, roll up your sleeves, kick off your shoes, and jump in full force. Sure, you may on a few rare occasions overreact or plunge your hand into catsup instead of blood . . . but good, genuine Samaritans aren't all that prim and proper. People who get involved are motivated by selfless compassion, a burden of concern that won't stay folded and creased in a book.

With biting honesty James asks:

> If you have a friend who is in need . . . and you say to him, "Well, good-bye and God bless you; stay warm and eat hearty," and then don't give him clothes or food, what good does that do? (James 2:15-16 TLB).

John probes even deeper when he asks:

> But if someone who is supposed to be a Christian . . . sees a brother in need, and won't help him—how can God's love be within him? (1 John 3:17 TLB).

Hard questions. And too stubborn to shrug and walk out of our heads . . . too tough to smile and let us off the hook.

It's one thing to do a word study on *agape*. Or diagram the sentence structure in Luke 10. Or mouth a lot of high-powered stuff about the humble, Spirit-filled life. But it's something else entirely to see and support an Eleanor Bradley in broad daylight. Or jump to your feet and defend an Andrew Mormille. Or care enough about a Kitty Genovese to at least call the cops, fast. To do anything less is so unchristian. So wrong.

Sometimes dead wrong.

COME ASIDE

Go out on a limb: Ask God to let you help someone in urgent distress in the immediate future. Be sensitive . . . He's going to answer your request!

And take extra time today to thank Him for the constant protection you enjoy from Him, allowing you to reach out confidently to others (read Psalm 121:7-8). Be ready!

SUSPICION

f the truth were known, there's a secret "detective spirit" in most of us. With the best of the paperback and TV detectives, we vicariously probe for motives, analyze the evidence, and ponder the killer's next move. Our curiosity forces us to investigate things that are just slightly irregular.

Even a child is known to pry deeper because of a built-in bent to inquire. It often leads to danger, but nobody would deny that that inquisitive nature is proof of a keen (often creative) mind. As growth occurs, this desire to question and challenge increases . . . often exasperating lazy-minded adults and easily threatened parents. While I would agree that it *can* be overdone, I am nevertheless convinced that Curiosity and Challenge are the healthy twins in the Discernment family. They are dressed alike until they grow up and become more refined and distinct.

But there is a difference between the expressions of discernment and raw suspicion. The difference may be veiled, but it is real. It lies in the realm of motive. Suspicion is the act of suspecting something wrong without proof or evidence. It is mistrust . . . doubt . . . skepticism . . . extreme or negative caution.

Curiosity sees a cast on a leg and asks, "What happened?" Suspicion wonders if *anything* happened.

Curiosity listens to a speaker and thinks, "How did he come up with that—what's his technique?" Suspicion doubts the validity of the statement or the motive of the speaker . . . or *both*.

Curiosity observes an irregularity and challenges simply, "Why?" Suspicion entertains the immediate idea, "What's wrong here? Who's to blame—who's at fault?"

Curiosity analyzes with neutral, unprejudiced wisdom while suspicion frowns and looks for deception and subterfuge. Curiosity listens to logic, common sense, and reason . . . suspicion looks for something hidden, something held back.

Both curiosity and suspicion may be terribly persistent, but one stays with the facts while the other strays beyond the facts—and in so doing, develops *without* the facts.

It was with commendable curiosity Moses investigated the burning bush in the Midian desert:

> "I must turn aside now, and see this marvelous sight, why the bush is not burned up" (Exodus 3:3).

But it was with an entirely different spirit Saul observed David in the king's court:

Saul looked at David with suspicion from that day on. (1 Samuel 18:9).

What a remarkable contrast!
Moses saw and then couldn't imagine . . . Saul imagined and then couldn't see.

—SUSPICION BLINDS US—

Moses' investigation resulted in hearing God . . . Saul's imagination resulted in condemning David.

—SUSPICION BINDS US—

Moses turned aside because a bush kept burning . . . Saul changed within because *he* kept burning.

—SUSPICION BURNS US—

COME ASIDE

In Proverbs 2:1-11, take a good look at the curiosity that leads to godly wisdom. What can you do today to exercise this kind of curiosity about God's treasures?

Insensitivity

y kids pulled a fast one on me one Christmas years ago. They teamed up, pooled their vast financial resources, and bought me a little motto to set on my desk. It was more than cute . . . it was convicting. In bold, black letters it read:

DIETS ARE FOR PEOPLE WHO ARE THICK AND TIRED OF IT

At first you thmile . . . then it makes you thad. Especially if you're not thick of being thick!

There's another thickness that's just as bad. We could call it an "inner thickness." I'm referring to *insensitivity* . . . being unaware, out of touch, lacking insight, failing to pay attention. The Hebrew Scriptures occasionally mention those who are foolish and simple, as in the book of Proverbs (1:22-33). The original term means "thick, dull, sluggish." It's the picture of mental dullness, one who is virtually blind toward others. . . failing to feel others' feelings, think others' thoughts, sense others' needs.

Professional insensitivity is painfully common. To some physicians you're case number twenty-three today . . . a body, weighing so much . . . a mouth, saying words . . . a gall bladder, needing removal.

And how about insensitive teachers or speakers? Talk about painful! A block of information is dumped into your ears from their mouth. Whether it's interesting or well thought through is unimportant. The whole episode is about as memorable as changing a flat.

And have you come across an insensitive salesperson lately? You can feel the thickness. Your exasperation leads to gross impatience . . . and then, finally, confusion. You're not sure if the individual understands only Swahili . . . or is recovering from advanced lockjaw.

Perhaps the most tragic shades of insensitivity occur in the home. Between mates, to begin with. Needs in the heart of a wife long to be discovered by her husband. She hides them until an appropriate moment . . . but it never arrives. He's "too busy." What cursed words! "Other things are more important." Oh, really? Name one.

A husband wrestles with a matter down deep . . . in the "combat zone" of his mind. Lacking perception, the preoccupied wife drives on—never pausing, never looking into his eyes, his soul-gate, reading the signs that spell

I A-M H-U-R-T-I-N-G.

Parental sensitivity rates desperately low these days. It's part of the fallout of our rapid pace. Solomon tells us that our children "make themselves known" by their deeds, their actions. He then reminds us that we have ears and eyes that ought to hear and see (Proverbs 20:11-12). But again, it takes time to do that. And again, we're "too busy."

Let's think that over. A basic task you accepted when you became a parent was the building of self-esteem and confidence into your offspring. Without coming out and saying it, they look to you to help them know how to believe in themselves, feel worthwhile, valuable, secure in a threatening world. In dozens of ways they drop hints that ask for help. The sensitive parent spots the hint, deciphers the code, and wisely brings reinforcement.

In his fine book *Hide or Seek*, Dr. James Dobson lists the five most common barriers that cause our children to doubt their worth—even when they are deeply loved. The first barrier on the list is "parental insensitivity." Our challenge is to counteract the world's value system, which requires of our little ones either high intelligence or physical attractiveness. It's impossible to shut out this value system entirely, but we must keep things in proper perspective—especially if our kiddos are neither smart nor beauties! Failure to do so can easily result in struggles with inferiority.

The key, I repeat, is *sensitivity*—tuning into the thoughts and feelings of our kids, listening to the clues they give us, and reacting appropriately. The sensitive heart rubs its fingers along the edges, feeling for the deep cracks . . . the snags . . . taking the time to hear . . . to care . . . to give . . . to share.

To be thick is understandable. To be thick and tired of it is commendable. To be thick and tired of it but unwilling to change—is inexcusable.

COME ASIDE

God's hatred of human insensitivity resounds in Obadiah 10-15, in which the nation of Edom is condemned for its treatment of God's people during their distress. Get close to God's heart as you read these piercing words.

THE LEGACY OF LEARNING

lice it any way you wish, ignorance is *not* bliss. Dress it in whatever garb you please, ignorance is *not* attractive. Neither is it the mark of humility nor the path to spirituality. It certainly is not the companion of wisdom.

On the contrary, it is the breeding ground for fear, prejudice, and superstition . . . the feeding trough for unthinking animals . . . the training field for slaves. It is blind and naked (Tennyson), the mother of impudence (Spurgeon), it brings despairing darkness (Shakespeare), never settles a question (Disraeli), nor promotes innocence (Browning). And yet it remains the favorite plea of the guilty, the excuse of the lazy—and even the Christian's rationalization for immaturity.

We dare not fall into that trap! Our spiritual fathers didn't. Trace your heritage back to Moses and you find that the people were given the Truth of God in written form that they might *know* and that their children might *know* the right path to follow.

In Samuel's day a "school of the prophets" was formed to dispel the ignorance among the people.

This philosophy carried into the New Testament as Jesus frequently rebuked His listeners for not reading, not knowing the underlying principles for living. How often Paul expressed similar convictions with such strong words as, "I would not have you to be ignorant. . . ." Dr. Luke commended the church at Berea because they were "examining the Scriptures daily to see whether these things were so" (Acts 17:11).

Our own nation saw the need for being knowledgeable . . . for perpetuating an educated, well-trained body of godly people who could proclaim God's message with intelligence, authority, and conviction. Our oldest institution of higher learning—founded only sixteen years after the landing at Plymouth—was established for the purpose stated on its cornerstone. That marker still stands near an iron gate that leads to the campus of Harvard University:

> After God had carried us safe to New England and we had builded our houses, provided necessaries for our livelihood, reared convenient places for God's worship and settled the civil government, one of the next things we longed for and looked after was to advance learning and perpetuate to posterity, dreading to leave an illiterate ministry to the churches when our present ministers shall lie in the dust.

This continued until European liberalism, with its subtle narcotic of humanism and socialism, began to paralyze the nerve centers of theological thought and educational philosophy. Doubt and despair replaced certainty and hope. Mental discipline, honed on the wheel of exacting academic requirements and intellectual integrity, began to lag. Permissiveness became the order of the day. This evolved into a mentality that now considers deep thought and thorough study a joke. Thank God, there are some exceptions. But they are *precious* few . . . especially among the saints.

To be sure, there are dangers connected with being knowledgeable. Solomon warns us of the worst in Ecclesiastes: *pride*—the wearying, futile pursuit of knowledge, a flesh trip that can cause a head to outgrow a heart. Mere intellectualism can be only "striving after wind" (1:17).

But my single desire is to support the premise that knowledge, rather than being an enemy of the faith, is an ally . . . perhaps one of our strongest. I call upon C. S. Lewis to state my cause, and with him I rest my case:

> If all the world were Christian it might not matter if all the world were uneducated. But, as it is, a cultural life will exist outside the Church whether it exists inside or not. To be ignorant and simple now—not to be able to meet the enemies on their own ground—would be to throw down our weapons, and to betray our uneducated brethren who have, under God, no defense but us against the intellectual attacks of the heathen.
>
> Good philosophy must exist, if for no other reason, because bad philosophy needs to be answered. The cool intellect must work not only against cool intellect on the other side, but against the muddy heathen mysticisms which deny intellect altogether. Most of all, perhaps, we need intimate knowledge of the past . . . the learned life then is, for some, a duty.

COME ASIDE

Daniel and his three fellow Hebrews mentioned in Daniel 1 provide one of many biblical examples of human intellect employed for God's purposes. Read 1:17-20 and also Daniel's prayer of praise in 2:19-23, and notice the quality and the source of Daniel's intellect.

What can you do to receive fully the mental riches God makes available to you? How can you get started today?

LABELS

et's Label.

That's a favorite parlor game among Christians.

The rules are easy to remember. Any number can play. But it's especially appealing to those who are given to oversimplification and making categorical comments. Name-droppers thrive on this game. And it helps if you speak with a measure of authority . . . looking somewhat pious and pronouncing your words very distinctly, very dogmatically. You'll gain stature in the group if you look down and frown a little as you affix the label to the person in question.

Labels vary. There are "temperament" labels. "She's a *choleric*, poor thing . . . married to a *melancholic*!"

These are akin to "emotional" labels. "Well, you know her—she's *nervous*" . . . or "He's a classic *neurotic*, a *perfectionist* to the core."

Of course, "doctrinal" labels are most popular among evangelicals. One guy is tagged a *liberal*, another *neo-evangelical* . . . and still others *conservative*—with a host of in-between shades. If a person mentions the sovereignty of God too much, we label the jar *Calvinist*. If he seems uneasy regarding local church organization, *Plymouth Brethren* is the tag. If she's convinced that God's future program is clearly spelled out in Daniel and Revelation, we brand her *premillenialist*. If one thinks that the Bible sets forth distinct eras during which man's relationship with God has unique characteristics, the label is *dispensationalist*, a sinister-sounding term very few people even understand! Another label that's now on the scene is *neo-fundamentalism* . . . a title that includes basic tenets and life outlooks that, in the mind of the "labeler," are unrelated to the fundamentals of the faith.

Now then, to be completely honest about it, it is occasionally helpful to lick a label and stick it on. It saves a bundle of time and it can communicate a fairly clear mental picture. However—it is important that we guard against using a wrong label, thus damaging that individual's true image or position in others' eyes. That is the main danger in playing *Let's Label*. It often means you set yourself up as judge and jury, declaring information that is exaggerated or thirdhand or just plain untrue. When that happens, we have stopped playing a game and started to slander.

Being alert and discerning, basing one's opinion on the absolute truth, is a sign of maturity, a mark of excellence in a life. But pasting labels on people and churches and schools with only partial facts, feelings, and opinions to back those statements up is worse than unfair . . . it's unchristian.

The game needs another name . . . like, *Let's Judge*.

COME ASIDE

How is labeling like lying? Can you find any clues in Proverbs 12:17-23?

Sunday Listening

ost of us were born hearing well, but all of us must learn to *listen* well. Listening is a skill, an art that is in need of being cultivated.

Dr. Ralph Nichols, considered by many to be an authority on the subject, believes that we think four, perhaps five times faster than we talk. This means that if a speaker utters one hundred twenty words a minute, the audience thinks at about five hundred words a minute. That difference offers a strong temptation to listeners to take mental excursions . . . to think about last night's bridge game or tomorrow's sales report or the need to get that engine tune-up before next weekend's trip to the mountains . . . then phase back into the speaker's talk.

Research at the University of Minnesota reveals that in listening to a ten-minute talk, hearers operate at only a twenty-eight percent efficiency. And the longer the talk, the less we understand, the less we track with our ears what somebody's mouth is saying. That could be downright frightening to guys like me who preach from forty to fifty minutes a crack! That also explains why some wag has described preaching as "the fine art of talking in someone else's sleep."

Good communication is tricky business. We are all busy people with heavy mental anchors dragging across our brains at every waking moment. It's hard work for any preacher to seize our attention, then hold it for an extended period of time—especially since we can think so much faster than he can talk.

Which brings up the seldom-mentioned secret of a good sermon. Aside from God's vital part in the whole thing, there are two crucial ingredients that make it happen. First, the one who speaks must speak well. Second, the one who listens must listen well. Neither is automatic. *Both* are hard work. I should also add that just because a Bible is open and religious words are being tossed around, there is no magical spell of sustained interest guaranteed. And difficult as it may be for us preachers to accept this, sincerity in the heart is no excuse for being dry, dull, and boring in the pulpit.

But let's think about the pew for a change. What can be done by the listener to keep the sermon interesting? Instead of thinking about how the preacher could improve, let's turn the record over to the flip side and consider how we could improve our listening skills. I'm indebted to Haddon Robinson, president of Denver Seminary (and a Ph.D. in the field of communication) for these four "don'ts" that are worth remembering.

Don't assume the subject is dull. When the topic is announced, avoid the habit of thinking, "I've heard that before" or "This doesn't apply to me." Good listeners believe they can learn something from everyone. Any message will have a fresh insight or a helpful illustration. A keen ear will listen for such.

Don't criticize before hearing the speaker out. All speakers have faults. If you focus on them, you will miss some profitable points being made. Those who listen well refuse to waste valuable time concentrating on the negatives. They also refuse to jump to conclusions until the entire talk is complete.

Don't let your prejudices close your mind. Some subjects are charged with intense emotions. Effective listeners keep an open mind, restraining the tendency to argue or agree until they fully understand the speaker's position in light of what the Scriptures teach.

Don't waste the advantage which thought has over speech. Remember the gap between speech-speed and thought-speed? Diligent listeners practice four skills as they mentally occupy themselves:

- First, they try to guess the next point.
- Second, they challenge supporting evidence.
- Third, they mentally summarize what they have heard.
- Fourth, they apply the Scripture at each point.

Writing down the outline and a few thoughts during the sermon also keeps the mind from drifting off course.

Young Samuel took the advice of Eli the priest, and as a result, he heard what God wanted him to learn. The message was riveted into Samuel's head so permanently, he never forgot it. And it all started with:

"Speak, for Thy servant is listening."

Try that next Sunday. A few seconds before the sermon begins, pray that prayer. You will be *amazed* how much more you hear when you work hard to listen well.

COME ASIDE

Meditate quietly and at length on 1 Samuel 3:1-10. Imagine God calling you by name just as He called Samuel.

Store up these thoughts, mentally installing them for quick recall when you're next in the presence of a teacher or preacher of God's Word.

No Place for Islands

obody is a whole chain. Each one is a link. But take away one link and the chain is broken.

Nobody is a whole team. Each one is a player. But take away one player and the game is forfeited.

Nobody is a whole orchestra. Each one is a musician. But take away one musician and the symphony is incomplete.

Nobody is a whole play. Each one is an actor. But take away one actor and the performance suffers.

Nobody is a whole hospital. Each one is a part of the staff. But take away one person and it isn't long before the patient can tell.

Cars are composed of numerous parts. Each one is connected to and dependent upon the other. Even a tiny screw, if it comes loose and falls out of the carburetor, can bring the whole vehicle to a stop.

You guessed it. We need each other. You need someone and someone needs you. Isolated islands we're not. To make this thing called life work, we gotta lean and support. And relate and respond. And give and take. And confess and forgive. And reach out and embrace. And release and rely.

Especially in God's Family . . . where working together is Plan A for survival. And since we're so different (thanks to the way God built us), love and acceptance are not optional luxuries. Neither is tolerance. Or understanding. Or patience. You know, all those things you need from others when your humanity crowds out your divinity.

In other words:

> Love each other with brotherly affection and take delight in honoring each other. Never be lazy in your work but serve the Lord enthusiastically.

> Be glad for all God is planning for you. Be patient in trouble, and prayerful always. When God's children are in need, you be the one to help them out. And get into the habit of inviting guests home for dinner or, if they need lodging, for the night (Romans 12:10-13 TLB).

Why? Because each one of us is worth it. Even when we don't act like it or feel like it or deserve it.

In a rare moment of remarkable insight, the *Wall Street Journal* dedicated an entire page to this very subject. It's like a modern-day application of the Romans 12 passage:

116

How Important
Are You?
More than
you think.
A rooster
minus a hen
equals
no baby chicks.
Kellogg minus
a farmer
equals
no corn flakes.
If the nail
factory closes
what good is the
hammer factory?
Paderewski's
genius wouldn't have
amounted to much
if the
piano tuner
hadn't shown up.
A cracker maker
will do better
if there's a
cheesemaker.
The most skillful
surgeon needs
the ambulance driver
who delivers the
patient.
Just as Rodgers
needed Hammerstein
you need someone
and someone
needs you.

Since none of us is a whole, independent, self-sufficient, supercapable, all-powerful hotshot, let's quit acting like we are. Life's lonely enough without our playing that silly role.

The game's over. Let's link up.

COME ASIDE

Read Romans 15:1-7. Who needs your help today—your understanding, your encouragement, your acceptance?

 Observation

small bottle containing urine sat upon the desk of Sir William Osler. He was then the eminent professor of medicine at Oxford University. Sitting before him was a classroom full of young, wide-eyed medical students listening to his lecture on the importance of observing details. To emphasize his point, he reached down and picked up the bottle. Holding it high, he announced:

> This bottle contains a sample for analysis. It's often possible by tasting it to determine the disease from which the patient suffers.

Suiting action to words, he dipped a finger into the fluid and then into his mouth, as he continued—

> Now I am going to pass the bottle around. Each of you please do exactly as I did. Perhaps we can learn the importance of this technique and diagnose the case.

The bottle made its way from row to row as each student gingerly poked his finger in and bravely sampled the contents with a frown. Dr. Osler then retrieved the bottle and startled his students with the words:

> Gentlemen, now you will understand what I mean when I speak about details. Had you been observant you would have seen that I put my index finger into the bottle but my middle finger into my mouth!

There is much to be learned from that true story, especially regarding you and your Bible. Time and again I have heard the complaint, "But I just don't get anything out of the Bible. I read it and ask God to show me His truth, but nothing happens!" Or people will occasionally say, "When I read that passage you preached on today, I wondered, 'How in the world will he get anything out of this?' I really can't understand why I can't see what is there."

I've got good news—*you can*! But you will have to open your eyes and think. You will need to force yourself to observe, to take notice, to read the Scriptures like a detective examining the evidence, to discipline yourself to become saturated with the particulars of the passage. Since such attention to details will supply you with the raw materials you must have to interpret God's Word accurately, I strongly advise you to *begin today*.

Think of your eyes as searchlights. Become a glutton for details in everyday life. Don't glance at birds—see sparrows. Don't smell flowers, observe the hyacinth, the fuchsia, the tulip. Don't consider a tree—look at a willow or a birch. Don't watch cars, notice Fords or Pontiacs and Toyotas. Don't simply hear others' words—listen for feelings and picture detailed concepts. Stop collecting the garbage of generalities and start stretching your mental muscles in the gymnasium of in-depth perception.

Most folks read through the Bible and casually notice birds, plants, trees, and wind. But not you! Aim higher than that.

Open the Song of Solomon and hear the liquid call of the turtledove.

Taste the pungent mandrakes of Genesis 30.

Smell the sweet cedarwood in 1 Kings.

Feel the salty blast of *Euraquilo*—that violent northeastern wind sweeping across the pages of Acts 27.

And when you stand in a hallowed place like Gethsemane, be aware! That Man who kneels among the gnarled and twisted trunks of the ancient olive trees is doing more than praying—He is pouring out His very soul before the Father. Don't leave until you see His blood mingle with sweat and tears. Those are *your* sins He faces—it is the prospect of *your* punishment that tears at His soul. Don't just glance at that scene—*see Him!*

The eternal Book of all books deserves a second look.

COME ASIDE

Write down all your observations as you gaze on the scene at Gethsemane in Matthew 26:36-56. Strain to see what you've never noticed before.

BACKING OFF

ids are nutty.

Some friends of ours in Texas have two little girls. The younger child is constantly on the move, rarely winding down by bedtime. So the nightly affair has become something of a familiar routine. A story from her favorite book. A drink of water. A prayer. A song. Her doll. Another drink of water. A kiss. A hug. A third sip of water. A trip to the bathroom. A warning. Another kiss. You know, the whole bit.

One night her dad decided he'd be Mr. Nice Guy, the epitome of patience and tolerance. He did it all. Not once did he lose his cool. When Miss Busybody finally ran out of requests, her daddy slipped out of the room, heaved a sigh of relief, and slumped into his favorite chair by the fireplace. Before he could stretch out and relax, however, there was a piercing scream from the jitterbug's room. Startled, he dashed down the hall and rushed to her bedside. Great tears were rolling down the little girl's face.

"What's wrong? What happened?"

"I burnt my tongue."

Baffled, he tried again, "You what?"

"I burnt my *tongue!*" she yelled.

"How in the world did you do that?" he asked.

"I licked my night-light."

That really happened. She couldn't control her curiosity. She simply had to discover how it would feel to lick that little thing that glowed so warmly and serenely by her bed. Rude was her awakening to the fact that lights are strictly for lighting . . . not licking. And tongues are made for tasting . . . not testing. You and I realize that the best thing our little friend could have done was to stay in bed, keep her tongue to herself, and allow the light to fulfill its appointed function.

But she didn't—and she got burned.

In the book of Ecclesiastes, Solomon, the wise, passes along to us a list of various types of "appointed times" on earth. Among them he mentions

> a time to heal . . . a time to shun embracing . . . a time to give
> up as lost . . . a time to be silent . . .

I see in these words of counsel one strong undercurrent of advice: BACK OFF! It is often wise to relax our intensity, refuse to force an issue, allow nature to take its course, "let sleeping dogs lie." Backing off, says Solomon, provides opportunity for healing to occur, opportunity for perspective to break through the storm clouds of emotion and illuminate a difficult situation with a fresh understanding.

When the time is right, things flow very naturally, very freely. To rush or force creates friction-scars that take years to erase. Intensity leads to futility. Like the little boy who plants the seed and then nervously digs it up every day to see if it is growing. Waiting is as necessary as planting and fertilizing.

When the fish aren't biting, banging on the water with an oar won't help. You can't get sap out of a hoe handle. Nor can a relationship be corrected by legislation and force. Remember, God says there is a "time to shun embracing" just as there are times to embrace. "Giving up as lost" may, on some occasions, be the wisest response, though extremely painful. Sometimes that means simply being silent and allowing God to work. In other words, *back off* so God can move in. This is never more essential than among family members in a home. Allowing some slack in the rope is, at the right time, a mark of real wisdom.

What a difficult pill for up-tight parents to swallow! Kept edgy by impatience, rigidity, and unbending determination, they foolishly rush in where angels loathe to tread. The result? Exasperated kids. Rooms choked with threats and irritating pressure.

Young guys can do this with girls they date. She wants room to breathe, some space to think things out for herself, but he continues to smother. We can do this with people we have offended. They need time to reason, freedom to forgive without being hurried. To push for a quick closure is like a hard-sell salesman pressing you to buy when you are trying to decide what's best. The faster he talks and the harder he pushes, the less interested you become in buying—even something you *need*. The wise salesman knows when to allow you the privilege of deciding for yourself—when to back off and leave you alone.

Nobody is able to eat while they're weeping. Serving more food isn't the answer. The appetite will return when the agony subsides . . . and not until. That takes time.

Stop and think. Think first about your family. Then your other friends. Are you being wise or foolish? Are you using force or providing freedom? Are you being pushy or patient? Are you intimidating by your intensity . . . or backing off and relaxing? Are you allowing the ground fog to roll back or are you launching blindly into dangerous flight?

Take it from one who has learned this difficult lesson the hard way— keep a tight bridle on your tongue, relax, and settle for a good night's sleep. Otherwise, you're going to get pushy, you're going to get caught with your tongue in the wrong place . . . and you're going to get burned.

COME ASIDE

Read John 7:1-14 and notice how Jesus "backed off" on occasion. Study closely His words throughout John 7 to find the keys for knowing when to back off and when not to.

QUESTIONS

om Skinner, the gifted black evangelist, penned a book a few years ago with a title that won't let me go:

*If Christ Is the Answer,
What Are the Questions?*

I like that . . . not only because it's creative, but because it strikes a chord in my soul that harmonizes well with the voices of many searchers in society.

Far too many sheep in the fold have turned a deaf ear to the questions of goats outside the gate. We are busily engaged in a mutual admiration campaign, complimenting one another's wool . . . or gloating over our position in the pen. The fence that separates us from the goats is all too often more like a sound-resistant one-way glass. This "glass fence" produces two serious and sad results:

1. It absorbs and muffles the outside sounds so that what we hear are not the actual questions goats are asking.

2. It reflects back to the goats not only their own hopeless appearance, but a distinct silence that says, in effect, "Sorry, we have no answer," or "We'll just ignore that, since you're not teachable and only want to argue."

Oh sure, there are exceptions . . . but you've got to agree with me that most sheep have *stopped considering the questions* and have *started analyzing the answers* .

Now, I'm not saying we never make a stab at it. I am saying, however, that our stabs are usually quick thrusts of doctrinal daggers in technical verbiage familiar mainly to sheep, not careful throws of javelins in the jargon of the goats, that hit the target with a telling effect. Sheep are satisfied, it seems, to bleat out answers to questions nobody's asking . . . or beat goats about the head and shoulders with dull biblical clubs backed up by a defensive, threatened attitude. My fellow sheep—that simply will not lead to a harvest of grateful goats. Bleeding, assaulted goats don't submit, they fight or flee.

Christianity is completely credible. Objective, honest, historically documented evidence in favor of the basics of our faith is massive in fact and impressive in volume. But there is many a goat who is hung up on some question(s) that tethers him outside the fold. His search is often genuine, his thinking is usually logical . . . and he is looking for evidence that makes sense, facts that hold up under intelligent investigation.

These questions are like ropes tossed over the fence. They are not necessarily designed to create an argument or slam our faith to the mat. They are often intellectual inquiries—occasionally theoretical—that force us to *think* (which many sheep stopped doing when they walked through the gate). If we view these ropes as lifelines, we'll grab hold and not let go. If we consider them as foolish arguments or an unimportant waste of time, we may miss choice, irreplaceable opportunities.

The apostle Peter put it this way:

> . . . always being ready to make a defense to everyone who asks you to give an account for the hope that is in you, yet with gentleness and reverence (1 Peter 3:15).

He precedes this command with a reminder that we should feel neither troubled nor intimidated. The slightest noise gives woolies the willies. No need! Especially if we are "ready to make a defense."

Sheep on the front lines today are those who have come to know and love the Answer . . . but are able to handle the questions with wisdom and gentleness. This means that we must stay inquisitive and alert.

I close today's reading by casting my vote for that seldom-heard-of American editor, Frank Colby, whose essays were released shortly after his death in 1925. In the first volume he wrote:

> Every man ought to be inquisitive through every hour of his great adventure down to the day when he shall no longer cast a shadow in the sun.

Maybe the reason we've stopped *answering* questions is because we've stopped *asking* them.

COME ASIDE

List ten good questions that might logically occur to a non-Christian who was exposed to Colossians 1:15-20 for the first time. Don't try to answer the questions—just ask them.

FIGHTING THE FAST FADE

s you waved goodbye to your friends at church last Sunday, what mental darts were left stuck in the target of your thinking?

Can you remember those pointed challenges from the man who stood before you with Bible in hand? How many hours since you sat there, opening your ears and heart to counsel from God's always-relevant Book? A few dozen maybe?

Ah, but it's starting to fade, isn't it? Those incisive, potentially life-changing principles are swimming away in a sea of fog and mist. What a frustration! Why can't we hang on to those mental, spiritual handholds we need so desperately as we cling to the face of this cliff called "daily living?"

Jesus illustrates this struggle so vividly in Mark, chapter 4. Do you remember? The seed is carefully sown. Yet shortly after God's Word is heard, the enemy of our souls, Satan himself, comes and snatches away the biblical insights that have been deposited in our hearts.

Isn't it the truth? Before the freshly baked cake is cool, he comes and licks off all the frosting. Before the new bike is ridden, he sneaks up and lets all the air out of the tires. Before the dress is worn, he slips up and jerks out the hem and jams the zipper. Before we crank up the car at 12:20, he's stolen the stuff we heard at 11:45.

Amazing! But you gotta remember, he's been at it since he winked at Eve in the garden. He's the first when it comes to rip-off experts.

There are others who follow in his train. Like a basketball fan discovered at the Portland airport awaiting the arrival of the Trailblazers following a victory over the Lakers. He was attempting to scalp a couple of tickets to the next game—for *a hundred and fifty bucks each*. As he wormed through the crowd, he located a well-dressed man who listened to his offer.

"How much?" asked the gentleman.

"One hundred fifty," he replied under his breath. "Not a cent lower."

"Do you realize you're talking to a plain-clothes officer of the law?" the man asked the scalper. "I'm going to turn you in, fella."

Suddenly the seller began to backpedal. He talked about how large a family he had . . . how much they needed him . . . how he'd never ever do it again.

Looking both ways, the well-dressed man said: "Just hand over the tickets and we'll call it even . . . now get out of here and I had better *never* catch you here again!"

But the worst was yet to come. The well-dressed man was no officer at all. Just a quick-thinking guy who used a little ingenuity to land two

choice seats to the next playoff game. He anonymously a
the local newspaper several days later.

Satan's strategy is just as ingenious and effective. He hears what we
hear and in the process plans his approach. He baits the rip-off trap,
then sets it up with just the right hair trigger. Here are several:

- an immediate argument in the car after church is over on
  where to go for dinner
- lots of activity, talking, and needless noise Sunday afternoon
- preoccupation with some worrisome, plaguing problem
  during the message
- a personality conflict with another church member
- irritation over how far away you had to park
- pride—that says, "I'm so glad Doo Dad is here. He really
  needs to get straightened out."

All those (there are more) are satanic rip-offs. Like a lion, he prowls
silently, camouflaged in the garb of our physical habits and our mental
laziness, seeking to devour. At the precise moment when it will have its
greatest impact, he snatches away the very truth we need the most, leaving us with hardly a memory of what God said earlier. It occurs *every*
Lord's Day in every language on every continent . . . at every local
church where the Scripture is declared.

In case you question the effectiveness of his strategy, think back just
two or three weeks . . . or *one* will do. Try your best to remember merely
a message title . . . or an outline . . . or for that matter, a couple applica-
tory principles.

You see, this isn't theory! It's warfare. And the battle is being waged
this very minute. Don't fight it alone. Your Commander is ready with
powerful reinforcement. Remember what Jesus said?

> "But the Helper, the Holy Spirit, whom the Father will send
> in My name, He will teach you all things, and bring to your
> remembrance all that I said to you" (John 14:26).

It's a promise worth remembering.

COME ASIDE

Read prayerfully through Lamentations 3:19-33. Ask the Spirit of
God to help you choose *one verse* here that you can cling to and continually recall during the next twenty-four hours.

P A R T   I I

Mid-Winter's Blast

WHEN PERSEVERANCE STEADIES OUR COURSE

Mid-Winter's Blast

have never been inside a Siberian work camp.

I have not sailed the North Atlantic in January. Neither have I clung to a sled behind a team of huskies barking their way across the Yukon. Nor was I a part of the combat Marine outfit that braved the notorious "frozen Inchon" in Korea.

But I have been cold. Frighteningly cold.

From frigid ice storms in the Rockies to bitter blizzards in Iowa and Illinois, Minnesota and Massachusetts, I have leaned hard against the wind, wondering if my face would ever regain its feeling. Those traumatic times have taught me to listen to things like weather warnings and wind-chill factors. There's a name for folks who don't: victim. That numbing, vicious blast when winter releases her fury may be given a fantasy label like "wonderland" by poet-and-artist types . . . but the rawboned realists who have survived those freezing winter winds that roar like a lion and sting like a whip have a healthy, awesome respect for blizzards. The best place to be during midwinter's blast is inside. Away from the cold . . . under a pile of thick, soft, cozy blankets . . . near a fireplace full of burning timber.

But I have been cold even there, frighteningly cold, when winter blew inside and refused to leave.

Feeling broken, bruised, and—worst of all—barren, like the scene outside. Asking why. Wondering when it would end. Struggling to go on. Windwhipped within, I have honestly thought at those times about packing it in.

Such midwinter miseries, I have come to realize, are not mine alone. You've had them too, haven't you? That's one of the reasons you picked up this book, isn't it? You long to persevere through the pits, but you find yourself running shy on hope. Hope . . . that midwinter mirage others talk about, but you fail to see. Believe me, I understand. It's faded from my eyes many times.

I've got some things to say especially to you in the pages that follow. Perhaps you will stumble across a statement or the turn of a phrase, maybe one particular word that will light a spark and bring back the warmth you've lacked in the midst of the blast. It's possible, you know. Hope doesn't require a massive chain where heavy links of logic hold it together. A thin wire will do . . . just strong enough to get us through the night until the winds die down.

If God should use something I have written to steady your course and help you cope with at least today's bitter battle, thank Him. The byproduct of hope's sudden breakthrough is called perseverance . . . a rare commodity in today's shallow times. But oh, so essential! It is all you need to take the chill out of the air.

It's the stuff of which pioneers were made and other hearty types . . . like those who endure Siberia, sail the North Atlantic, cross the Yukon, fight with frozen feet at Inchon . . . and even those who regain enough hope to press on when only moments ago they had written out and rehearsed their resignation from the human race.

CAN'T...OR WON'T?

o offense, but some of you don't have any business reading this today. Normally I do not restrict my words to any special group of people. But now I must. This time it is *for Christians only*. Everything I write from now to the end of this reading on excuses is strictly for the believer in Christ. If you're not there yet, you can skip on to the next page because you lack a major ingredient: the power of God. Non-Christians are simply unable to choose righteous paths consistently. That divine response upon which the Christian can (and *must*) draw is not at the unbeliever's disposal. That is, not until personal faith in Jesus Christ is expressed. This is one of those now-not-later issues that's limited to believers only.

Now then, if you know the Lord, you are the recipient of limitless ability . . . incredible strength. Just read a few familiar lines out of the Book, *slowly* for a change:

> I can do all things through Him who strengthens me (Philippians 4:13).

> "My grace is sufficient for you, for power is perfected in weakness." Most gladly, therefore, I will rather boast about my weaknesses, that the power of Christ may dwell in me (2 Corinthians 12:9).

> For this reason, I bow my knees before the Father . . . that He would grant you, according to the riches of His glory, to be strengthened with power through His spirit in the inner man (Ephesians 3:14,16).

> He has granted to us His precious and magnificent promises, in order that by them you might become partakers of the divine nature . . . (2 Peter 1:4).

And one more:

> No temptation has overtaken you but such as is common to man; and God is faithful, who will not allow you to be tempted beyond what you are able, but with the temptation will provide the way of escape also, that you may be able to endure it (1 Corinthians 10:13).

Wait a minute now. Did you read every word—or did you skip a line or two? If so, please go back and *slowly* graze over those five statements written to you, a Christian. It's really important.

Okay, what thought stands out the most? Well, if someone asked me that question, I'd say, "Special strength or an unusual ability from God." In these verses it's called several things: strength, power, divine nature, ability. God has somehow placed into the Christian's insides a special something, that extra inner reservoir of power that is more than a match for the stuff life throws at us. When in operation, phenomenal accomplishments are achieved, sometimes even *miraculous*.

Let's get specific.

It boils down to the choice of two common words in our vocabulary. Little words, but, oh, so different! *Can't* and *won't*. Christians need to be very careful which one they choose. It seems that we prefer to use *can't*.

"I just *can't* get along with my wife."

"My husband and I *can't* communicate."

"I *can't* discipline the kids like I should."

"I just *can't* give up the affair I'm having."

"I *can't* stop overeating."

"I *can't* find the time to pray."

"I *can't* quit gossiping."

No, any Christian who takes seriously those five passages we just looked at (there are dozens more) will have to confess the word really should be *won't*. Why? Because we have been given the power, the ability to overcome. Literally! And therein lies hope in hoisting anchors that would otherwise hold us in the muck and mire of blame and self-pity.

One of the best books you can read this year on overcoming depression is a splendid work by two physicians, Minirth and Meier. The volume is appropriately entitled *Happiness Is a Choice*. These men agree that:

> As psychiatrists we cringe whenever [Christian] patients use the word *can't*. . . .
>
> Any good psychiatrist knows that "I can't" and "I've tried" are merely lame excuses. We insist that our patients be honest with themselves and use language that expresses the reality of the situation. So we have our patients change their *can'ts* to *won'ts*. . . .
>
> If an individual changes all his *can'ts* to *won'ts*, he stops avoiding the truth, quits deceiving himself, and starts living in reality . . .

"I just *won't* get along with my wife."

"My husband and I *won't* communicate."

"I *won't* discipline the kids like I should."

"I just *won't* give up the affair I'm having."

"I *won't* stop overeating."

"I *won't* find the time to pray."

"I *won't* quit gossiping."

Non-Christians have every right and reason to use *can't*, because they really can't! They are victims, trapped and bound like slaves in a fierce and endless struggle. Without Christ and His power, they lack what it takes to change permanently. They don't because they can't! It is a fact . . . a valid excuse.

But people like us? Hey, let's face it, we don't because we won't . . . we disobey because we want to, not because we have to . . . because we choose to, not because we're forced to. The sooner we are willing to own up realistically to our responsibility and stop playing the blame game at pity parties for ourselves, the more we'll learn and change and the less we'll burn and blame.

Wish I could find a less offensive way to communicate all this, but I just can't.

Oops!

COME ASIDE

If there's a "won't" in your life that you've been calling a "can't," talk it over now with God. Use any or all of these short passages to help you find God's perspective as you pray: Psalm 105:4, Isaiah 43:18-19, Habakkuk 3:19, and Hebrews 10:35-39.

IS TRAUMA TERMINAL?

he definition reflects devastation:

Trauma: An injury (as a wound) to living tissue caused by an extrinsic agent . . . a disordered psychic or behavioral state resulting from mental or emotional stress . . .

Like potatoes in a pressure cooker, we century-twenty creatures understand the meaning of stress. A week doesn't pass without a few skirmishes with those "extrinsic agents" that beat upon our fragile frames. They may be as mild as making lunches for our kids before 7:30 in the morning (mild?) or as severe as a collision with another car . . . or another person. Makes no difference. The result is "trauma"—a two-bit word for nervous. You know, the bottom-line reason Valium remains the top seller. Our emotional wounds are often deep. They don't hemorrhage like a stabbing victim, but they are just as real and just as painful . . . sometimes more.

Remember the stress test carried on by Dr. Thomas Holmes and his colleagues? They concluded that an accumulation of two hundred or more "life change units" in any year may mean more disruption—more trauma—than an individual can stand. On their scale, death of a spouse equals one hundred units, divorce represents seventy-three units . . . and Christmas equals twelve units! That helps explain the idea behind "something snapping" inside certain people when the final straw falls on them. Our capacity for trauma has its limits.

Joseph Bayly could certainly understand. He and his wife lost three of their children—one at eighteen days (after surgery); another at five years (leukemia); a third at eighteen years (sledding accident plus hemophilia). In my wildest imagination, I cannot fathom the depth of their loss. In the backwash of such deep trauma, the Bayly couple stood sometimes strong, sometimes weak, as they watched God place a period *before* the end of the sentence on three of their children's lives. And their anguish was not relieved when well-meaning people offered shallow, simple answers amidst their grief.

H. L. Mencken must have had those situations in mind when he wrote:

There's always an easy solution to every human problem—neat, plausible, and wrong.

Eyes that read these words might very well be near tears. You are trying to cope without hope. You are stretched dangerously close to the "200-unit" limit . . . and there's no relief on the horizon. You're bleeding and you've run out of bandages. You have moved from mild tension to advanced trauma.

Be careful! You are in the danger zone, emotionally. You're a sitting duck, and the adversary is taking aim with both barrels loaded, hoping to open fire while you are vulnerable. Bam, *"Run!"* Boom! *"Think suicide."*

Listen carefully! Jesus Christ opens the gate, gently looks at you and says:

> Come to Me, all you who labor and are . . . over burdened,
> and I will cause you to rest—I will ease and relieve and re-
> fresh your souls (Matthew 11:28 Amplified Bible).

Nothing complicated. No big fanfare, no trip to Mecca, no hypnotic trance, no fee, no special password. Just *come*. Meaning? Unload. Unhook the pack and drop it in His lap . . . now. Allow Him to take your stress as you take His rest. Does He know what trauma is all about? Remember, He's the One whose sweat became like drops of blood in the agony of Gethsemane. If anybody understands trauma, He does. Completely.

His provision is profound, attainable, and right. He's a master at turning devastation into restoration.

COME ASIDE

Probe closely into God's heart—go ahead, He won't mind!—as you read His words to His people in Joel 2:18-32.

Then look at His invitation in Matthew 11:28-30, and accept it again with all your heart.

PERSISTENCE

ersistence pays.

It's a costly investment, no question about it. But the dividends are so much greater than the original outlay that you'll almost forget the price. And if the final benefits are *really* significant, you'll wonder why you ever hesitated to begin with.

A primary reason we are tempted to give up is other people . . . you know, the less than twenty percent whose major role it is in life to encourage others to toss in the towel. For *whatever* reason. Those white-flag specialists never run out of excuses you and I ought to use for quitting. The world's full of "why-sweat-it" experts.

I'm sure Anne Mansfield Sullivan had a host of folks telling her that the blind, seven-year-old brat wasn't worth it. But Anne persisted—in spite of temper tantrums, physical abuse, mealtime madness, and even thankless parents. In her heart she knew it was worth all the pain. Was it ever! Within two years the girl was able to read and write in braille. She ultimately graduated *cum laude* from Radcliffe College (where Miss Sullivan had "spelled" each lecture into her hand), and Helen Keller devoted the rest of her life to aiding the deaf and the blind.

Want another 'fer instance? Well, this particular man was told that if he hadn't written a book by age thirty-five, chances were good he never would. He was almost forty, I should add. There were others who reminded him that for every book published, ninety-five became dust-collecting manuscripts. But he persisted. Even though he was warned that stories like he wanted to write weren't popular. Nor were they considered worthy of top prizes in the literary field (his work later won the Pulitzer). Hollywood hotshots also told him such a book certainly held no dramatic possibilities. But James Michener hung tough. He refused to wash the desire out of his hair as he persisted and presented to the public *Tales of the South Pacific*. Oh, by the way, the Broadway critics had warned, "It'll *never* make a musical."

How many military battles would never have been won without persistence? How many men and women would never have graduated from school . . . or changed careers in midstream . . . or stayed together in marriage . . . or reared a retarded child? Think of the criminal cases that would never have been solved without the relentless persistence of detectives. How about the great music that would never have been finished, the grand pieces of art that would never have graced museums, cathedrals, and monuments the world over? Back behind the impeccable beauty of each work is a dream that wouldn't die mixed with the dogged determination of a genius of whom this indifferent world is not worthy.

Think also of the speeches, the sermons, the books that have shaped thinking, infused new hope, prompted fresh faith, and aroused the will to win. For long and lonely hours away from the applause—even the *awareness*—of the public, the one preparing that verbal missile persisted all alone with such mundane materials as dictionary, thesaurus, historical volumes, biographical data, and a desk full of other research works. The same could be said of those who labor to find cures for diseases. And how about those who experiment with inventions?

This past week I heard about a couple of men who were working alongside the inventor Thomas Edison. Weary to the point of exasperation, one man sighed, "What a waste! We have tried no less than seven hundred experiments and *nothing* has worked. We are not a bit better off than when we started."

With an optimistic twinkle in his eye, Edison quipped, "Oh, yes, we are! We now know seven hundred things that *won't* work. We're closer than we've ever been before." With that, he rolled up his sleeves and plunged back in.

If necessity is the mother of invention, persistence is certainly the father.

God honors it. Maybe because He models it so well. His love for His people, the Jews, persists to this very day, even though they have disobeyed Him more often than they have loved Him in return. And just think of His patient persistence in continually reaching out to the lost, ". . . not wishing for any to perish, but for all to come to repentance" (2 Peter 3:9b). And how about His persistence with *us*? You and I can recall one time after another when He could have (and *should* have!) wiped us out of the human race, but He didn't. Why? The answer is in Philippians 1:6:

> He Who began a good work in you will continue until the day of Jesus Christ—right up to the time of His return—developing [that good work] and perfecting and bringing it to full completion in you (Amplified Bible).

The One who began *will* continue right up to the end. Being the original finisher, He will persist. I'm comforted to know He won't be talked out of a plan that has to do with developing me. I need help!

Okay, since we are to be "imitators of God" (Ephesians 5:1), seems to me we oughta be about the business of persistence. Sure is easy to bail out theologically. You know, the age-old sovereignty cop-out. "If God wants such-and-such to happen, He's gonna have to do it all. I'm unable in myself." Now there may be a few occasions where that is an appropriate game plan; but by and large, His Spirit is willing, but our flesh is weak—dare I say lazy and indifferent? Unlike our Father, we tend to fade in the stretch.

May I get painfully personal? A proper, nutritional diet and a realistic program of exercise. Most folks I know have lost *hundreds* of pounds in their lifetime, only to put 'em on again. They all started well . . . but just about the time persistence was paying off, they quit. Believe me, I understand. That was the story of my life for about twenty years. But one day—one eventful, life-changing day—I stopped all the excuses (glands, stress, travel, reward for hard work, expensive wardrobe, not as heavy as a rhino, Cynthia's good cooking, etc.) and began a sensible process of taking off *and keeping off* fifty-five unwanted and unhealthy pounds of fat.

People didn't help much. Can't remember the number of times they warned me about being too thin, I shouldn't take such "risks." I was "looking ill." A rumor spread that I had cancer. Some thought I'd died. Would you believe that my wife got several sympathy cards expressing sorrow over my death? But I stayed at it. By the grace and power of Almighty God, I persisted.

All because of a simple, personal decision. Simple, yes . . . but easy? You gotta be kidding. Perhaps the single toughest decision of my adult life. Personal, yes . . . but automatic? It's still an everyday battle—no, three-times-a-day—battle. And my relentless commitment to conditioning gets tougher every month, I openly confess. But every mile I pound out on my *New Balance 990s*, I cast another vote for persistence.

Enough about me—you've got the winter stretching out in front of you. Think of these weeks as a time framework for your own investment. Choose an objective carefully, state it clearly in writing, then, with the persistence of an athlete training for the twenty-fourth Olympiad, *go for the goal!*

Trust me, when winter gives way to spring—and summer—you'll be so glad you did. And by then you'll have a new two-word motto to take you into the fall:

Persistence pays.

COME ASIDE

Use Ezekiel's call from the Lord in Ezekiel 2:1-8 to motivate your persistence in completing the tasks God has given you.

And don't forget to write down your objectives in clear language.

STARTING WHERE YOU ARE

o start over, you have to know where you are. To get somewhere else, it's necessary to know where you're presently standing. That's true in a department store or a big church, on a freeway or a college campus . . . or in *life*, for that matter. Very, very seldom does anybody "just happen" to end up on the right road. The process involved in redirecting our lives is often painful, slow, and even confusing. Occasionally it seems unbearable.

Take Jonah. (No one else wanted to.) He was prejudiced, bigoted, stubborn, openly rebellious, and spiritually insensitive. Other prophets ran to the Lord. He ran *from* Him. Others declared the promises of God with fervent zeal. Not Jonah. He was about as motivated as a 600-pound grizzly in mid-January.

Somewhere down the line the prophet got his inner directions crosswired. He wound up, of all places, on a ship in the Mediterranean Sea bound for a place named Tarshish. That was due west. God had told him *Nineveh*. That was due east. (That's like flying from Los Angeles to Berlin by way of Honolulu.) But Jonah never got to Tarshish, as you may remember. Through a traumatic chain of events, Jonah began to get his head together in the digestive tract of a gigantic fish.

What a place to start over! Slopping around in the seaweed and juices inside that monster, fishing for a match to find his way out, Jonah took a long, honest look at his short, dishonest life. For the first time in a long time, the prophet brushed up on his prayer life. He yelled for mercy. He recited psalms. He promised the Lord that he would keep his vow and get back on target. Only one creature on earth felt sicker than Jonah—the fish, in whose belly Jonah bellowed. Up came the prophet, who hit the road running—*toward Nineveh*.

One of the most encouraging things about new years, new weeks, and new days is the word *new*. Friend Webster reveals its meaning: "refreshed, different from one of the same that has existed previously . . . unfamiliar." Best of all, it's a place to start over. Refresh yourself. Change directions. Begin anew.

But that requires knowing where you are. It requires taking time to honestly admit your present condition. It means facing the music, standing alone inside the fish and coming to terms with those things that need attention, fishing in the seaweed for a match. *Before you find your way out, you must determine where you are*. Exactly. Once that is accomplished, you're ready to start over.

Just as there are few atheists in foxholes, so there are few rebels in fish stomachs. Perhaps you can identify rather easily with Jonah. This hasn't been your all-time-spiritual-high-plateau year, right? You've dodged and ducked, squirmed and squeaked your way through one Tarshish trip after another. But no more. You're tired. *Exhausted* says it better. Swallowed alive by your circumstances says it best. You feel oppressed, guilty, overused, and underdeveloped. You're not that old . . . but you've run a long way. Few moons but many miles. A subtle whisper in your ear says, "You're through. Finished. Burned out. Used up. You've been replaced . . . forgotten."

That's a lie! A carefully-timed deception by the enemy of your soul. Look at what the prophet Joel writes to all the Jonahs who may be reading this book. God is speaking:

> I will make up to you for the years that the swarming locust has eaten . . . (Joel 2:25a).

If God can take a disobedient prophet, turn him around, and set him on fire spiritually, He can do the same with *you*. He is a Specialist at making something useful and beautiful out of something broken and confused.

Where are you? Start *there*. Openly and freely declare your need to the One who cares deeply. Don't hide a thing. Show God all those locust bites. He's ready to heal every one . . . if you're ready to run toward that Nineveh called *tomorrow*.

COME ASIDE

To help you start anew, personalize the Scripture by praying through Hebrews 10:15-25.

OPERATION ARRIVAL

hen most people think of Christmas, they envision brightly wrapped gifts, the manger scene, kids wearing bathrobes in traditional pageants, and Bing Crosby singing "White Christmas." Not me. Like my friend Jay Kesler, I think of *Fords and Chevys*.

For the longest time I didn't understand the new car industry. I had always thought it worked like this. When a guy wanted a car, he dropped by the local dealership, kicked a few tires, slammed some doors, and fiddled around with radios, hoods, and trunk lids. Then he would rap with the salesman, dicker over prices, choose his favorite color, and place the order. I figured that when headquarters got the specs, they'd scurry around the shop finding the right steering wheel, engine, chrome strips, and hub caps, then make sure all that stuff got stuck on correctly before it was shipped. You know, kind of like whipping up a last-minute meal with grub from the kitchen.

But that's not the way it is at all. To my amazement I discovered that a computer card puts into motion dozens of contacts all over the country. One spot makes only engines. Another, the glass and plastic parts. Some other outfit does the steering wheels, and yet another the carpet and vinyl. As the order is placed, it triggers action in all these related areas. And—hopefully—at just the right time the special things arrive at the assembly plant where it all comes together—everything from bumper bolts to windshield wipers. And within a relatively short period of time, a shiny new car is punched out, rolled onto a transport truck, and sent to its proper destination.

What a remarkable arrangement ingenious Americans have devised! And none of it was even thought of a hundred years ago.

Now then—if man can come up with an organizational plan as complex as all that, think of how much *more* efficient God's arrangement was . . . almost 2000 years ago. I'm referring to the perfectly synchronized events surrounding the Savior's birth. For sure, it was no afterthought.

Scripture assures us that

> . . . when the fulness of the time came, God sent forth His Son . . . (Galatians 4:4).

Fantastic statement!

At just the right moment, precisely as God arranged it, in keeping with a plan we might dub "Operation Arrival," enter *Messiah*.

Micah said it would be in Bethlehem, Judah. It was. But I thought

Joseph and Mary were of Nazareth, Galilee. They were. Aren't those places miles apart? Yes, in those times *days* apart. Then . . . how? Well, you see, that's just a small part of the plan, nevertheless amazing. Especially when you consider Mary was almost "term" in her pregnancy. To get them down south in time required fairly good roads—unheard of prior to the Roman takeover. And they certainly needed to be forced to travel . . . hence a required census from Caesar Augustus (Luke 2:1) that forced Joseph to register in person in the city of his family roots, Bethlehem (Luke 2:4).

But before a Savior could be born, there also needed to be some natural means of common communication—a familiar tongue that would quickly spread the news. No problem. Thanks to Alexander the Great, the father of *koine* Greek, that language was ripe and ready for rapid dissemination of the gospel message through the pen of the evangelists and apostles from then on.

Thanks to good roads, a decision in Rome, and a bothersome census, it happened at just the right place. At just the right time . . . with an articulate language as the perfect verbal vehicle. A little baby that the world hardly noticed arrived. Rome was too busy building and conquering. Augustus thought he was hot stuff prancing about the palace demanding that census. In reality, he was little more than a wisp of lint on the prophetic page . . . a pawn in the hand of the Commander of "Operation Arrival."

The next time you drive away in a new car, think of Christmas. The things God pulled off to get His Son delivered on time twenty centuries ago would make the pride of American ingenuity look like an organizational afterthought by comparison.

COME ASIDE

One of the best summaries of Operation Arrival is found in an old man's words in Luke 1:68-75. Read and enjoy.

THE CRY FROM A CAVE

he Cave of Adullam was no Holiday Inn.

It was a wicked refugee camp . . . a dark vault on the side of a cliff that reached deeply into a hill. Huddled in this clammy cavern were 400 losers—a mob of miserable humanity. They came from all over and wound up all together. Listen to the account:

> And everyone who was in distress, and everyone who was in debt, and everyone who was discontented, gathered. . . . there were about four hundred men . . . (1 Samuel 22:2).

The original Mafia. They all had one thing in common—a bad record. The place smelled like the Rams' locker room and sounded like an Army barracks. You can bet not one of those guys ever heard Gothard's principles on handling irritations. They were so tough they'd make Al Capone sleep with a night light. They were gross. Anybody who got near that gang stayed as quiet as a roomful of nuns. They had a quaint name for those who crossed their paths . . . *victims.*

Except for David. That's right. *David.* It became his responsibility to turn that mob into an organized, well-disciplined fighting force . . . mighty men of valor. Talk about a challenge! These weren't the filthy five, nor the nasty nine, nor the dirty dozen. Remember—there were 400 of these hard-luck hooligans. Shortly thereafter, their numbers swelled to 600. And David was the den mother for these desperados. He was general, master sergeant, and chaplain all rolled into one. David, "the sweet psalmist of Israel," became David the drill instructor. Needless to say, his battalion of 600 is not to be confused with the 600 who "rode into the valley of death" in Tennyson's *Charge of the Light Brigade.* The only place these guys had ridden was out of town, chased by their creditors . . . which turned David's men into predators.

Did he pull it off? Could a shepherd from Bethlehem assume command of such a nefarious band of ne'er-do-wells? Did he meet the challenge?

Indeed!

In a brief period of time he had the troops in shape—combat ready. Incredible as it seems, he was doing battle against the enemy forces using strategic maneuvers before the year was up. These were the very men who fought loyally by his side and gave him strong support when he became the king of Israel. They were called "the mighty men," and many of their names are listed in the Bible for heroism and dedication.

All of us face a challenge. For some of you, it's a business that has all the earmarks of disaster. For others, it's the challenge of schooling without adequate money, or a houseful of young lives to shape, or a wounded relationship, or a prolonged illness that lingers and hurts. Still others of you find yourself in leadership over a group of people who need constant direction and encouragement . . . and you're tired of the demands. Some of you endure employment in a company that lacks a lot.

Be encouraged! If David could handle that cave full of malcontents, you can tighten your belt and take on the challenge in *your* cave. Do you need strength? Peace? Wisdom? Direction? Discipline? Ask for it! God will hear you. He gives special attention to cries when they come out of caves.

COME ASIDE

Use Ephesians 6:14-18 as a checklist for facing the challenges that confront you today.

"THE MOST OF YOUR TIME"

he same old elusive, irretrievable phantom winks at us about this time of the year *every* year. He stabs us awake with such things as a Christmas card from a friend separated from us by many miles, whom we've not contacted for many moons. If this doesn't do it, a photograph is his next approach. Tucked away in the card or letter is a snapshot of Jimmy So-and-so or the Watcha-ma-callit family.

"My, he's aged," we say.

Or, "Have they had *two* more kids since we last heard from them?"

Or perhaps, "Say, Honey, I think I detect a touch of gray in Jimmy's hair."

(And you wonder how come everyone else shows the wear and tear while *you* escape it year after year.)

Oh yes . . . Time has asked you to move over and allow him to take a seat, even if his sitting makes you uncomfortable. It's his rather brusque way of saying: "Howdy, I'm still here!"

In one sense, that's a *relief*. If he weren't, you wouldn't be either. In another sense, that's a *reminder*. Time is your slave, completely available and cooperative. He hasn't a lazy streak in his entire makeup. What's more, he provides you with an equal break every day you live, for no one else has *more* or *less* time than you when any day or week begins. His reminder is expressed beautifully in one of Paul's letters:

> Be very careful, then, how you live—not as unwise but as wise, making the most of every opportunity, because the days are evil (Ephesians 5:15-16 NIV).

Our goal, then, is not to *find more time* but to *use time more wisely*. You see, we really aren't responsible for our capacity . . . but we are certainly responsible for the strategic investment of our time. The literal rendering of Ephesians 5:16 is "redeeming the time."

That's worth a moment of meditation. Time must be purchased. We pay for it through selected activities and occupations, important or otherwise. And when it comes right down to it, the great difference between one person and another lies largely in his or her use of time.

The application of this is not: Go faster, get in a hurry, rush through each day! Nor is it: Refuse to relax, never take a break, don't look up! I cannot recall one place in any of the four Gospels where Jesus Christ was said to have been in a hurry . . . or labored continuously, day and night, without proper refreshment or rest. After all, that wouldn't be "making the most of your time" by any stretch of the imagination.

Listen—God has given you (as He gave His Son) sufficient time in each day for you to fulfill His perfect plan—including the interruptions! If you're fudging on your sleep or becoming a frantic, nail-biting, hurried Christian, then you are adding to your day too many things that simply are not His will for you. Check the seventeenth verse in Ephesians 5—you'll be glad you did.

All I ask is that you make an honest appraisal of your week. If there are leaks in your time dike, why not plug them?

If your priorities should be sifted more clearly from the trivia, that would be to your advantage.

If a simple plan would help to organize your day, that's only playing it smart.

If you should give a kind but unqualified, unexplained "No" more often, do it.

It's easy to forget that time is our slave, not our sovereign, isn't it?

When the new year becomes a reality at midnight, December 31, give God your year afresh and anew. Down deep—down in the depths of your spirit—dedicate yourself to Him as though for the first time in your life. Tell Him you are *His* and His *alone* . . . and that you want the new year to be His year for you through and through.

It just may be that Time will vanish from your life sometime in the next twelve months—and Eternity will take his place . . . as you take your place before your Redeemer. Face to face. *And time shall be no more.*

God's timing for Christ's return may very well occur before you tear one more sheet off that new calendar . . . and then again, it may not. Ephesians 5:15-16 applies either way.

Look at it this way:

God's part . . . the time of my Redeemer.

My part . . . the redeeming of my time.

COME ASIDE

Meditate on Hosea 10:12 to help you dedicate to God your use of time.

PAIN

They called him "Old Hickory" because of his tenacity and grit. His mother chose "Andrew" on March 15, 1767, when she gave birth to that independent-minded South Carolina rebel. Wild, quick-tempered, and disinterested in school, Andrew answered the call for soldiers to resist the British invasion at age thirteen. Shortly thereafter, he was taken prisoner. Refusing to black an enemy officer's boots, he was struck with a saber—Andrew's introduction to pain.

Although he bore the marks of the blow for the rest of his life, Andrew's fiery disposition never waned. A fighter to the core, he chose to settle arguments in duels and lived most of his days with two bullets painfully wedged in his body. After he distinguished himself on the battlefield, his name became a national synonym for valor and stern persistence. When politics nodded in his direction, "Old Hickory" accepted the challenge: first the Senate, then nomination for President. The shadow of pain appeared again in another form as he lost a narrow race with John Quincy Adams.

Four years later, however, he ran again . . . and won! But pain accompanied the victory. Two months before he took office he lost his beloved wife, Rachel. Grief-stricken, the President-elect pressed on. Even as he was being sworn into office as our nation's seventh President, he fought the anguish of a raging fever caused by an abscess in the lung.

Some time later one of the bullets within him had to be surgically removed. He endured that operation—done without anesthetic—in typically courageous fashion. Even his political career was painful. A nasty scandal split his cabinet and critics clawed at him like hungry lions. Although he stood firm for many months, the telling signs of pain began to manifest themselves. He was one of the few men who left office, however, more popular than when he came. "For once, the rising was eclipsed by the setting sun," wrote a contemporary sage. And it was pain, more than any other single factor, which drew the qualities of greatness out of Andrew Jackson.

Pain humbles the proud. It softens the stubborn. It melts the hard. Silently and relentlessly, it wins battles deep within the lonely soul. The heart alone knows its own sorrow, and not another person can fully share in it. Pain operates alone; it needs no assistance. It communicates its own message whether to statesman or servant, preacher or prodigal, mother or child. By staying, it refuses to be ignored. By hurting, it reduces its victim to profound depths of anguish. And it is at that anguishing point that the sufferer either submits and learns, developing maturity and character; or resists and becomes embittered, swamped by self-pity, smothered by self-will.

I have tried and I cannot find, either in Scripture or history, a strong-willed individual whom God used greatly until He allowed him to be hurt deeply.

It was just such a person who wrote these words for all to read:

Guests

Pain knocked upon my door and said
That she had come to stay,
And though I would not welcome her
But bade her go away,
She entered in.
Like my own shade
She followed after me,
And from her stabbing, stinging sword
No moment was I free.
And then one day another knocked
Most gently at my door.
I cried, "No, Pain is living here,
There is not room for more."
And then I heard His tender voice,
"'Tis I, be not afraid."
And from the day He entered in,
The difference it made!

Martha Snell Nicholson

COME ASIDE

Jeremiah 20 is a short but vivid picture of a prophet's pain—both inward and outward. Feel your way through this passage. Try to identify with Jeremiah, especially in his highly emotional words of verses 7-18. What can you learn from this hurting man of God?

Innovation

ebster defines it: "The introduction of something new . . . a new idea, method, or device." When we innovate, we change, we flex. We approach the standard operating procedure, not like a soft-footed Indian scout sneaking up on a deer by the brook, but rather like Wild Bill Hickok in a saloon with both guns blazing.

It takes guts to innovate, because it requires creative thinking. Thinking is hard enough, but *creative* thinking—ah, that's work! To get the juices squirting, you have to be dissatisfied with the status quo.

Take photography, for example. For years, the same old procedure . . . which required long periods of delay. Nobody even thought about hurrying up the process. Not until a guy named Edwin Land, who formed a company with a funny name— *Polaroid*.

Sometimes innovation is forced on us. Take December 7, 1941. We got caught with our military pants down. Before American planes could get airborne, or even out of the hangar, most of them were destroyed. We were forced to ask the obvious: "How can we get the planes out of the hangars *fast*?"

A fellow by the name of Mitchell solved the problem in a most innovative way. He simply turned the question upside down and asked the unobvious: "How can we get the hangar away from the planes—*fast*?" The result (after the inevitable laughter and rejection) was a two-piece hangar. Each section was mounted on wheels with sufficient power to separate the two at thirty-five miles an hour . . . which enabled the fighter planes to take off in several different directions. *Fast*.

Now, you're thinking: Land and Mitchell are geniuses. And you are ready to toss in Newton and Bell and Edison and Ford and the Wright brothers. And you're also telling yourself that there aren't many of those gifted people spread around. Granted, those might very well qualify as geniuses . . . but if you ask them, they'll tell you another story. J. C. Penney once observed, "Geniuses themselves don't talk about the gift of genius; they just talk about hard work and long hours." It's the old one percent inspiration and ninety-nine percent perspiration answer.

Let's have four "greats" take the stand and testify. These are their actual words:

> *Michelangelo*: "If people knew how hard I worked to get my mastery, it wouldn't seem so wonderful after all."
> *Carlyle*: "Genius is the capacity for taking infinite pains."

Paderewski: "A genius? Perhaps, but before I was a genius I was a drudge."
Alexander Hamilton: "All the genius I may have is merely the fruit of labor and thought."

Are innovative people really that rare? Not if you listen to Sheldon David, TRW vice president:

The capacity to exercise a relatively high degree of imagination, ingenuity, and creativity in the solution of organizational problems is widely, not narrowly, distributed in the population.

You know what that says to me? It says there are a whole lot more innovative people (who currently see themselves only as "drudges") than any of us can imagine. In fact, *you* may very well be one of them!

Let's take a little test and see. I have Earl Nightingale to thank for this list of twenty-five traits generally found in creative, innovative people. Now, relax. You don't need all twenty-five . . . but if you have most of them, you may be closer than you think.

Drive—a high degree of motivation
Courage—tenacity and persistence
Goals—a sense of direction
Knowledge—and a thirst for it
Good health
Honesty—especially intellectual
Optimism
Judgment
Enthusiasm
Chance taking—willingness to risk failure
Dynamism—energy
Enterprise—willing to tackle tough jobs
Persuasion—ability to sell
Outgoingness—friendly
Patient yet impatient—patient with others, yet impatient with the status quo
Adaptability—capable of change
Perfectionism—seek to achieve excellence
Humor—ability to laugh at self and others
Versatility—broad interests and skills
Curiosity—interested in people and things
Individualism—self-esteem and self-sufficiency

Realism/idealism—occupied by reality but guided by ideals
Imagination—seeking new ideas, combinations, and re-lationships
Communication—articulate
Receptive—alert

Okay, that's enough. I told you creative thinking was hard work! But there is something even harder . . . and that's *change*. It's admitting the need, being honest and humble enough to face the facts, then secure enough to consider "new ideas, methods, or devices," to pull it off. Swallowing our pride shouldn't be that difficult, since that's what we eat all day.

Go ahead and give it a whirl. Take one of those many things that keeps dragging you under and search for a creative way to solve the problem. And don't quit until it's done . . . and that smile of relief returns to your face.

I know you can do it! You did it before and it worked. And that problem was so huge you could hardly continue. Then came the change . . . the most important decision you ever made based on the most innovative combination ever devised. A man. A cross. Blood. And belief.

God defines it: "The introduction of something new . . . a new birth."

COME ASIDE

What basic principles in innovation does Jesus give in his parable in Luke 5:36-39?

Keep them in mind as you creatively tackle a big problem you've encountered.

THE HAMMER, THE FILE, AND THE FURNACE

t was the enraptured Rutherford who said in the midst of very painful trials and heartaches:

Praise God for the hammer, the file, and the furnace!

Let's think about that. The hammer is a useful and handy instrument. It is an essential and helpful tool, if nails are ever to be driven into place. Each blow forces them to bite deeper as the hammer's head pounds and pounds.

But if the nail had feelings and intelligence, it would give us another side of the story. To the nail, the hammer is a brutal, relentless master—an enemy who loves to beat it into submission. That is the nail's view of the hammer. It is correct. Except for one thing. The nail tends to forget that both it and the hammer are held by the same workman. The workman decides whose "head" will be pounded out of sight . . . and which hammer will be used to do the job.

This decision is the sovereign right of the carpenter. Let the nail but remember that it and the hammer are held by the same workman . . . and its resentment will fade as it yields to the carpenter without complaint.

The same analogy holds true for the metal that endures the rasp of the file and the blast of the furnace. If the metal forgets that it and the tools are objects of the same craftsman's care, it will build up hatred and resentment. The metal must keep in mind that the craftsman knows what he's doing . . . and is doing what is best.

Heartaches and disappointments are like the hammer, the file, and the furnace. They come in all shapes and sizes: an unfulfilled romance, a lingering illness and untimely death, an unachieved goal in life, a broken home or marriage, a severed friendship, a wayward and rebellious child, a personal medical report that advises "immediate surgery," a failing grade at school, a depression that simply won't go away, a habit you can't seem to break. Sometimes heartaches come suddenly . . . other times they appear over the passing of many months, slowly as the erosion of earth.

Do I write to a "nail" that has begun to resent the blows of the hammer? Are you at the brink of despair, thinking that you cannot bear another day of heartache? Is that what's gotten you down?

As difficult as it may be for you to believe this today, the Master knows what He's doing. Your Savior knows your breaking point. The bruising

156

and crushing and melting process is designed to reshape you, *not ruin you*. Your value is increasing the longer He lingers over you.

A. W. Tozer agrees:

> It is doubtful whether God can bless a man greatly until He has hurt him deeply.

Aching friend—stand fast. Like David when calamity caved in, strengthen yourself in the Lord your God (1 Samuel 30:6). God's hand is in your heartache. Yes, it is!

If you weren't important, do you think He would take this long and work this hard on your life? Those whom God uses most effectively have been hammered, filed, and tempered in the furnace of trials and heartache.

COME ASIDE

Take time to thank your Master for any trials and heartaches in this season of your life. And meditate afresh on James 1:2-12.

RADICAL ADJUSTMENTS

xtreme dilemmas are usually solved by radical adjustments. It used to be called "fighting fire with fire." Minor alterations won't do. If the situation is getting completely out of hand, a slight modification won't cut it. It's get-with-it time.

- If the tumor is the size of a grapefruit, taking a handful of vitamins three times a week isn't the answer.
- If the foundation has shifted so much that the walls are cracking and the windows won't close, the place needs more than a paint job.
- If the ship is sinking and the storm is getting stronger, it's time to do something much more decisive than dialogue.
- If the church is emptying because needs are going unmet, singing hymns and preaching longer sermons won't do the trick.
- If the family isn't talking, serving more meals is hardly the way to turn things around.

The most radical alternative may sometimes be the most practical. These will *not* be the most popular or enjoyable decisions . . . or the most diplomatic.

Radical adjustments make waves, not friends. Heads sometimes roll and hearts often break. The uninvolved public seldom understands or agrees, especially at the outset. But the strange thing is that radical adjustments, more often than not, make pretty good sense when reconsidered through the rearview mirror. After the fact, stone-throwing critics ultimately nod their approval . . . calling the decision "courageous" or even "visionary." What the critics usually overlook is just how painful the drastic decision really was.

On October 12, 1972, a Fairchild F-227 of the Uruguayan Air Force was chartered by an amateur rugby team. The plan? To fly from Montevideo to Santiago, Chile . . . a flight pattern which required flying over the rugged Andes. There were forty-five on board, including the crew. Bad weather brought the plane down in Mendoza, a small Argentinian town. Since the weather improved the following morning, the Fairchild set off again, flying south to the Planchon Pass. They would never make their destination.

- ◆ At 3:21 P.M. the pilot reported to Air Traffic Control in Santiago that he was over the Pass of Planchon.
- ◆ At 3:24 P.M. he reported their plane was over a small town in Chile named Curico. He was authorized to turn north and begin his descent to the airport of Pudahuel.
- ◆ At 3:30 P.M. he reported his height—15,000 feet.
- ◆ When Santiago control tower spoke to the F-227 one minute later, there was no reply . . . nor would there be for the next ten weeks. An extreme dilemma had transpired.

Several things made search attempts futile. The Andes are a vast, treacherous, and confusing range. The top of the plane was white, making it impossible to spot from the air. Heavy snowfalls caused the vessel to blend into its surroundings. There was little chance that the plane would ever be found, and less chance still that any of the forty-five passengers and crew could have lived through the fall.

Ten weeks later, a Chilean peasant tending his cattle in a remote valley deep in the Andes spotted two gaunt, bearded figures in the distance. They made wild gestures. They fell to their knees as though in supplication, but the peasant, fearing they were terrorists, fled the scene. The next day, however, he returned and noticed the two strangers were still there across the river. He approached the bank of the river, wrapped some paper and a pen into a handkerchief and tossed it to the other side.

When it was thrown back by the bedraggled figures, these words had been written with a quivering hand:

> I come from a plane that fell in the mountains. I am Uruguayan . . .

Those who endured the ordeal had done so because of a radical adjustment. *They had become cannibals.* Instead of starving to death, they decided to strip thin layers of skin off the frozen bodies of the victims and survive by eating the flesh of those who had once been their friends and teammates. It was literally a life-or-death, albeit painful, decision. But because of it, sixteen survived and were rescued. Their story is told in a book that bears an appropriate one-word title—*Alive*.

It's possible that you find yourself cornered today. Although you are not lost in the foreseen Andes, you feel gripped with fear because your situation is extreme. It's time to get control of your finances. Or break off that compromising relationship. Or say yes to God's clear leading. Or come to terms with your priorities. Or get your career in gear. It's no time for a mild and easy shift. The dilemma is extreme and the only solution is a radical one. You've thought it through and you've considered all the alternatives. Your throat is sore from praying and your eyes burn from weeping. You know it's right, but you're scared. *Really* scared. Initially, somebody won't understand and you'll not be able to explain. Yet you are convinced it's best . . . it will glorify God . . . it can be supported by scriptural principles . . . and it's right.

So? So quit procrastinating and do it.

Had Christ not taken a drastic step, sinners like us would've never survived the fall. We would never have been rescued. We would be permanently lost. The cross was God's incredible response to our extreme dilemma. Christ did something radical.

Now it's your turn. Get with it.

COME ASIDE

Commit again to the Lord the radical step which you believe He wants you to take. As you do, listen to His words to His servant in Joshua 1:9.

MISCOMMUNICATION

on't garble the message!"

If I heard that once during Marine boot camp, I must've heard it four dozen times. Again and again, our outfit was warned against hearing one thing, then passing on a slightly different version. You know, changing the message by altering the meaning a tad. It's so easy to do, isn't it? Especially when it's filtered through several minds, then pushed through each mouth. It is amazing how the original story, report, or command appears after it has gone through its verbal metamorphosis.

Consider the following:

A colonel issued this directive to his executive officer:

> Tomorrow evening at approximately 2000 hours, Halley's Comet will be visible in this area, an event which occurs only once every seventy-five years. Have the men fall out in the battalion area in fatigues, and I will explain this rare phenomenon to them. In case of rain we will not be able to see anything, so assemble the men in the theatre and I will show them films of it.

Executive officer to company commander:

> By the order of the colonel, tomorrow at 2000 hours, Halley's Comet will appear above the battalion area. If it rains fall the men out in fatigues; then march to the theatre where the rare phenomenon will take place, something which occurs only once every seventy-five years.

Company commander to lieutenant:

> By order of the colonel in fatigues at 2000 hours tomorrow evening, the phenomenal Halley's Comet will appear in the theatre. In case of rain in the battalion area, the colonel will give another order, something which occurs once every seventy-five years.

Lieutenant to sergeant:

> Tomorrow at 2000 hours, the colonel, in fatigues, will appear in the theatre with Halley's Comet, something which

161

happens every seventy-five years. If it rains, the colonel will order the comet into the battalion area.

Sergeant to squad:

> When it rains tomorrow at 2000 hours, the phenomenal seventy-five-year-old General Halley, accompanied by the colonel, will drive his Comet through the battalion area theatre in fatigues.

Garbled messages aren't unique to the military. They provide the perfect fuel for gossip sessions and just the right ingredient for slanderous slams. Exaggerate this detail or rearrange that fact and you've got a recipe that'll make more mouths water than hot fudge on a rainy night. Don't be too careful with numbers, omit a few specifics, leave room for a subtle innuendo or two, and for sure, add some color to make the things more interesting. Then when you sense the listener is sufficiently misinformed, don't bother to correct the mistake. Stay quiet. Calm yourself with the thought that nothing more (?) will be said to anyone else. I mean, you didn't rob a bank or something. You just forgot to mention a couple of tiny tidbits that don't make that much difference, right? How in the world could that hurt? Why be such a stickler? Well, let me ask you a few related questions.

- How accurate do you expect your physician to be when he talks about what he found during surgery? Do words matter that much?
- How about that contract? Are you going to bother with stuff like terms and implications and amounts of money and percentages?
- Do you feel comfortable with a car or insurance salesperson who tells you one thing today and a slightly different comment day after tomorrow?
- Ever dated a guy who had a little problem telling the same story the same way each time? Did the thought of marrying him make you a little nervous?
- What about a minister or counselor who told you not to worry about *exactly* what the Bible says? What if he didn't seem to think that each one of those "Thus saith the Lord" statements was very important?

Speaking of which, God's style of communication doesn't seem to leave much margin for generalities. He told more than one prophet to say it painfully straight and make it obviously clear. He gave Moses precisely ten commandments, not "a dozen or so." He told Jonah to go directly to Nineveh, not "whichever city seems fair to you, pal." He mentions His interest in every jot and tittle of His Word, not "just the part that's easy to read and fun to do."

The God who expects His children to behave doesn't leave for the weekend with a note on the door that says, "Whatever turns you on . . ." The preservation of an inerrant text assumes respectful treatment and accurate communication.

Do you remember what Paul wrote to the Corinthians who had begun to scramble the Scripture with weird and senseless sounds? Drawing upon the analogy of music, he asks:

> Even in the case of lifeless things that make sounds, such as the flute or harp, how will anyone know what tune is being played unless there is a distinction in the notes? Again, if the trumpet does not sound a clear call, who will get ready for battle? (1 Corinthians 14:7-8 NIV).

The battle is raging. If ever we needed "a clear call" from the bugler, it is now. Are you responsible for passing on information? Tighten your lips! Hit the right note! *Don't garble that message!*

COME ASIDE

Observe God's style of communication in the ringing message of Micah 4:1-7, a model of clarity.

If there's something you've been trying unsuccessfully to communicate to someone, take time now to write it down as clearly as you can.

ACTING DECISIVELY

ow then, revere the LORD, and serve Him in sincerity and truth. Reject the gods which your ancestors served beyond the river and in Egypt, and serve the LORD. However, if it seems wrong in your eyes to serve the LORD, choose today whom you will serve—whether the gods whom your fathers served beyond the river or the gods of the Amorites in whose land you live. Nevertheless, I and my house, we shall serve the LORD" (Joshua 24:14-15 MLB).

I like Joshua's style. Like a good leader, he laid out the facts. He exhorted those about him to get off the fence and get their spiritual act together. He encouraged personal authenticity and strong commitment . . . but not once did he pull rank and fall back on intimidation to get his way. He risked being ignored and rejected when he left the final decision up to them. He respected their right to follow his advice or walk away when he told them, in so many words, "Make up your mind!" But there was never any question where he stood. He had weighed the evidence, considered the alternatives, and come to a settled conviction—he and his family were going to serve the Lord God, no question about it. But what others would do was strictly up to them. They would have to decide for themselves.

Unusual combination. A strong leader who knew where he was going, but gave others the space they needed to choose for themselves. No threats. No name-calling. No public put-downs. No exploitation or manipulation or humiliation. He didn't play on their emotions or attack their alleged ignorance or use some gimmick to gain strokes in defense of his position. He knew what God would have him do, and he realized the consequences of their choosing differently . . . but they needed to weigh those issues for themselves. It needed to be their decision, not his. At that point, he backed off and said, "Now you decide."

That's not only smart, it's an evidence of two admirable virtues: security in himself and respect for others. Today, it is clear to all of us that Joshua made the right decision back then. From our objective perspective, he chose the correct alternative . . . as they also did later on. But note again that he didn't hurry his people to opt for his position. Joshua knew that if they didn't wrestle with the issues on their own, the resulting decision might be superficial . . . fragile . . . a commitment that might very well melt under the inevitable heat of difficulty and trial.

Nevertheless, there will always be some who want others to make their decisions for them. Many individuals in Christendom are continually looking for some evangelical guru or superstar pastor or bionic authority figure to cosign for their lives. As David Gill wrote:

> We want heroes! We want reassurance that someone knows
> what is going on in this mad world. We want a father or a
> mother to lean on. We want revolutionary folk heroes who
> will tell us what to do until the rapture. We massage the egos
> of these demagogues and canonize their every opinion.

It takes the restraining power of the Holy Spirit to withstand such tempting invitations to take control. It is helpful to remember that every time we yield to that destructive desire for power we retard others' growth toward maturity. Making one's own decisions develops healthy mental muscles. But I repeat, there will always be a few who crave to be told what to do. They are the ones who remain so indecisive their favorite color is plaid.

A major reason some prefer to be indecisive is laziness. Decision making is hard work. Peter Drucker is correct when he says:

> A decision is a judgment. It is a choice between alternatives.
> It is rarely a choice between right and wrong. It is at best a
> choice between "almost right" and "probably wrong"—but
> much more often a choice between two courses of action,
> neither of which is probably more nearly right than the
> other.

That may sound like a tongue-twister, but in reality it's a mind-boggler, requiring a painful, exacting process rare to many . . . a process called *thinking*.

How much easier it is to adopt a list, to click off the answers one, two, three, four, five. You don't have to think. All you need to do is follow instructions. Don't weigh the consequences. Don't sweat the details. Just do as you are told and leave the driving to "us," namely a few guys at the top. Don't think it through and decide . . . just submit.

If that is the approach you prefer, let me remind you of two words, just two words—*Watergate* and *Jonestown*.

Decisiveness in both of those tragedies was replaced with blind obedience, unquestioned authority, and absolute loyalty. Somebody, somehow, at some time in each of those outfits convinced the troops that Tennyson's battle cry for the Light Brigade was the standard operating procedure for them:

Theirs not to make reply.
Theirs not to reason why.
Theirs but to do and die.

There is a place for that philosophy in the military where there isn't time to stop and think. Discussion groups aren't too popular in combat when the objective is survival.

But in day-to-day living, when issues are not clearly spelled out in Scripture, when there is a lot of gray instead of black and white, we need to learn a lesson from Moses' mature successor.

Think wisely. Weigh the alternatives. Choose for yourself. Decide now.

COME ASIDE

Study Paul's recollection in Galatians 2 of a crucial point in his life. How and why did he exhibit decisiveness here?

Explanations

nce upon a time life was simple and uncomplicated. Oh sure, there were struggles and problems, but they weren't all that complex. Good and evil did battle with each other. So did will-power and laziness. Right fought against wrong in the main event and not too many folks remained neutral. There was a clear, unmistakable line between winning and losing . . . victory and defeat . . . accomplishment and failure . . . actual war between opposing forces and peace, real peace—not smoldering, game-playing peace.

Sometimes we hated ourselves and we openly confessed our guilt and shame. On other occasions we tightened our belts, did the hard thing, and we made it happen. We felt proud of our determination and we passed on that pride to our young. They even believed in us! A marriage was for keeps. A job was for work. A crime was for punishment. Irresponsibility was frowned on, a broken promise was inexcusable, adultery was a scandal, hardship was endured, extra effort was admired and applauded.

Then, ever so slowly, the fog rolled in.

All the evils of the world, once black as tar, turned strange shades of gray. Instead of our seeing them clearly as wrong or someone's fault, they became fuzzy . . . and ultimately "explainable." Which, being interpreted, means "excusable." And the outworking of all this is a remarkable twist, a subtle switching of roles.

It's now the guilty (you'll excuse the expression) who is more protected than the victim. It's the one who protests an act of violence who is frowned upon, not the doer of the deed. It's the guy who uses words like *discipline* and *diligence* and *integrity* and *blame* and *shame* who is the weirdo, not the one who has developed the scientific gift of explanation and rationalization.

"If a drunk driver kills my wife or cripples my kids, how dare I hate him? We all know alchoholism is a disease and nobody gets a disease on purpose. But if I do hate him and if I'm caught up with such rage that I kill the driver, you can't be angry with me. After all, wasn't I suffering from temporary insanity? (That's a brief disease . . . like the flu.)"

Explanations abound, everything from poor toilet training and unfair parents to oppressive work conditions and governmental rip-offs. I smiled when I encountered Rex Julian Beaber's words recently. He's a clinical and forensic psychologist who teaches family medicine at UCLA Medical School. With tongue in cheek he writes:

Now don't worry if you find yourself angry with your spouse or boss. You just have an emotional problem. Eating too much? That's OK, you're simply suffering from obesity. Certainly you needn't concern yourself with any lack of will power. As we have learned, your food problem is really just repressed sexuality, or maybe you don't have enough pineapple in your diet. . . . The one thing that is clear is that the problem isn't your fault and the solution could never be as simple as "Just stop eating so much."

Are you bored with work? You probably suffer from burnout, one of the newest pet diseases of the middle class. Remember the old days when you thought they called it work because it was difficult, unpleasant and boring? Remember when you believed the reason you were being paid was to do your job whether you liked it or not? Those days are over. Remember when drug or alcohol abuse was a product of some combination of hedonism and foolishness? That era has ended too. Now you're an addict. You have no will, so you are not to blame; the disease got you.

Sometimes in my more maddening moments I entertain crazy "what if" ideas. What if we were suddenly stripped of our century twenty maladies and "scientific" explanations? What if there was a resurgence of such dated phrases as:
"I have decided to . . ."
"I will . . ."
"I will no longer . . ."
"I am wrong . . ."
"Starting today, I won't . . ."
That would mean saying farewell to foggy terms like:
"I am thinking about it . . ."
"I'm working on it . . ." and,
"Someday I plan to . . ."
which psychologists, pastors, and counselors worth their salt realize mean little more than, "I'm working out some great excuse for *not doing it.*"

How do I know? I've learned those phrases, too! And occasionally when I get cornered by a hard set of facts, I dip into my bag just like you do—especially if I'm not ready to come to terms with my own responsibility. Out come those handy little guilt-relieving "explanations."

Little by little I'm learning just how enamored I was of all those catch phrases that made me forget I was on a sinking ship.

Let me level with you. And I say this for one reason only—to encourage you to replace explanations with decisions and actions. If I had continued giving in to those lame excuses, my marriage would not have held together, my ministry would have become mediocre, I would never have finished one book I wanted to write, I would not have a close friend, I would have jumped from job to job because of the pressure, and I would still be a fat slob.

Jesus was right. After telling His disciples how to live fulfilled lives, He put the clincher on it by adding, "If you know these things, happy are you if you *do* them."

COME ASIDE

Read with complete openness James 1:22-25. And don't let another day slip by without taking action on that issue about which you know God has been prompting you.

SACRAMENT OF BROKEN SEED

hances are running high that you're in a hurry today. Am I right? Your "To Do" list stretches on and on. If you're reading this in the morning, you're wondering how in the world you'll get it all done. If the day has already slipped away as you read these words, you're wondering where in the world the hours *went*.

Yeah, I can identify. It's been that kind of week. Really, that kind of *month*. But let's take five and ponder a word that gets overlooked in the midst of a breakneck schedule. Just a simple word . . . *helping*.

Think about that. About being of assistance . . . your arm around the hunched shoulder of another . . . your smile saying "try again" to someone who's convinced it's curtains . . . your cup of cool water held up to a brother's cracked lips, reassuring and reaffirming.

Every time I pick up my pen, the thought of helping urges me to push ink into words. There are enough—more than enough—specialists in body blocks and pass defense and tackling those with the ball, causing fumbles, bruises, and injuries. I'd much rather run interference. Open up holes. Slap some fanny and say, "You can do it, now git at it!" I couldn't agree more with Philip Yancey, a man who models his own advice:

> C. S. Lewis once likened his role as a Christian writer to an adjective humbly striving to point others to the Noun of truth. For people to believe that Noun, we Christian writers must improve our adjectives.

Whether in the sweltering heat of summer or during winter's bitter blast, I'd like to think that some carefully selected turn of a phrase, some pointed story, even the choice of a single word I used reached over to your hand with a grip of fresh hope. The Noun is so attractive, so satisfying, we dare not get sloppy with our adjectives.

It's all part of helping folks "hold fast the confession of our hope without wavering . . . " and being committed to "stimulate one another to love and good deeds" (Hebrews 10:23-24).

I hope that the following mid-winter poem will stimulate you to reach beyond the safe bounds of your private, fenced-off territory. It's called "At the Winter Feeder," a perceptive piece by John Leax, professor of English and poet-in-residence at Houghton college:

His feather flame doused dull
by icy cold,
the cardinal hunched
into the rough, green feeder
but ate no seed.

Through binoculars I saw
festered and useless
his beak, broken
at the root.

Then two: one blazing, one gray,
rode the swirling weather
into my vision
and lighted at his side.

Unhurried, as if possessing
the patience of God,
they cracked sunflowers
and fed him
beak to wounded beak
choice meats.

Each morning and afternoon
the winter long,
that odd triumvirate,
that trinity of need,
returned and ate
their sacrament
of broken seed.

If birds had souls, I have no doubt that that cardinal would, long before springtime, yield to the God of his friends. Attractive adjectives plus unselfish verbs equal faith in the Noun of truth.

It's an axiom that holds true at the winter feeder.

COME ASIDE

Feed on Titus 3:3-8.

Then, before this time tomorrow, give special help to someone you know.

Dress your dreams in denim

ome collegians think manual labor is the president of Mexico ... until they graduate. Suddenly, the light dawns. Reality frowns. And that sheltered, brainy, fair-skinned, squint-eyed scholar who has majored in medieval literature and minored in Latin comes of age. He experiences a strange sensation deep within his abdomen two weeks after framing his diploma. Hunger. Remarkable motivation accompanies this feeling.

His attempts at finding employment prove futile. Those places that have an opening don't really need a guy with a master's in medieval lit. They can't even spell it. Who cares if a truck driver understands European poetry from the twelfth century? Or what does it matter if the fella stocking the shelves at Safeway can give you the ninth letter in the Latin alphabet? When it comes to landing a job, most employers are notoriously pragmatic and unsophisticated. They are looking for people who have more than academic, gray wrinkles between their ears. They really couldn't care less about how much a guy or gal knows. What they want is someone who can *put to use* the knowledge that's been gained, whether the field is geology or accounting, engineering or plumbing, physics or barbering, journalism or welding.

That doesn't just happen. People who are in great demand today are those who can see it in their imaginations—then pull it off. Those who can think—then follow through. Those who dress their daring dreams in practical denim workclothes. That takes a measure of gift, a pinch of skill, and a ton of discipline! Being practical requires that we traffic in reality, staying flexible at the intersections where stop-and-go lights flash. It also demands an understanding of others who are driving so as to avoid collisions.

Another mark of practicality is a constant awareness of time. The life of a practical person is fairly uncomplicated and usually methodical. The practical mind would rather meet a deadline and settle for limited objectives than accomplish the maximum and be late.

The favorite expressions of a practical soul often begin with "what?"

What does the job require?
What do you expect of me?
What is the deadline?
What are the techniques?

Or "how" . . .

> How does it work?
> How long will it take?
> How much does it cost?
> How fast can it go?

Dreamers don't mix too well with pragmatists. They irritate each other when they rub together . . . yet both are necessary. Take away the former and you've got a predictable and occasionally dull result. Remove the latter and you've got creative ideas without wheels, slick visions without handles . . . and you go broke trying to get it off the runway.

The Bible is full of men and women who dreamed dreams and saw visions. But they didn't stop there. They had faith, they were people who saw the impossible, and yet their feet were planted on planet earth.

Take Nehemiah. What a man! He had the task of rebuilding the stone wall around Jerusalem. He spent days thinking, praying, observing, dreaming, and planning. But was he ever practical! He organized a mob into work parties . . . he faced criticism realistically . . . he stayed at the task without putting out needless fires . . . he met deadlines . . . and he maintained the budget.

Or take Abigail. What a woman! She was married to a first-class fink, Nabal by name, alias Archie Bunker. Because of his lack of wisdom, his greed, prejudice, and selfishness, he aroused the ire of his employees. They laid plans to kill him. Being a woman of faith, Abigail thought through the plot, prayed, and planned. Then she did a remarkable thing. She catered a meal to those hungry, angry men. Smart gal! Because of her practicality, Nabal's life was saved and an angry band of men was calmed and turned back.

It is the practical person, writes Emerson, who becomes "a vein in times of terror that commands the admiration of the wisest." So true. Amazing thing about the practical person—he may not have the most fun or think the deepest thoughts, but he seldom goes hungry!

Just now finishing school? Looking for a job? Is this the reason you're discouraged? Remember this—dreams are great and visions are fun. But in the final analysis, when the bills come due, they'll be paid by manual labor. *Labor* . . . hard work forged in the furnace of practicality.

I encourage you . . . get with it. Be practical, that is.

COME ASIDE

Get a feel for Nehemiah's good mix of vision and practicality by reading as much as you can in chapters 2, 6, and 13 in his book.

What were this man's strengths, and how can you emulate them?

"LITTLE" PEOPLE, "BIG" PEOPLE

od makes some people large, others moderate in stature. Still others are small in size. We frequently make the mistake of calling small folks "little," but that is an unfortunate and unfair tag. I'm not picking at terms . . . there is a great deal of difference between being small and being little. If you don't think so, just ask someone who is less than average height. They won't hesitate telling you they may be small, but they're definitely *not* little.

Being "little" implies much more than being short. It suggests being petty, lacking in great-heartedness, having a mind that is restrictive, suspicious, envious, spiteful. "Little" people (regardless of their physical size) find it extremely difficult to applaud another's achievement, especially if the accomplishments bear the marks of success and excellence. While there are many who are big enough to appreciate outstanding work, there is always the "little" world comprising those who frown, depreciate, question, doubt, criticize, and forever search for the flaw.

Sixty-eight years ago there was a young, small company in Detroit, Michigan. The odds against its surviving were heavy. But this struggling firm was determined not to lower its standard. Excellence and quality craftsmanship would not be compromised—*period*. There would be no tolerance for mediocrity, no winking at a cheap and shoddy "let's-just-get-by" philosophy. At that time it wasn't part of a huge corporation (that came later), and even though it was eclipsed by much larger and more powerful competitors, this resilient, independent company stayed by its standard. Interestingly, it slowly gained recognition as a leader. The company published an advertisement in *The Saturday Evening Post*, January 2, 1915. Here is what it said:

The Penalty of LEADERSHIP

In every field of human endeavor, he that is first must perpetually live in the white light of publicity. Whether the leadership be vested in a man or in a manufactured product, emulation and envy are ever at work. In art, in literature, in music, in industry, the reward and the punishment are always the same. The reward is widespread recognition; the punishment, fierce denial and detraction. When a man's work becomes a standard for the whole world, it also becomes a target for the shafts of the envious few. If his work be merely mediocre, he will be left severely alone—if he achieve a masterpiece, it will set a million tongues a-wagging.

Jealousy does not protrude its forked tongue at the artist who produces a commonplace painting. Whatsoever you write, or paint, or play, or sing, or build, no one will strive to surpass or slander you, unless your work be stamped with the seal of genius. Long, long after a great work or a good work has been done, those who are disappointed or envious continue to cry out that it cannot be done.

Spiteful little voices in the domain of art were raised against our own Whistler as a mountebank, long after the big world had acclaimed him its greatest artistic genius. Multitudes flocked to Bayreuth to worship at the musical shrine of Wagner, while the little group of those whom he had dethroned and displaced argued angrily that he was no musician at all. The little world continued to protest that Fulton could never build a steamboat, while the big world flocked to the river banks to see his boat steam by.

The leader is assailed because he is a leader, and the effort to equal him is merely added proof of that leadership. Failing to equal or to excel, the follower seeks to depreciate and to destroy—but only confirms once more the superiority of that which he strives to supplant.

There is nothing new in this. It is as old as the world and as old as the human passions—envy, fear, greed, ambition, and the desire to surpass. And it all avails nothing. If the leader truly leads, he remains—the leader. Master-poet, master-painter, master-workman, each in his turn is assailed, and each holds his laurels through the ages. That which is good or great makes itself known, no matter how loud the clamor of denial. That which deserves to live—lives.

I am aware that all sorts and sizes of people will read this piece. A few of you are "little," hard as it may be to face it. But I'm convinced that many more of you are "big," which, being translated, means visionary, courageous, bold, secure, productive, unafraid of hard work, and unintimidated by the odds. Good for you! Press on. Grow even bigger. Stand tall. Run hard as you set a new pace. Refuse to reduce your stride. Embrace quality and excellence and determination. Without fudging one inch on integrity and humility, push on . . . lead on. Ignore the "little" world of onlookers who are too petty to produce, too suspicious to affirm, too envious to acknowledge greatness. Go hard after your goal, get on with it!

Isn't that the essence of Paul's charge to the Corinthians?

. . . continue to be firm, incapable of being moved, always letting the cup run over . . . because you know that your labor in the service of the Lord is never thrown away (1 Corinthians 15:58 Williams).

It's certainly what the apostle had in mind when he challenged young Timothy to "Take pains with these things, be absorbed in them, so that your progress may be evident to all. Pay close attention to yourself . . . persevere!"

Regardless of your stature, in spite of your current circumstances, age, status, occupation, location, limitations, or background, aim high . . . way up there where the ranks are as thin as the air. And the next time you're tempted to listen to those who would penalize you, remember that little company in Detroit, determined to succeed over seven decades ago. Oops, not "little," small.

Come to think of it, I've never heard anyone call the Cadillac Motor Car Company "little."

COME ASIDE

Check your aim. Is it too low?

Use John 14:12-14 to help you think about it, and then make any necessary adjustments.

PROPHET SHARING

ave you noticed? Some people have the uncanny ability to see so far into tomorrow, you feel like you're operating in the shadows of yesterday. While you and I are evaluating where we've been, those forward-thinking people are forever exploring where we're going. Instead of reacting, they're on the offense . . . probing, innovating, analyzing, and warning—always warning. While we search for ways to settle in and find comfort on our sofa-like surroundings, they are confronting the consequences of reality, facing the music before we even realize the prelude has begun.

Prophets, I suppose we could call them . . . seers who frown while others yawn . . . restless, troubled, contemplative souls. They're not unlike the characters in a thought-jabbing cartoon published years ago. The whole message is contained in a single frame as the figures of a man and a woman are falling upside down through space.

"Gertrude," says the man, "we can't go on living like this!"

Those who slumber in the sleepy, warm twilight of sundown, finding a great deal of security in the mediocrity and predictability of sameness, cannot bring themselves to see either potential danger or possible tragedy. But those who see their world adrift, moving all too rapidly toward a bleak and disastrous dawn, shout across the chasm of complacency, "We can't go on living like this!"

Perhaps they are not upside down after all. They just seem that way. Thinking ahead keeps them topsy-turvy in their heads. While chatty, laughing tourists are taking snapshots of the lowlands with rose-colored filters, those lean, tough-minded climbers have scaled the rugged peaks. It gives them a stark view of what's ahead. Tomorrow's storm keeps them from enjoying today's lull. They're hard to live with, sometimes impossible to understand.

Robert Greenleaf recalls a story which grew out of Beethoven's composition, the C# Minor Quartet, Opus 131. When first played in the composer's lifetime, it appeared to be unlike anything the master had ever written before. "Ludwig," a friend asked, "what has happened? We don't understand you anymore." It is reported that Beethoven, with a sigh, replied, "I have said all that I have to say to my contemporaries; now I am speaking to the future."

If you are one of those seers, a tomorrow-thinker in a world of yesterday-dwellers, take heart. Realize that you must be true to yourself. While you may not be applauded for your warnings, you will be rewarded for your efforts. Just be patient with those who lack your zest and zeal. Say your piece, make your contribution, shout, if you must . . . but keep in mind that prophets were seldom heeded, rarely thanked, and never popular.

A legend dated around A.D. 89 states that the apostle John lost the first transcription of his apocalyptic vision. The account was preserved only by word of mouth, since the document was lost during the persecution of Dioletian. In it a *fifth* horseman emerged. This rider actually led the other four, says the legend. You remember the other four: War, Pestilence, Famine, and Death. As the lead rider became nauseated by the deeds of his fellows, he pressed far ahead of them. He entered every village, every city, with a great cry and terrifying predictions. To the rulers of each place he warned of those who came hard behind him, and as proof, he showed them the blood on his own horse's hooves. Then, as always, he went on, for his urgency was great.

Behind him citizens fell into profound arguments. Some called him a liar. They said the blood was that of goats, not humans. Others considered him insane . . . and a few claimed he had not passed that way at all; they merely imagined him there. Theological, philosophical, and political debates abounded. In the end, no one said, "A prophet has been among us," so his warnings did not prevail. The four horsemen ultimately arrived, and as predicted, slew their three times tens of thousands.

Meanwhile, the legendary fifth horseman came to the outermost reaches of the earth and turned about, satisfied with his work. However, as he revisited one city after another—all now destroyed and desolate—he realized nothing he had said had made one bit of difference. Unrepentant, arrogant, indifferent, and disobedient, they had refused to act upon the truth they had been told. The legend concludes with the fifth horseman rejoining his companions. Together they slew all mankind and destroyed their cities.

And the identity of him who led? The name of him who warned, according to the legend?

Reality.

COME ASIDE

Read the words God spoke through a great prophet in Amos 3:7-8.

Have you heard the Lion roar? If so, what will you do?

THE GHOST OF EPHRAIM

salm 78 is a hymn of history. Being a *Maskil* psalm, it is designed to instruct those who ponder its message. The opening words command us to *listen . . . to incline our ears* to what the composer, Asaph, has to say. Immediately we realize that he is recounting the unhappy days of disobedience which characterized the Jews during their rebellion and wandering. Throughout the psalm, Asaph contrasts God's faithfulness and patience with Israel's failure and unbelief. The ancient hymn was, no doubt, sung in a minor key.

My eye fell upon verse 9 recently as I was on a safari through the Scriptures. I was intrigued by a strange stroke of the psalmist's pen:

> The sons of Ephraim were archers equipped with bows, yet they turned back in the day of battle (Psalm 78:9).

These men of Ephraim were adept with bow and arrow. Furthermore, they had sufficient hardware to handle the enemy's attack. They possessed both skill and supplies in abundance . . . but you couldn't tell it! On the "day of battle" (that is, the first day of the fray) they "turned back." Like foxes hunted by hounds, they ran. The sound of battle made them as nervous as a longtailed cat in a room full of rocking chairs. Although well-armed and capable with their weapons, they lacked in steadfastness. On the surface they were a highly-polished, impressive-looking, rugged company of muscular men. They were as smooth as a Marine drill team, running through the manual of arms like a fine-tuned machine. No one faulted "E" Company at inspection. Everyone's sandals shone like polished chrome. But underneath the dress-blues, written across their soft underbelly, was a more accurate description— *coward*. The fastest maneuver they ever accomplished was the waving of the white flag. The only weapon they ever used to restrain the enemy was a cloud of dust as they retreated *en masse*, in a hurry.

What an indictment! The sons of Ephraim loved Memorial Day parades and target practice, but as soon as the going got tough, they ran out of their shiny sandals heading back to the barracks. The original *quitters*. Discipline and guts were nasty words in the Ephraim camp. Their watchword was *ease* and their slogan was "Make a good appearance." But behind the thin veneer of valor was the brittle, plastic shell of surrender.

Ephraimites live on, you know. They have invaded the ranks of churches and families, and until difficulty comes, you cannot spot them.

They ape the lifestyle of heroic saints to perfection. Their words and prayers, verses and vows shine like Ephraim's arrows at dawn. But let the hot rays of hardship beat upon their backs and they melt like butter on the back burner. They "just can't handle the battle" . . . they "can't take the pressure" . . . they opt for the easy way out. They run. They come for counsel but reject the demands of Scripture. They want a medicine man with a quick cure, not direct advice to repent, reestablish biblical relationships, and restore God's method for living.

On a Los Angeles radio talk show, author Anna Sklar uncovered an incredible statistic from her book, *Runaway Wives*. Ten years ago for every wife or mother who walked away from her home and responsibilities . . . 600 husbands and fathers did so. Today, for each man who now does that, two women do.

Selah! Pause and let that sink in.

Understand, I'm not advocating either, nor taking sides that one is better than another. I am simply amazed at the unbelievably rapid rise in modern-day women who choose escape as a favorite method of "coping." Contrary to our great American heritage, many of today's citizens would rather switch than fight . . . or, quite honestly, quit than stick. That which was once not even an option is now standard operating procedure—the preferred plan to follow. Homes and churches across the country are haunted by ghosts of the Ephraimites.

The quitting habit creates a strange undertow which complicates rather than corrects our difficulties. The ability to "turn off" responsibilities is now in vogue. There was a time when the going got tough, the tough got going. No longer! Now it's, "If you start to sink, *jump*, don't bail." It's, "If it gets hard, *quit*, don't bother."

"Let's just quit" are household words. A marriage gets shaky and hits a few hard jolts—"Let's just quit." When a personal dream or goal in life is met with hurdles and hardship—both goal and dream are soon forgotten. Before long we begin to resemble Rome in its last days—a magnificent mask of outward, impressive stature . . . devoid of inner strength . . . soft and mushy at the core, desperately lacking in discipline and determination.

There is not an achievement worth remembering that isn't stained with the blood of diligence and etched with the scars of disappointment. To run, to quit, to escape, even to *hide* solves nothing . . . it only postpones a reckoning with reality. It may feel good now, but it's disaster when the bills come due.

Are you facing some difficult battle today? Don't run! Stand still . . . and refuse to retreat. Look at it as God looks at it and draw upon His power to hold up under the blast. Sure, it's tough. Nobody ever said the Christian life was easy. God never promised you a Disneyland. He offers something better—His own sustaining presence through any trouble we may encounter.

I've never been much of an admirer of Harry S. Truman—but I did, at times, appreciate his gristle. The battle often raged during his presidency and on one occasion he responded to it with the words:

"If you don't like the heat, get out of the kitchen!"

I've not met anyone who was able to stay strong without some time in the kitchen. Ephraimites are terribly undernourished. So my advice is a little different from Truman's:

If you don't like the heat—stay in the kitchen and learn to handle it!

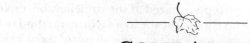

COME ASIDE

In whatever battle that bears down on you today, write down five reasons why you should NOT surrender.

For inspiration, look at 1 Timothy 6:11-16 and 2 Timothy 4:5-8.

WORKAHOLICS

trange creatures roam the land these days. Being efficient, diligent, and productive, they are remarkably impressive . . . but beneath the surface they are suffering from a miserable malady. Compulsively driven with an obsessive desire to achieve, these creatures give themselves to labor like alcoholics give themselves to booze.

Workaholics.

You will find them in every imaginable occupation, and unfortunately, they are usually successful. I say "unfortunately" because success only increases their drive. In sales, they are always at the top. In school, they are always in the books. In sports, they are always in the lead. In subjects, they are always in the know. To these creatures there is one *and only one* reason for existence— *WORK*.

This applies even to vacations! Give a workaholic an opportunity to get away for a few days and he will find a dozen logical reasons why it isn't possible. *Force* him to do so and he will wear himself down planning out each day, each mile, each step of the trip. Once there, he will begin to feel anxious after ten minutes of quiet relaxation. To the workaholic, unplanned moments are lethal . . . rest is *senseless* . . . enjoyable fun times are "irresponsible activities for children!" With a long, stinging whip, guilt—the inner taskmaster of the workaholic—pounds him into daily submission, whether he is at work, at home, at church, or at school.

This creature finally begins to show the cracks of his stress-ridden conscience. He becomes increasingly more demanding of himself and others—especially those nearest him. This neurotic intolerance slowly begins to isolate him. Muscular tics appear. His smile erodes into a frown. Performance and greater achievement become his security . . . and any setback or failure fractures his equilibrium.

As I write this I think of the need for balance. A measure of efficiency and discipline in life is absolutely healthy and necessary. Being faithful and dedicated to our work is commendable. "Redeeming the time" is biblical. But there is a point where we no longer enjoy ourselves. We can go to strange extremes—extremes that create inner functional disorders which turn us into slaves. We find ourselves blinded to *other* areas of life which are just as significant as our work—sometimes more! Harold R. Nelson, director of the Department of Pastoral Care at the Swedish Covenant Hospital in Chicago, describes this tendency that gives birth to workaholics:

> All of us have our own ways of hating or degrading ourselves.
> You may do it by being a hard-working perfectionist, and I

may do it by being a disorganized, lazy nonconformist. If all you know is "work and achieve," you may be consciously or unconsciously trying to prove your worth to yourself and others.

Well, let's discover if *you* are one of these strange creatures, okay? The following chart should help you determine the answer. Numbers one and two pretty well describe a workaholic. Number three is fairly well balanced. Numbers four and five—you've got other problems, but you are definitely *not* a workaholic.

Quality of Work
1) Leaps tall buildings with a single bound.
2) Must take a running start to leap over buildings.
3) Can leap over only short buildings.
4) Crashes into building when attempting to leap.
5) Cannot recognize buildings at all.

Timeliness
1) Is faster than a speeding bullet.
2) Is as fast as a speeding bullet.
3) Not quite as fast as a speeding bullet.
4) Would you believe a *slow* bullet?
5) Wounds self with bullet when attempting to fire.

Initiative
1) Is stronger than a locomotive.
2) Is stronger than a bull elephant.
3) Is strong as a bull.
4) Shoots the bull.
5) Smells like a bull.

Communication
1) Talks with God directly.
2) Talks with angels.
3) Talks to himself.
4) Argues with himself.
5) Loses those arguments.

COME ASIDE

What need for balance in our work-life can you detect in Paul's teaching in 2 Thessalonians 3:6-13? (Read carefully!)

SLEEPING IN CHURCH

really feel sorry for Eutychus. It was bad enough for the fella to fall asleep in church while Paul was preaching . . . he even fell out the window to his death three stories below! But *then*, of all things, Dr. Luke included the incident for all the world to read down through the centuries. Think of that! The only time Eutychus got his name in Scripture was when he died while sleeping in church. Makes you glad the Bible is complete, doesn't it?

Listen to the story:

> On Sunday, we gathered for a communion service, with Paul preaching. And since he was leaving the next day, he talked until midnight! The upstairs room where we met was lighted with many flickering lamps; and as Paul spoke on and on, a young man named Eutychus, sitting on the window sill, went fast asleep and fell three stories to his death below (Acts 20:7-9 TLB).

If the same thing happened to sleepers today, every church would have to build a *morgue* in the basement. There isn't an experienced preacher who hasn't faced the most incredible (sometimes *hilarious*) slumbering saints in the pew. I've seen them bump their heads on the back of the pew in front of them . . . snore out loud . . . stay seated when everyone else stood up . . . drool on their Bible . . . and even drop their hymnbook, then jump when it hit the floor.

I've watched couples nod in magnificent rhythm, perfect timing. One student used to come to a church I formerly pastored and sit right down front . . . and be sound asleep in a matter of *seconds*. He was there every Sunday, resting his eyes. I honestly used to wonder why he bothered to get dressed and come to church in the first place. And then there was the lady who had the strangest wheeze and smile when she exhaled while snoring—a shrill, stutter-like sound that reminded you of a chattering chimpanzee. She kinda looked like one when she slept, come to think of it.

Why? Now there's the question worth answering. Why do people sleep in church? Let me suggest several reasons.

Tradition. That's right. We are often *trained* to do it. As children we stretched out on the pew beside 'our parents and were *encouraged* to sleep rather than make a disturbance. Habits are hard to break.

Physical factors. Occasionally a church is not well ventilated, or gets too warm and stuffy, almost "cozy." This was part of the problem Eutychus had. The flickering lamps brought warmth up where he was sitting plus a hypnotizing "spell" in the room. Poor lighting and obstructions of vision are additional causes.

Personal factors. Lack of sufficient sleep during the week—or especially Saturday night—creates drowsiness on Sunday. Some medication makes us sleepy . . . as well as low-thyroid problems or low blood sugar. Concentration is broken and soon our minds start to drift and doze.

Indifference. Although it would be pleasant to ignore this, it is nevertheless another real reason. People are sometimes turned off spiritually. Sleep allows them to tune out the input. Carnality—or lack of salvation entirely—creates an indifferent attitude.

Dull, boring messenger. We preachers can be guilty of not organizing our material clearly and concisely. This leads to rambling and mumbling . . . unnecessary details not essential to the message. A failure to present the Word of God with genuine enthusiasm accompanied by fresh, specific illustrations and set forth in an unpredictable yet appropriate manner can cause boredom. A monotonous voice only adds another dose of *Sominex* to those fighting the battle of the eyelids. In all honesty, the messenger can be as guilty as the hearer, sometimes *more*.

So much for diagnosis . . . what about a prescription to overcome "the slumbers"?

It must be a *team* effort. Three parts must work together. The *building* must be comfortable and conducive to worship . . . yet altogether unlike a funeral parlor. That's so important. Then the *listener* must be prepared—physically, spiritually, emotionally—for worship. It takes good habits of health to cultivate a spiritual appetite. Last, the *speaker* must be alert and sensitive. Not a clown or a candidate for head cheerleader — but ever aware of the most effective ways to combat plainness, sameness, and tameness.

Think it over. See you Sunday. If you sit in the balcony and get sleepy, watch out! Eutychus, "being dead, yet speaketh."

COME ASIDE

Practice going through Psalm 65 as a personal warmup for heartfelt, joyful worship.

JEALOUSY

ike an anger-blind, half-starved rat prowling in the foul-smelling sewers below street level, so is the person caged within the suffocating radius of selfish jealousy. Trapped by resentment and diseased by rage, he feeds on the filth of his own imagination.

"Jealousy," says Proverbs 6:34, "enrages a man."

The Hebrews used only one word for jealousy as the Old Testament was being written: *qua-nah*, which meant "to be intensely red." The term was descriptive of one whose face flushed as a sudden flow of blood announced the surge of emotion. To demonstrate the grim irony of language, "zeal" and "ardor" come from the same word as "jealousy."

Here is the way it works. I love something very much, indeed, *too much*. I pursue it with zeal. I desire, in fact, to possess it completely. But the thing I love slips out of my hands and passes into another's. I begin to experience the gnawing pangs of jealousy. Strangely, the feelings of zeal and love begin to change. By the dark, transforming power of sin, my love turns to hate. Once I was open, happy, filled to the brim with exquisite delight, but no longer! Now I am closed within a narrow compass of inner rage, intensely and insanely angry.

Jealousy and envy are often used interchangeably, but there is a difference. Envy begins with empty hands, mourning for what it *doesn't* have. Jealousy is not quite the same. It begins with full hands but is threatened by the loss of its plenty. It is the pain of losing what I have to someone else, in spite of all my efforts to keep it. Hence, the tortured cry of Othello when he fears that he is losing Desdemona:

> I had rather be a toad
> And live upon the vapor of a dungeon,
> Than keep a corner in the thing I love
> For other's uses (Othello III,iii. 270).

This was Cain's sin. He was jealous of Abel. He resented God's acceptance of his brother. No doubt his face was red with emotion and his eyes filled with rage as God smiled on Abel's sacrifice. Not until Abel's warm blood poured over Cain's cruel hands did jealousy subside. Solomon might well have written the epitaph for Abel's tombstone:

> Jealousy is cruel as the grave.
> Its flashes are flashes of fire
> (Song of Solomon 8:6 RSV).

Anyone who has experienced deliverance from this damnable parasite knows only too well the extent of its damage. Jealousy will decimate a friendship, dissolve a romance, and destroy a marriage. It will shoot tension through the ranks of professionals. It will nullify unity on a team . . . it will ruin a church . . . it will separate preachers . . . it will foster competition in a choir, bringing bitterness and finger-pointing among talented instrumentalists and capable singers. With squint eyes, jealousy will question motives and deplore another's success. It will become severe, suspicious, narrow, and negative.

I know what I'm saying. I lived many of my earlier years in the dismal, gaseous subterranean pipelines of jealousy, breathing its fumes and obeying its commands. It was gross agony.

But finally, by the grace of Jesus Christ, I realized that I didn't have to live in darkness. I crawled out . . . and the releasing sunlight of freedom captured my heart. The air was so fresh and clean. Oh, the difference it has made! It is utter delight.

Ask my wife.

COME ASIDE

The terrible bitterness of jealousy is reflected even in Old Testament Law. Read Numbers 5:11-31, and contrast the tone and content of this passage with 1 Corinthians 13:4-7.

Which do you want in your life? Why?

DETERMINATION

recent issue of *Sports Illustrated* featured a lengthy article on Tom Landry, coach of the Dallas Cowboys. Those who know me won't be surprised to hear that I read every word of it.

I was living in Dallas when the Cowboys were formed into a team and Tom Landry was first introduced as the head mentor of that original, rag-tag bag of unknown athletes. The first few years were bleak, to say the least. The crowds were sparse and instead of cheers there were groans. One losing season led to another, and as you can imagine, the public soon made Landry the target of their savage verbal assaults. Sports writers added insult to injury in their vicious criticisms, as did the broadcasters who implied and stated that the team needed a coach with more outward enthusiasm, more flair, and more creativity. Landry quietly plugged on. Maligned and plagued with mis-understanding, he hung in there with bulldog determination, refusing to succumb to public pressure. *Quit* wasn't in Landry's vocabulary. The idea of ditching when the going got rough was never a consideration. His disciplined determination paid off—again and again—as his Cowboys rode into pro football legend.

Now they're calling Landry a legend . . . but he hasn't changed within. With the same inner tenacity of undaunted, untiring determination, Tom Landry gives God the glory and claims that the life of the apostle Paul is an example we all should follow. How true.

Our day, unfortunately, has made quitting fashionable.

After all, if you can quit a job or a team when the road gets bumpy, why not apply that philosophy to *everything*. Like a diet or a class or a church or a marriage or parenthood. The fog of failure clouds the issues and the cramp of criticism sucks away the motivation. Conviction is now being viewed as a neurotic tendency. Discipline is considered somewhat sadistic. Determination is, in the minds of the mesmerized masses, that which characterizes a stubborn fool . . . a quality not needed and not wanted by those who seek public approval.

Ah, but what then are we left with?

Take away conviction, discipline, and determination and you have cut the heart out of real living. You have eliminated the challenge that keeps the game of life exciting and rewarding. You have settled for nothing better than a tie with the opponent. You have erased the very things that made the Pattons, the MacArthurs, the Pullers, the Kellers, the Churchills, the Beethovens, the Lombardis, and the Landrys giants amidst dwarfs.

I can assure you that the gospel was laid in the lap of Europe because Paul was ablaze with sufficient determination to proclaim it—no matter the sacrifice or cost. When he wrote to the Corinthians, "Be on the alert, stand firm in the faith, act like men, be strong" . . . he knew whereof he spoke! In case you question that, you've not read his autobiography recently . . . written in blood (2 Corinthians 11:22-33). His final words reflect the same heart-throbbing determination:

> I have fought the good fight, I have finished the course, I have kept the faith (2 Timothy 4:7).

Show me a company that is efficient, progressive, dynamic, and organized—and I'll be willing to guarantee that behind the scenes, somewhere near or at the top of that company is a well-disciplined, determined leader. The same applies to a Christian organization or a school, a hospital, a home, a ball team, a city, a military outfit, a bank, or any other enterprise.

Let me close by making this personal . . . to *you*. Are you lagging behind in areas of determination? Are you becoming negligent, for example, in your financial obligations . . . or in some personal discipline . . . or in the quality of work you do . . . or in your study habits . . . or in your correspondence . . . or in your promptness . . . or in finishing the tasks you begin? Believe me, this is a rebuke to *me* as much as anyone . . . and not an easy thing for any of us to fulfill—but it is essential!

The history of man is strewn with the litter of nameless people who faced calamity and hardship, suffering and criticism—and gave up. Or—in the words of Psalm 78—"They turned back."

To you who are tempted to turn back . . . I urge you instead to stand firm . . . act like men . . . be strong! The benefits of determination far outweigh the alternate course.

Ask Tom Landry.

COME ASIDE

Confess to God negligence or laziness which His Spirit is revealing to you, and vow to press on.

For motivation along the way, uncover the secret of Paul's determination by reading Acts 20:22-24.

WITCH HUNTING

lip Wilson's line, "De debil made me do it," is designed to be funny, not phony. Whether the comedian believes in an actual Satan is, for the moment, immaterial. All he is interested in is getting a laugh. But the thing that makes it so effective is the real-to-life scenario the guy is acting out.

Here's this character who has done something bad. No one can deny it, it is wrong. But instead of taking the blame, owning up to the full responsibility of wrong, he cops out by pointing an accusing finger at "de debil." Why do we laugh? It's obvious . . . and in light of his hilarious routine, it's also excusable. We're not just laughing at him, we're laughing at ourselves—at one of our favorite indoor sports, The Blame Game. And since he is altogether wicked and invisible (and therefore unable to challenge our accusation in audible tones) there's no better scapegoat than the adversary himself.

But when this practice becomes a daily habit, it stops being funny and starts being phony. The comedy routine belongs on a stage, in front of an audience, where everybody understands that the character is just acting a nut. It's when we become escape artists, dodging the responsibility of our own disobedience, that we carry the thing too far.

There is a general heading under which all this falls. It's called "witch hunting." Not just blaming Satan for every evil action, but finding him in every nook and cranny . . . thinking that he is the subtle force behind *all* wicked events and encounters.

It's the age-old conspiracy mentality. There are those, for example, who see and hear the devil in certain levels of music. They tell us to play the tapes backwards and we can hear the subliminal satanic message . . . which seems a lot like reading a book in a mirror to detect its evil connotation. Strange. They warn us against Proctor and Gamble because the beard of a face in the tiny logo includes 666.

Don't laugh. So many believed this that a boycott of P & G products was strongly encouraged. The antagonism became so shrill the company was forced to spend a fortune trying to combat fears of a satanic connection. Half a dozen lawsuits were filed back in 1982 by P & G, claiming that they were being slandered by certain preachers and a few media personalities. And the beat goes on.

A Christian lady in Kansas City went to court to get her license plate changed from CPG 666 (note the P and G) on the grounds that her fellow church members were shunning her.

While I'm on the subject, the 666 scare stuff is getting downright ridiculous. The fact is that those three digits can be uncovered in almost anybody's name, if you're willing to work at it hard enough. Using the code A = 100, B = 101, and so on, *Hitler* adds up to 666. With a simpler code of A = 1, B = 2, and multiplying each letter-value by 6, *Sun Moon* adds up to 666. The same technique works on *Kissinger*, as well as the word *computer* (*that* I can believe).

Are you game for more? It's possible to uncover 666 in the names of some evangelical leaders. By adopting the so-called "devil's code" (a favorite ploy of numerologists, whereby the alphabet is numbered *backward* from zero; Z = 0, Y = 1, X = 2 . . .) and multiplying each letter-value by 6 (whew!), Moral Majority founder Jerry Falwell's last name equals 666. Billy Graham requires a more elaborate numerical treatment . . . but if you want to bad enough, you can make him out to be antichrist. Why? I just read it in a magazine:

> His initials are W. F. G. (William Franklin Graham). Using the A = 1 code, the letters add up to 36. The sum of the counting numbers from 1 through 36 is 666, and 36 = 6x6.
>
> Mischievous Democratic numerologists stung by the recent election point out that each of the President's names, Ronald Wilson Reagan, has six letters. That's not all. Using the A = 100 code, the letters of the three names total 1984, the year of the President's landslide reelection. And what about Walter Mondale? In the A = 1 code, W = 23, and M = 13, adding up to 36, from which 666 is obtained by the method applied to Billy Graham (*Discover*, February 1985).

Talk about nuts! Several years ago I had a guy use a similar code, showing me (with tongue in cheek) how *my* name resulted in 666. That did it! I was able to hide no longer. I've even had a well-meaning believer claim he had the demon of nail-biting and another the demon of overeating. Next thing I know, I'll hear I have the demon of preaching too long.

Hold it! You know what I'm going to say, don't you? Since that's true, I won't need to say as much. You and I know there is a devil and a host of demons . . . an authentic "prince of the power of the air," whose sole goal is to infect and influence with evil. He is on the prowl (1 Peter 5:8), diabolical in nature and deceptive in method (2 Corinthians 11:3). He is responsible for much wickedness, but not *all of it*—there's also the world and the flesh, remember (1 John 2:15-16). If he cannot get us entrapped in one extreme, where he's an imaginary prankster with horns, pitchfork, and a red epidermis . . . then it's the other, where he's everywhere, in everything, embodying everyone, and we start listening to music backwards and sniffing out signs of 666 in labels, license plates, and leaders.

C'mon, Christian, let's wise up. We look foolish enough in the eyes of the lost without giving them fuel for the fire. Leave the funny stuff for Flip and the phony stuff for fanatics. We've got our hands full maintaining a sensible balance on the tightrope of truth. If there's one thing "de debil" can't stand, it's the truth.

COME ASIDE

What are the best things we can learn from Luke 11:14-28?

TOUGH DAYS

ou've heard them. Those all-too-familiar cries of exasperation. Maybe a couple have crossed *your* mind today sometime between the too-early clang of the alarm and the too-late racket of the neighbors next door.

Going from bad to worse.

Jumping from the frying pan into the fire.

Between a rock and a hard place.

He said, "Cheer up, things could get worse." So I cheered up—and sure enough, things got worse!

My mother told me there would be days like these, but she never said they would run in packs.

Tough days. We all have them. Some are worse than others. Like the one the hard-hat employee reported when he tried to be helpful. Maybe you heard about it, too; the account actually appeared on a company accident form. Bruised and bandaged, the workman related this experience:

When I got to the building I found that the hurricane had knocked off some bricks around the top. So I rigged up a beam with a pulley at the top of the building and hoisted up a couple barrels full of bricks. When I had fixed the damaged area, there were a lot of bricks left over. Then I went to the bottom and began releasing the line. Unfortunately, the barrel of bricks was much heavier than I was—and before I knew what was happening the barrel started coming down, jerking me up.

I decided to hang on since I was too far off the ground by then to jump, and halfway up I met the barrel of bricks coming down fast. I received a hard blow on my shoulder. I then continued to the top, banging my head against the beam and getting my fingers pinched and jammed in the pulley. When the barrel hit the ground hard, it burst its bottom, allowing the bricks to spill out.

I was now heavier than the barrel. So I started down again at high speed. Halfway down I met the barrel coming up fast and received severe injuries to my shins. When I hit the ground, I landed on the pile of spilled bricks, getting several painful cuts and deep bruises. At this point I must have lost my presence of mind, because I let go of my grip on the line.

194

> The barrel came down fast—giving me another blow on my
> head and putting me in the hospital.
> I respectfully request sick leave.

Yeah! I would imagine!

Some days you honestly wonder why you ever crawled out from under the covers that morning . . . and later, if you will ever make it back to bed that night. Most of us have little difficulty fielding a couple or three problems during the day, but when they start coming down like hail, with no relief, rhyme, or reason, we get jumpy. More often than not we also get grumpy. Invariably there are those who love us and really want to help. But try all they like, tough days are usually solo flights. Others only complicate matters.

Take the four guys who decided to go mountain climbing one weekend. In the middle of the climb, one fella slipped over a cliff, dropped about sixty feet, and landed with a thud on the ledge below. The other three, hoping to rescue him, yelled, "Joe, are you okay?"

"I'm alive . . . but I think I broke both my arms!"

"We'll toss a rope down to you and pull you up. Just lie still!" said the three.

"Fine," answered Joe.

A couple of minutes after dropping one end of the rope, they started tugging and grunting together, working feverishly to pull their wounded companion to safety. When they had him about three-fourths of the way up, they suddenly remembered he said he had broken *both* of his arms.

"Joe! If you broke both your arms, how in the world are you hanging on?"

Joe responded, "With my TEEEEEEEEEEEETH . . . "

No, other people can't help much on tough days. They may be good companions, but they sure can't stop the pain. Holding hands and singing during an earthquake is small comfort.

Some would advise, "Just get in there and keep busy—work harder." But that doesn't help much either. When the barn's on fire, slapping a coat of paint on the other side doesn't make much sense. If the tires are flat, driving faster is pretty dumb.

So—what's the answer? How can we handle tough days when the Enemy works overtime to persuade us that God doesn't care? Just recently, I have found solid encouragement from four threads woven into the fabric of Galatians 6. See if you don't agree.

1. *Let us not lose heart* (v. 9). On tough days, you gotta have heart. Don't quit, whatever you do. Persevere. Stand firm. Be strong, resilient, determined to see it through. Ask God to build a protective shield around your heart, stabilizing you.

2. *Let us do good* (v. 10). Our tendency will be anything but that. Instead of good, we will feel like doing evil. Fume. Swear. Scream. Fight. Pout. Get irritated. Burn up all kinds of emotional BTU's. Rather than parading through that shop-worn routine, stay quiet and consciously turn it *all* over to the Lord.

3. *Let no one cause you trouble* (v. 17). Superb advice! Refuse to allow anyone (or *anything*) to gain mastery over you. That throne within you belongs only to the Lord Jesus Christ. Stop leasing it out!

4. *Let grace be with your spirit* (v. 18). Allow the full impact of grace to flow through your thoughts, your attitudes, your responses, your words. Open the gates and let those good things stampede freely across your tough day. You sit on the fence and relax.

It works. It *really* does.

Even on sick leave.

COME ASIDE

Think again about Galatians 6:9-10 and 6:17-18. How would you have handled differently your latest "tough day," following the guidelines in these verses?

CRITICISM

Looking for a role model on how to handle criticism? It would be worth your while to check out the book of Nehemiah. On several occasions this great-hearted statesman was openly criticized, falsely accused, and grossly misunderstood. Each time he kept his cool . . . he rolled with the punch . . . he considered the source . . . he refused to get discouraged . . . he went to God in prayer . . . he kept building the wall (Nehemiah 2:19-20; 4:1-5).

One of the occupational hazards of being a leader is receiving criticism (not all of it *constructive*, by the way). In the face of that kind of heat, there's a strong temptation to "go under," "throw in the towel," "bail out." Many have faded out of leadership because of intense criticism. I firmly believe that the leader who does *anything* that is different or worthwhile or visionary can count on criticism.

Along this line, I appreciate the remarks made by the fiery president of a past generation, Theodore Roosevelt:

> It is not the critic who counts; not the man who points out how the strong man stumbled or where the doer of deeds could have done them better. The credit belongs to the man who is actually in the arena; whose face is marred by dust and sweat and blood; who strives valiantly; who errs, and comes short again and again, because there is no effort without error and shortcoming; who does actually try to do the deed; who knows the great enthusiasm, the great devotion and spends himself in a worthy cause; who, at the worst, if he fails, at least fails while daring greatly.

> Far better is it to dare mighty things, to win glorious triumphs even though checkered by failure, than to rank with those poor spirits who neither enjoy nor suffer much because they live in the gray twilight that knows neither victory nor defeat.

To those words I add a resounding *amen*.

A sense of humor is of paramount importance to the leader. Many of God's servants are simply too serious! There are at least two tests we face that determine the extent of our sense of humor:

◆ the ability to laugh at ourselves
◆ the ability to take criticism

Believe me, no leader can continue effectively if he fails these tests! Equally important, of course, is the ability to sift from any criticism that which is true, that which is fact. We are foolish if we respond angrily to *every* criticism. Who knows, God may be using those words to teach us some essential lessons, painful though they may be.

Isn't this what Proverbs 27:5-6 is saying?

> Better is open rebuke
> Than love that is concealed.
> Faithful are the wounds of a friend,
> But deceitful are the kisses of an enemy.

And let me call to your attention the word *friend* in these verses. Friendship is not threatened but strengthened by honest criticism. But—when you are criticized by one who hardly knows you, filter out what is fact . . . and ignore the rest!

Nehemiah did that . . . and he got the wall built.

———— ✦ ————

COME ASIDE

Evaluate how King David handled a particularly bothersome critic in 2 Samuel 16:5-14 and 19:15-23.

How much do you think you should follow his example as you deal with criticism?

LETTERS OF REFERENCE

September 12, A.D. 61
Dear Paul:

We are considering a man to serve as a manager in the copper plant of our growing company, Corinthian Chariots, Inc. We are an aggressive, innovative firm with plans for expansion into major metropolitan regions like Rome, Athens, Antioch, and Jerusalem. We are looking for future employees who would fit into a visionary business like ours. Because you have worked with him for several years, I have chosen to write you and ask if you would be so kind as to send us a letter of recommendation regarding this individual. He comes highly recommended to us by others, but none have worked as closely or known him as well as you. Your opinion would be greatly appreciated. His name is Alexander, the coppersmith.

Sincerely,
Sosthenes Agrippus, Personnel Director

It would be interesting to discover how the apostle would have answered such a query. Knowing what he knew about Alexander (1 Timothy 1:18-20; 2 Timothy 4:14-15), I wonder if he would've said the hard thing.

Probably so. Even though he was "the apostle of grace," Paul would have done the company no favor by fudging with the facts. Being committed to grace in no way suggests turning a deaf ear to reality.

Dear Abraham:

Your nephew Lot has applied for a rather large loan with our agency. His plans are to develop a full-scale cattle ranch on property he inherited from you in the Jordan Valley near Sodom. It is our custom before making our final decision to pursue an investigation of the potential borrower's background to determine the advisability of granting a loan. What we are asking for is a character reference from you regarding Lot. He has given us your name. An immediate reply would be most appreciated.

Very truly yours,
Shanib Zuzim
Oaks of Mamre Savings and Loan Agency, Gomorrah

Another intriguing situation. Abraham would be faced with additional pressure in that it was a family member who was in question. What would the patriarch have done? Would he have hedged . . . said only nice things . . . all the while being fully aware of Lot's irresponsible and short-sighted lifestyle (Genesis 13:11-13)? No, I doubt it. Even though a much-respected friend of God, Abraham would be required by the sheer facts of his firsthand observations to say it straight, regardless.

How about this one?

> 3 February A.D. 97
> Dear John:
>
> Our church is giving serious consideration to asking a successful layman in our congregation if he is willing to be a candidate for our board of elders. He has recently moved from Ephesus to our new community here in Perga Estates along the Pamphylian coastline. We understand that you have worked alongside Mr. Diotrephes for several years, thus qualifying you to inform us of your opinion of him. We as a young church are in great need of strong, mature leadership, and he seems perfectly fitted for the role. All of us have been quite impressed with his knowledge of the Scriptures and his prior years of leadership in the Ephesian Evangelical Bible Assembly. Would you please respond and hopefully confirm our decision to pursue Mr. Diotrephes? Your reply will be held in strictest confidence. Thank you.
>
> Shalom en Christos,
> Stephanas Fortunatus
> Chairman, Board of Elders

Once again, honesty is on the line. From John's former experience with Diotrephes, he was only too aware of the man's savage style. Check out 3 John 9-10 if that sounds too strong. But time had passed. Would "the beloved apostle" simply let by-gones be by-gones or would he honestly mention the trail of grief that man had left in his wake? I suggest that John would have reported the inescapable and undeniable facts.

The next time you are asked to complete a letter of recommendation, a character reference, or simply answer a few pointed questions about someone, remember these imaginary cases. There's no need to dig up and parade every mistake from someone's past, but neither do we help a company or a church by ignoring character weaknesses or a faulty track record. Not idle gossip, mind you, but facts you are able to verify and document, if necessary.

Being a loving Christian doesn't excuse us from reporting the hard thing. The river of love must be kept within its banks. Truth on one side, discernment on the other.

COME ASIDE

John's third New Testament letter is short, but has much to tell of the apostle's character judgments about three men: Gaius, Diotrephes, and Demetrius. Study closely this brief epistle to see what criteria John used to evaluate these men.

WHY DO WE SUFFER?

f all the letters Paul wrote, Second Corinthians is the most autobiographical. In it the great apostle lifts the veil of his private life and allows us to catch a glimpse of his human frailties and needs. You need to read that letter in one sitting to capture the moving emotion that surged through his soul.

It is in this letter alone that he records the specifics of his anguish, tears, affliction, and satanic opposition. In this letter alone he spells out the details of his persecution, loneliness, imprisonments, beatings, feelings of despair, hunger, shipwrecks, sleepless nights, and that "thorn in the flesh"—his companion of pain. How close it makes us feel to him when we picture him as a man with real, honest-to-goodness problems . . . just like you and me!

It is not surprising, then, that he begins the letter with words of *comfort*—especially verses 3 through 11 (please stop and read).

Now then, having read those nine verses, please observe his frequent use of the term *comfort* in verses 3-7. I count *ten times* in five verses that the same root word is employed by Paul. This word is *para-kaleo*, meaning literally, "to call alongside." It involves more than a shallow "pat on the back" with the tired expression, "the Lord bless you . . ." No, this word involves genuine, in-depth understanding . . . deep-down compassion and sympathy. This seems especially appropriate since it says that God, our Father, is the "God of all comfort" who "comforts us in all our affliction." Our loving Father is never preoccupied or removed when we are enduring sadness and affliction! Read Hebrews 4:14-16 and Matthew 6:31-32 as further proof.

There is yet another observation worth noting in 2 Corinthians, chapter 1. No less than three reasons are given for suffering—each one introduced with the term "that." Can you locate them? Take a pencil and circle the "that" in verses 4, 9, and 11. Quietly, without a lot of fanfare, the Holy Spirit states reasons we suffer:

1. *"That we may be able to comfort those who are in any affliction . . ."* (v. 4). God allows suffering so that we might have the capacity to enter into others' sorrow and affliction. Isn't that true? If you have suffered a broken leg and been confined to crutches for weeks—you are in complete sympathy with someone else on crutches, even *years* after your affliction. The same is true for the loss of a child . . . emotional depression . . . an auto accident . . . undergoing unfair criticism . . . financial burdens.

God gives His children the capacity to understand by bringing similar sufferings into our lives. Bruises attract one another.

2. *"That we should not trust in ourselves . . ."* (v. 9). God also allows suffering so that we might learn what it means to depend on Him, not on our own strength and resources. Doesn't suffering do that? It *forces* us to lean on Him totally, absolutely. Over and over He reminds us of the danger of pride . . . but it frequently takes suffering to make the lesson stick. Pride is smashed most effectively when the suffering comes suddenly, surprisingly. The express trains of heaven are seldom announced by a warning bell; they dash suddenly and abruptly into the station of the soul. Perhaps that has been your experience recently. Don't resent the affliction as an intruder—welcome it as God's message to stop trusting in your flesh . . . and start leaning on Him.

3. *"That thanks may be given . . ."* (v. 11). Honestly—have you said, "Thanks, Lord, for this test"? Have you finally stopped struggling and expressed to Him how much you appreciate His loving sovereignty over your life? I submit that one of the reasons our suffering is prolonged is that we take so long saying "Thank you, Lord" with an attitude of genuine appreciation.

How unfinished and rebellious and proud and unconcerned we would be without suffering! Here are two statements on suffering I heard years ago and shall never forget:

> Pain plants the flag of reality in the fortress of a rebel heart.

> When God wants to do an impossible task, He takes an impossible individual—and crushes him.

May these things encourage you the next time God heats up the furnace!

COME ASIDE

Get the most out of 2 Corinthians 1:3-11, and make sure these truths lead you to praise today.

THE BIG PICTURE

On an average day in America,

- ◆ 500 million cups of coffee are consumed.
- ◆ School kids ride 12,720,000 miles on school buses.
- ◆ 10,205 people give blood.
- ◆ $54,794 is spent to fight dandruff.
- ◆ 10,000 passengers take their first airplane ride.
- ◆ 205 animals are buried in pet cemeteries.
- ◆ 3 million people go to the movies.
- ◆ 9,077 babies are born.
- ◆ 4,109 people parachute from planes.
- ◆ 679 million phone conversations occur (50 million are long distance).
- ◆ 5,962 couples get married.
- ◆ Each one of us produces nearly 6 pounds of garbage.
- ◆ 1,169,863 people take a taxi.
- ◆ $10 million is spent on advertising.
- ◆ 5,041 folks reach age 65.
- ◆ Motorists pay $4,036,000 in tolls.
- ◆ 10 doctors are disciplined by state medical boards.
- ◆ 88 million watch prime-time television.
- ◆ 63,288 cars crash.
- ◆ Industry generates nearly one pound of hazardous waste for every American.
- ◆ 1.1 million patients are in the hospital.
- ◆ 180,000 people buy new radios.
- ◆ 28 mail carriers are bitten by dogs (2,466 children are also bitten by dogs).
- ◆ 41 million people go to school.
- ◆ 19,178,000 snapshots are taken by amateurs.
- ◆ 240 patents are issued.
- ◆ 38,690 go to hear a major symphony orchestra.
- ◆ 21,000 gallons of oil are spilled from tankers and barges.

So what? That's trivia, right? Dull stuff nobody really cares about. Well, think of it this way. When you multiply all those things by 365, you get the general idea that there's a fair amount of energy, money, activity, and trauma going on in a year's time. And that's just in America—representing only a portion of the world's population. We may not be big, but we're busy. In fact, we are *so* busy it's easy to get selfishly swept up in the whirlwind of our own little playground sandwiched between the Pacific and the Atlantic Oceans . . . blessed beyond measure and rich beyond comparison.

Every so often it's helpful to stop the annual merry-go-round, get off, look objectively, and think clearly. It's not only helpful, *it's essential* for the Christian. In this circus-like American lifestyle of ours, we tend to be deafened by the blare of our own band and blinded by the lights of our own spots, shining—always shining—on the ring of our own choice.

That needs to change. We need to hear the voice of the Ringmaster as He raises His hand to stop the band:

> "We interrupt this program to bring all of you a re-minder that the world in which you live is not the whole world . . . but only a very small part of the world for which I died."

The Great Commission is still "the Great Commission," not "The Limited Agreement for My Corner of America." He still looks out across a wide world and weeps over men and women and children who do not know—have never heard—His healing, life-giving Name.

Can you feel His pain?

What could you do this week to reach farther, see wider, feel deeper? What could help you kindle a greater understanding, perspective, and compassion for this vast hurting world of ours?

Taking a missionary out for coffee?

Reading—really absorbing—a good missions magazine?

Writing a letter to some battle-weary missions veteran in the trenches of a distant country?

Making friends with a lonely international student?

Writing a check so that a hungry third world family finds hope for another day?

Praying that the Lord would give you an opportunity to serve Him in a cross-cultural experience—even for one year?

Sound risky? Maybe. But I've got a hunch that when the score is added up one day as we stand before our Lord, many of us will wish we'd played a lot more *Risk* . . . and a lot less *Trivial Pursuit*.

COME ASIDE

Read Matthew 9:36-38. How far was Jesus seeing?

RELEVANCE

e was a hated man. He was therefore maligned, threatened, publicly criticized, and privately rebuked. By his own admission he struggled vigorously with sins of the flesh. Especially outrageous anger. His debating disposition, wrote one biographer, caused his writings to "smell of powder; his words are battles; he overwhelms his opponents with a roaring cannonade of argument, eloquence, passion, and abuse." Sarcasm dripped from his pen.

He insulted a colleague by deliberately and repeatedly misspelling his name. He piled such vulgarity on him that one reputable historian said he could not translate its meaning into decent English. "One massive thunderclap" is an apt description of the man's style.

You may be surprised to know he was a Christian. He was, in fact, *clergy*. Once he admitted:

> I never work better than when I am inspired of anger; when I am angry I can write, pray, and preach well.

His maverick spirit led to his being excommunicated by the Pope when he was only thirty-eight. Rubbing salt into the ecclesiastical wound, he married a nun (in the sixteenth century, no less!) and became the talk of every monastery in Europe. Unintimidated, he stood alone like a bull in a blizzard . . . but silent *he wasn't*.

As is true of all such notorious characters, exaggeration and extravagance swarm around his story. It is difficult to filter out myth from truth, but one thing is for certain, Martin Luther was not irrelevant. Irreverent, yes; irrelevant, no. Out of step, yes; out of touch, no. Off base, yes; off target, no. Insulting and offensive, yes; impertinent and tedious, no.

With all his faults, Luther could never be criticized for being dull and distant. His philosophy could be summed up in his own timely words:

> If you preach the gospel in all aspects with the exception of the issues which deal specifically with your time—you are not preaching the gospel at all.

Don't misunderstand, he wasn't advocating a "social gospel," but rather a word from God that contains the solid ring of relevance. The gospel isn't to be changed. It is not ours to tamper with. But it *is* to cut into each generation like a flashing sword, sharpened on the stone of Scripture, tempered in the furnace of reality and need.

Of all the reactions a person may have to the gospel, I can think of none worse than a yawn . . . a sleepy "So what?" A bored "Who cares?"

I find it refreshing that Jesus Christ met people where they were. His words touched nerves. There was a lot more here-and-now than then-and-there in his talks. His attack on the hypocrisy and prejudice of religious phonies came through loud and clear. He met people as they *were*, not as they "ought to" be. Angry young men, blind beggars, proud politicians, loose-living streetwalkers, ignorant fishermen, naked victims of demonism, and grieving parents were as clearly in His focus as the Twelve who hung on His every word.

His enemies misunderstood Him, but couldn't ignore Him. They hated Him, but were never bored around Him. Jesus was the epitome of relevance. Still is.

It is *we* who have hauled the cross back out of sight. It is *we* who have left the impression that it belongs only in the cloistered halls of a seminary or beneath the soft shadows of stained glass and marble statues. George MacLeod, who wrote the following piece, expresses my firm conviction.

> I simply argue that the cross be raised again
>   at the center of the market place
>   as well as on the steeple of the church,
> I am recovering the claim that
>   Jesus was not crucified in a cathedral
>   between two candles:
> But on a cross between two thieves;
>   on a town garbage heap;
>   At a crossroad of politics so cosmopolitan
>   that they had to write His title
>   in Hebrew and in Latin and in Greek . . .
> And at the kind of place where cynics talk smut,
>   and thieves curse and soldiers gamble.
> Because that is where He died,
>   and that is what He died about.
>   And that is where Christ's men ought to be,
>   and what church people ought to be about.

COME ASIDE

What motivation for reaching out to your world—and what guidelines—do you see expressed in Matthew 10:16-42?

Being what ya' are

In my more zany moments, I have been known to do some crazy things. I'm relieved that most of them are not known by most of you. If they were, I sincerely doubt that what little bit of dignified respect I may have earned over the years would remain intact.

Maybe that explains why I had such a struggle with the whole idea of entering the ministry in the first place. I mean this is the one profession least attractive to a guy whose background included absolutely unbelievable practical jokes, tricks played on preachers and teachers (especially very serious ones), hilarious fun in school, and endless hours playing sax in a jazz band with some guys who are probably strung out in the French Quarter today . . . or maybe they got their lives squared away (in San Quentin) and are now living nice 'n orderly. All I ask is that they don't squeal on me. My memory is enough to reduce me to putty, like the time I rode a motorcycle down the middle row of my high school English Lit class.

But I suppose that's the reason I have such trouble to this day with stuffed shirts who have made it to the top and work hard to impress. You know the kind . . . super-dignified types, smoke blowers, who give off airs, who play roles and drop names and look shocked when even tiny cracks of humanity peek out from under their world of formality. Small-talk people who hobnob with the hotshots and expect special treatment.

Sorry, I just have difficulty wading through all that swamp, especially if cannibalistic pride is on parade. And more often than not it is, isn't it? In such social settings, I find myself reverting to my younger years and wanting to make crazy faces across the room or set off a firecracker under the coffee table or smash somebody in the face with a cream pie or pass a note that reads "Who really cares?" to the loudmouth bragging about how much he cleared last year after taxes. But then, those things don't fit the clergy. We're supposed to calm the waves, not make 'em, right?

Well, that's hard to do. And it's doubly hard if you've got a background that's South Texas brown mud rather than Ivy League blue blood. And if your mom and dad were just plain folks, married during the depression, intent on hard work and honesty and content with little, whose home was full of song and whose hearts were full of love.

Life never got so intense that there wasn't time to listen or a funny story to enjoy. Can't remember a day passing when our family didn't laugh at *something*, even though our times were torn by international war and periodic personal disagreements. They didn't do it, but my parents could've hung this sign in our place: "Through these halls walk three of the most stubborn teenagers in the nation!" Hard times make for straight talk . . . and on many occasions I recall being told the importance of standing alone, setting my own agenda, not trying to be something I wasn't, and above all, walking humbly with my God.

"Pride will eat you up, son. *Just be what ya' are.*"

I cannot number the times I heard words of Scripture quoted to me that assaulted phony and faulty arrogance. Verses like:

> For who regards you as superior? And what do you have that you did not receive? But if you did receive it, why do you boast as if you had not received it? (1 Corinthians 4:7).

And:

> I say to every man among you not to think more highly of himself than he ought to think . . . (Romans 12:3).

And Solomon's great advice:

> Let another praise you, and not your own mouth; a stranger, and not your own lips (Proverbs 27:2).

Little did I then realize the value of such a small start in life! But I have now lived long enough to see that starting anywhere but at the bottom could have resulted in being dazzled—especially in the ministry—when snobs at the top bid me come along. No thanks. Not interested.

All this flashed back at me when I read the funny dialogue entertainer Sid Caesar includes in his autobiography, *Where Have I Been?* Carl Reiner, the airport reporter, is interviewing Caesar as Professor Von Houdinoff, an expert on magicians.

> REINER (confused): As I understand what you're trying to explain, your book is saying that there's a connection between the illusions of magicians and what happens to people in real life.
>
> CAESAR: You got it, fella.
>
> REINER: Can you give me an example?
>
> CAESAR: You vant an example of great illusionary power? . . . Hans Schnorkel . . . a Frenchman. He vas working on a trick mit a shark. So he got this shark . . . a two-thousand-pound tiger shark . . . und he put that shark in a tank mit

over a million gallons of sea vater. . . . Und then he stood on the side of the tank und he had himself handcuffed, behind his back. . . . There he vas, handcuffed mit just a bathing suit. . . . Und then, Hans threw himself into the tank mit the shark. . . . As soon as Hans hit the water, the shark spun around und started svimming slowly, slowly toward Hans. Und Hans, he just stood there in the tank and looked the shark right in the eye. . . . Und the shark just slowly stopped and looked Hans right back in the eye. . . . Und then, all of a sudden, the shark just rolled right over on his belly . . . und ate 'im.

REINER (incredulous): He *ate* him? What kind of an illusion is that?

CAESAR: It's a very good illusion. . . . But you gotta do it right. You see, don't start off rehearsing mit a shark. You start with a guppy, a goldfish, a nice herring, a piece of salmon is not bad . . . don't get crazy mit a shark right away.

REINER: That's an interesting story, Professor, but how does it apply to real life?

CAESAR: How? You can't see? You don't make the connection?

REINER: Sorry, Professor . . . I don't.

CAESAR: If you start out too big, you could let yourself be eaten up.

COME ASIDE

In 1 Corinthians 4:7-13, Paul uses irony to contrast two groups of people. Follow his message in these verses and see what it has to do with being who you really are.

SELF-CONTROL

ill-power is a forgotten word amidst most Christian circles today. Many of us are soft, flabby, and fat either outwardly or inwardly . . . or *both*.

The overindulgence and underachievement of our age have created a monster whose brain is lazy, vision is blurred, hands are greedy, skin is thin, middle is round, and seat is wide. Color him baby blue!

What has spawned this strange, pillowy product? The Greeks would say: "A serious lack of *enkrateia*." That isn't a vitamin, it's a virtue—self-control.

The word actually means "inner power or strength." Expanded, it includes such things as having mastery or possession of something, the controlling power of the will (under the operation of the Spirit of God), the inner strength to resist and refrain, the strength *not* to indulge, *not* to act on impulse.

Paul uses this term in 1 Corinthians 7:9 regarding the control of sexual desire. He refers to it again in 9:25 as he speaks of the athlete's control over his body and its wants during the period of time he is training for a contest. Rigid, severe discipline went into such training, mixed with separation and loneliness. Stern soul-discipline was a constant companion of the Greek athlete of the first century. *Enkrateia* became his middle name for ten long months.

In Galatians 5:23, this virtue occurs in the list of the fruit of the Spirit. But lest you think it is something God suddenly drops on you without any involvement on your part, allow me to quote 2 Peter 1:5-6 so as to keep everything in balance:

> Now for this very reason also, applying all diligence, in your
> faith supply moral excellence, and in your moral excellence,
> knowledge; and in your knowledge, self-control, and in your
> self-control, perseverance, and in your perseverance, godli-
> ness.

Observe two things, please. First, this is a series of commands to the Christian—this is *our* responsibility. Second, the fulfilling of the commands necessitates our "applying all diligence"—this will take sacrificial *effort* . . . emotional blood, sweat, and tears!

For the remainder of this reading I'd like to apply self-control to our lives just from the *neck up*.

Naturally, we are the product of what we think about. Our actions and our reactions originate in our minds. What do you think about?

211

Upon what do you spend most of your mental energy? How much independent, hard-core, no-nonsense, controlled mental input goes into your day on the average?

Those sorts of questions haunt me when I consider how a phenomenon like TV watching has so thoroughly saturated our society. Consider the following facts:

Ninety-five percent of American households—over 60 million homes—have televisions. An additional 100,000 sets are being added with every passing month. More than 106 million adults find themselves in front of the tube on an average week in America.

And how often do those TVs get turned on? The American average is 48 hours per week. The average male watches 26 hours per week, while the female watches 30 hours.

A national survey reports that the average American high school student spends more time in front of a television in his lifetime than the sum total spent before a teacher from kindergarten through high school.

I don't have to remind you that I am not anti-TV. I own one and I thoroughly enjoy viewing selected programs regularly as time permits. However, it is exceedingly serious when a nation like ours has become so lacking in self-control that we cannot turn a one-inch knob to "off" and provide our minds and eyes a needed rest from the blast of consistent cosmos propaganda.

It is a pity that many Christians have the TV schedule better memorized than a single chapter from God's precious Word. Due to our lack of mental self-control, our driving desire is to be entertained and amused, rather than challenged through reading or family discussions or silent meditation or personal planning and goal-setting.

I suggest that you attack this problem with a loaded rifle, not a sling shot. Take one needy area at a time and shoot it into submission with relentless prayer and determination as the Spirit provides the gunpowder. Let's meet at the rifle range. I think I hear a few shots already.

COME ASIDE

Don't fail to draw on the Lord's power as you work on self-control, knowing His strength is yours. Understand and believe Romans 8:9-14.

A SEASON TO
DRAW NEAR

r. Seuss wasn't thinking of me when he wrote *The Grinch That Stole Christmas.*

Charles Dickens would not have asked me to play Scrooge in his story. In spite of what you may read later . . . remember that! I'm not anti-Christmas nor do I brandish the overused bumper sticker, "Put Christ Back into Christmas." Our family has a tree every year. We exchange presents, play Christmas records, sing carols, enjoy the festivities, and even wish a few people "Merry Christmas." Believe me—I have no bone to pick with the yuletide season, unless it's off the turkey.

But you'll have to agree, the season is not without its unique problems and temptations. Our lovely land of plenty drifts dangerously near insanity three or four weeks every year, and it is to that issue I'd like to address myself.

There is a "cosmic lure" to Christmas in contemporary America—a compelling *something* that draws many like a magnet. Emotions, unpredictable and undisciplined, begin to run wild.

Nostalgia mixed with eleven months of guilt can prompt purchases that are illogical and extravagant.

Neighborhood pressure can cause houses to be strung with hundreds of lights.

Television advertising, Christmas bank accounts, and special "wish books" only increase the pull of the magnet that inevitably ends with the sound of the cash register or the hollow snap of the credit card.

I remind you . . . I'm not against the basic idea of Christmas nor the beauty of the scenery. My plea is for common sense and balance, that's all. We Christians need to be alert to the dangers . . . then think through a strategy that allows us to combat each one. I'll mention only four.

1. *Doctrinal danger* . . . substituting the temporal for the eternal.

A couple of scriptures give needed counsel here:

> . . . keep seeking the things above, where Christ is. . . . Set your mind on the things above, not on the things that are on earth. . . . Do not conform any longer to the pattern of this world . . . be transformed (Colossians 3:1-2 and Romans 12:2 NIV).

It's important that we rivet into our heads exactly what we're celebrating. It is our Savior's arrival, not Santa's. The significance of giving presents is to be directly related to God's presenting us the Gift of His Son—

and our kiddos need that reminder year in and year out.

2. *Personal Danger* . . . impressing but not imparting.

We represent the King. We are His chosen ambassadors, doing His business "in season and out of season." Then let's do it *this* season! People are wide open to the gospel these days. Forget about trying to impress others by what you buy. Spend more time imparting what you already possess.

3. *Economic Danger* . . . spending more than you have.

Before every purchase, *think*. Ask yourself some direct, penetrating questions: Is this within my budget? Is it appropriate? Is it really saying what I want it to say? Gifts you *make* are often much more appreciated and much less expensive than those you buy. Stretching the dollar usually involves planning ahead. A safe rule to follow is this: If you don't have the cash—don't buy it. For example, my wife and I decided years ago that Christmas cards had to go. No offense now. That's just an illustration of something God spoke to *us* about. We found it saved us many dollars and gobs of time.

4. *Psychological Danger* . . . getting built up for a letdown.

One of the most effective maneuvers of the world system is to create a false sense of excitement. The Christian can get "high" very easily on the crest of Christmas. But the cold that sweeps in on the tail of a fading afterglow can be a dangerous, depressing experience. Guard yourself. Keep a firm hand on the controls. Don't be deceived. Enjoy the 25th . . . but not at the expense of the 26th.

If you stay occupied with the Person, you'll seldom have to fight off the plague. Make Hebrews 12:3 your aim—consider Him. Fill your thoughts and desires and expectations with your unfailing Lord.

When the wrappings and ribbons are in the trash can and the manger scene is back in the attic and the friends and family have said goodbye and the house feels empty and so do you . . . there is One who waits to fill your heart and renew your hope. He was there on December 24. He'll be there on the 26th.

COME ASIDE

Use 2 John 7-11 to help you know how to respond to any Christmas custom or philosophy that discards Jesus.

Slow down!

he bumper sticker caught my eye. Made me think. Even aroused some guilt. I was on the freeway as his car was pulling off. My day had been full and it was far from over. Stuffed in my pocket was a list, most of the items not yet purchased. A little panic rushed over the back roads of my mind as I divided all the things yet to be bought into those few days left before Christmas. The guy didn't seem in much of a hurry, which irritated me a bit, yet it told me that his sign was for real. I began to study the words in my head. They started making sense.

I BRAKE FOR CHRISTMAS

Easing up on the accelerator and releasing my frown, I began to calm down my inner motor with questions like: Why the hurry? What's the rush? Could this explain the reason you've been unable to enjoy the spirit of the season?

Psalm 46:10 drifted into my mind like the sound of a distant bell on a clear morning.

Be still and know that I am God. . . .

Then I remembered a story Billy Rose, the syndicated columnist of yesteryear, once wrote. As I reflected on it, I began to get into the beauty and color and joy of Christmas. Maybe it will help you, too.

* * *

There was once a fellow who, with his dad, farmed a little piece of land. Several times a year they would load up the old ox-drawn cart with vegetables and go into the nearest city to sell their produce. Except for their name and the patch of ground, father and son had little in common. The old man believed in taking it easy. The boy was usually in a hurry . . . the go-getter type.

One morning, bright and early, they hitched up the ox to the loaded cart and started on the long journey. The son figured that if they walked faster, kept going all day and night, they'd make the market by early the next morning. So he kept prodding the ox with a stick, urging the beast to get a move on.

"Take it easy, son," said the old man. "You'll last longer."

"But if we get to market ahead of the others, we'll have a better chance of getting good prices," argued the son.

No reply. Dad just pulled his hat down over his eyes and fell asleep on the seat. Itchy and irritated, the young man kept goading the ox to walk faster. His stubborn pace refused to change.

Four hours and four miles down the road, they came to a little house. The father woke up, smiled, and said, "Here's your uncle's place. Let's stop in and say hello."

"But we've lost an hour already," complained the hotshot.

"Then a few more minutes won't matter. My brother and I live so close, yet we see each other so seldom," the father answered slowly.

The boy fidgeted and fumed while the two old men laughed and talked away almost an hour. On the move again, the man took his turn leading the ox. As they approached a fork in the road, the father led the ox to the right.

"The left is the shorter way," said the son.

"I know it," replied the old man, "but this way is so much prettier."

"Have you no respect for time?" the young man asked impatiently.

"Oh, I respect it very much! That's why I like to use it to look at beauty and enjoy each moment to the fullest."

The winding path led through graceful meadows, wildflowers, and along a rippling stream—all of which the young man missed as he churned within, preoccupied and boiling with anxiety. He didn't even notice how lovely the sunset was that day.

Twilight found them in what looked like a huge, colorful garden. The old man breathed in the aroma, listened to the bubbling brook, and pulled the ox to a halt. "Let's sleep here," he sighed.

"This is the last trip I'm taking with you," snapped his son. "You're more interested in watching sunsets and smelling flowers than in making money!"

"Why, that's the nicest thing you've said in a long time," smiled the dad. A couple of minutes later he was snoring—as his boy glared back at the stars. The night dragged slowly, the son was restless.

Before sunrise the young man hurriedly shook his father awake. They hitched up and went on. About a mile down the road they happened upon another farmer—a total stranger—trying to pull his cart out of a ditch.

"Let's give him a hand," whispered the old man.

"And lose more time?" the boy exploded.

"Relax, son . . . you might be in a ditch sometime yourself. We need to help others in need—don't forget that." The boy looked away in anger.

It was almost eight o'clock that morning by the time the other cart was back on the road. Suddenly, a great flash split the sky. What sounded like thunder followed. Beyond the hills, the sky grew dark.

"Looks like a big rain in the city," said the old man.

"If we had hurried, we'd be almost sold out by now," grumbled his son.

"Take it easy . . . you'll last longer. And you'll enjoy life so much more," counseled the kind old gentleman.

It was late afternoon by the time they got to the hill overlooking the city. They stopped and stared down at it for a long, long time. Neither of them said a word. Finally, the young man put his hand on his father's shoulder and said, "I see what you mean, Dad."

They turned their cart around and began to roll slowly away from what had once been the city of Hiroshima.

* * *

C'mon, slow down. Be still. This year let's give Christmas a brake.

COME ASIDE

Let Ecclesiastes 3:1-15 help slow you down today.

A BRIDGE CALLED CREDIBILITY

arch 11, 1942, was a dark, desperate day at Corregidor. The Pacific theater of war was threatening and bleak. One island after another had been buffeted into submission. The enemy was now marching into the Philippines as confident and methodical as the star band in the Rose Bowl parade. Surrender was inevitable. The brilliant and bold soldier, Douglas MacArthur, had only three words for his comrades as he stepped into the escape boat destined for Australia:

"I SHALL RETURN."

Upon arriving nine days later in the port of Adelaide, the sixty-two-year-old military statesman closed his remarks with this sentence:

"I CAME THROUGH AND I SHALL RETURN."

A little over two and a half years later—October 20, 1944, to be exact—he stood once again on Philippine soil after landing safely at Leyte Island. This is what he said:

"This is the voice of freedom, General MacArthur speaking. People of the Philippines: I HAVE RETURNED!"

MacArthur kept his word. His word was as good as his bond. Regardless of the odds against him, including the pressures and power of enemy strategy, he was bound and determined to make his promise good.

This rare breed of man is almost extinct. Whether an executive or an apprentice, a student or a teacher, a blue collar or white, a Christian or pagan—rare indeed are those who keep their word. The prevalence of the problem has caused the coining of terms painfully familiar to us in our era: credibility gap. To say that something is "credible" is to say it is "capable of being believed, trustworthy." To refer to a "gap" in such suggests a "breach or a reason for doubt."

Jurors often have reason to doubt the testimony of a witness on the stand. Parents, likewise, have reason at times to doubt their children's word (and vice versa). Citizens frequently doubt the promises of politicians, and the credibility of an employee's word is questioned by the employer. Creditors can no longer believe a debtor's verbal promise to pay, and many a mate has ample reason to doubt the word of his or her partner. This is a terrible dilemma! Precious few do what they *say* they will do without a reminder, a warning, or a threat. Unfortunately, this is true even among Christians.

Listen to what the Scriptures have to say about keeping your word:

> Therefore each of you must put off falsehood and speak truthfully to his neighbor (Ephesians 4:25 NIV).

> And whatever you do, whether in word or deed, do it all in the name of the Lord Jesus (Colossians 3:17 NIV).

> O LORD, who may abide in Thy tent?
> Who may dwell on Thy holy hill?
> He who walks with integrity . . .
> And speaks truth in his heart (Psalm 15:1-2).

> It is better not to vow than to make a vow and not fulfill it (Ecclesiastes 5:5 NIV).

> When a man . . . takes an oath to obligate himself by a pledge, he must not break his word but must do everything he said (Numbers 30:2 NIV).

Question: Judging yourself on this matter of keeping your word, are you bridging or widening the credibility gap? Are you encouraging or discouraging others?

Let me help you answer that by using four familiar situations.

1. When you reply, "Yes, I'll pray for you"—do you?
2. When you tell someone they can depend on you to help them out—can they?
3. When you say you'll be there at such-and-such a time—are you?
4. When you obligate yourself to pay a debt on time—do you?

Granted, no one's perfect. But if you fail, do you own up to it? Do you quickly admit your failure to the person you promised and refuse to rationalize around it? If you do you are *really* rare . . . but a person of genuine integrity. And one who is an encouragement and can encourage others.

I know another One who promised He would return. He, too, will keep His word. In fact, He's never broken one promise. There's no credibility gap with Him. He *will* return. I can hardly wait to see His smiling face.

COME ASIDE

Taste the encouragement in God's message to His people in Zephaniah 3:8-13—and chew especially His words about purified and truthful speech. Let them motivate you today to the highest standard—God's standard—of integrity.

HOPE FOR SURVIVAL

O riginally, it was this:

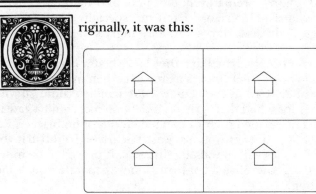

But later on, it was this:

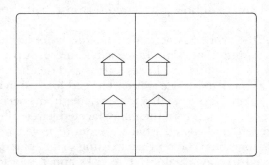

Understand, I wasn't living back then, but from what I read, that's actually what happened. It occurred when "Go west, young man!" was the challenge of America . . . when squatter's rights seemed the most advantageous way to pry families loose and dare them to brave the elements via the covered wagon.

So out they came, exchanging the crowded, soot-choked industrial cities back East for the open plains, clear skies, and fertile, albeit rugged, farmland of the West.

Predictably, those early settlers built their cabins or sod huts smack dab in the middle of their homestead, acres (often *miles*) from the nearest family. Strong, sturdy fences marked property lines as pride of ownership became the badge of courage. Words like *independence* and *private property* were common table talk as the young were taught how to fight for survival.

But as time passed all that began to change. As it was put to the test, isolationism proved to be a far cry from ideal. When photographers returned from those lonely houses, they showed pictures of wild-eyed women, stooped, gaunt, prematurely old men, and haunted-looking children. Life was hard making it on their own, especially through bitter winters, fighting off disease, starvation, and angry savages with bows and arrows.

More and more settlers learned that they had a better chance of making it if they would build their houses near each other, in the corner of their property rather than in the center. Four families could survive much easier if they loosened their grip on independence, built a gate in their fence, and relinquished their overstated emphasis on privacy. Enduring winter's blast or a lengthy illness wasn't nearly so frightful if you had three other families within walking distance. It proved to be much more fun coming together instead of living lonely, separate, touch-me-not lives of isolation.

From all this emerged a proverb:

"Shared joy is a double joy, shared sorrow is half a sorrow."

Seasons of the year became more colorful, more hopeful. Farming, harvesting, canning, and slaughtering became group projects. Weddings and worship, gains and losses, births and deaths became shared experiences as mere existence was exchanged for real living . . . entering into each others' joys as well as sorrows, neighbors becoming friends (then relatives!) . . . sharers in the many-faceted jewel called "living."

Those old settlers learned what we seem to have forgotten today: pulling closer together is better than existing so far apart. Sharing is still to be preferred to staying aloof. The risks and periodic hassles notwithstanding, four in a corner are better than one in the middle. I'm confident that's the whole point of Ecclesiastes 4:9-10,12 (TLB):

> Two can accomplish more than twice as much as one, for the results can be much better. If one falls, the other pulls him up; but if a man falls when he is alone, he's in trouble. . . . And one standing alone can be attacked and defeated, but two can stand back-to-back and conquer; three is even better.

A lot of us Western folk come from pioneering stock. The myth of "rugged individualism" dies a hard and bitter death. Our credo says:

> "I can handle it."
> "I'll tough it out somehow."
> "I don't need to lean on anyone."
> "I'll just hole up and lick my wounds; no one really cares anyway."

222

That may be good Western mythology, but it's rotten biblical theology. Chase the phrase "one another" through the last half of your New Testament and you'll see what I mean. *We really do need each other.* More profoundly, more desperately than we even begin to realize. As a matter of fact, we were *given* to one another by the Lord of the Body—because each one of us has a unique something to contribute—a piece of the divine puzzle no one else on earth can supply (see Ephesians 4).

Where is your sod hut? Out in the middle of some lonely, windswept acres? How long has it been since you've had some significant, openhearted, fences-down interaction with folks in a local Body? Too long? Maybe it's time you moved your hut to the corner of your field. Maybe it's time you installed a gate in that high, forbidding fence. It could make a big difference in your life.

For some of you, it may even mean survival.

COME ASIDE

Reflect on the example set by the original Christians in Acts 2:44-45 and 4:32. What do you have that you can share more of with other believers?

Winter's End

T H E   P R O M I S E   R E T U R N S

Winter's End

loundering with my father is among my most cherished childhood memories.

Armed with a beat-up Coleman lantern, two gigs, a stringer . . . and clothed in old sneakers, faded jeans, torn shirts, and funny hats, we'd get to the water. When the sky got nice 'n dark, we'd wade in. Not too far out, you understand, knee-deep was plenty. And off we'd stumble into the night to stab a few flat, brown creatures who chose our shoreline as the place for a shrimp supper.

Actually, my dad was more addicted to floundering than I. He went to get the fish. I went to be with him, which was fine for a while. By and by we'd round the point about a mile away from the bay cottage where the other members of the Swindoll tribe were. If we stopped and listened, we could hear them laughing like crazy. And here I was knee deep in muddy, cold salt water . . . with nothing but thick darkness in front of me.

To this day I still remember looking back wistfully over my shoulder toward that ever-so-tiny light at the cabin in the distance. A few steps further and it was out of sight. No light, no more sounds of laughter, just the glow of a lantern and the reassuring words of my dad, who somehow knew the fears of a little boy walking in darkness next to him.

Soon I began asking myself why. Why in the world had I agreed to come? Why didn't I stay back with the family? And how long? If I asked him once, I must have asked a dozen times, "How much longer, Daddy? When are we gonna turn around?" In tones that were mellow and quiet, he comforted me. I asked, "What if the mantle burns out?" We brought along a flashlight. "What if the batteries are dead?" He was very familiar with the path that would get us back. While he was searching for flounder, I was looking and listening for relief . . . those marvelous words, "Well, Son, this is far enough. Let's turn around."

Instantly, I found myself wading on tiptoes, caring nothing about finding some poor flounder—only that light, that tiny signal in the distance that assured me my dad really knew the way. Once it was spotted, my entire personality changed. My anxieties were relieved. My questions were answered. Hope lit the darkness like a thousand lanterns . . . thanks to one tiny light at the end of my childhood tunnel of fears.

Four long decades have passed since I trudged through the darkness with my father, but they have not erased from my mind the incredible importance of hope. Its significance seems larger than life to me today. How powerful is its presence!

Take from us our wealth and we are hindered. Take our health and we are handicapped. Take our purpose and we are slowed, temporarily confused. But take away our hope and we are plunged into deepest darkness . . . stopped dead in our tracks, paralyzed. Wondering, "Why?" Asking, "How much longer? Will this cold, dark winter ever end? Does He know where I am?"

Then the Father says, "That's far enough," and how sweet it is! Like blooms through melting snow, long-awaited color returns to our life. The stream, once frozen hard, starts to thaw. Hope revives and washes over us.

There is nothing like light, however small and distant, to put us on tiptoes in the darkness. Our whole personality changes when our Father utters those magical words, "Let's turn around!" His promises suddenly gain substance as reassuring hope warms us like the sun in late March.

Inevitably, spring follows winter. Every year. Yes, including this one. Barren days, like naked limbs, will soon be clothed with fresh life. Do you need that reminder today? Are you ready for some sunshine on your shoulders . . . a few green sprouts poking up through all that white? A light at the end of your tunnel?

Look! There it is in the distance. It may be tiny, but it's there. You made it! Your Father knew exactly where He was going. And why. And for how long. That cottage in the distance? Let's name it New Hope. You'll soon be there, laughing again with the family.

You may live to see the day when your journey into the darkness is among your most cherished memories.

DISCOVERIES

an you see anything?"

What a question to ask! Howard Carter's mouth and eyes were wide open when his aide asked it. His head was stuck into a timeless tomb. Beads of perspiration popped out on the British archaeologist's brow. For six straight years he had been digging. Endless trenches. Tons of rubble. Huge chunks of worthless debris. Nothing!

It was 1922. For more than a score of centuries, archaeologists, tourists, and tomb robbers had searched for the burial places of Egypt's pharaohs. It was believed that nothing remained undisturbed—especially in the Royal Valley where the ancient monarchs had been buried for over half a millennium. Because nobody felt there was anything left to be discovered, Carter carried on his pursuit, privately financed, with only a few scraps of evidence to keep him going. Somewhere . . . somehow . . . he was convinced there was one remaining tomb. Twice during his six-year search he was within two yards of the first stone step leading to the burial chamber.

Finally—EUREKA!

Can you see anything?

That was like pilot Michael Collins on July 20, 1969, asking Armstrong and Aldrin, "Do you feel anything?" as moon dust formed puffy white clouds around their boots.

Peering into silent darkness, Howard Carter saw what no modern man had ever seen: wooden animals, statues, chests, gilded chariots, carved cobras, unguent boxes, vases, daggers, jewels, a throne, the wooden figure of the goddess Selket . . . and a hand-carved coffin of a teenaged king. In his own words, he saw "strange animals, statues, and gods—everywhere the glint of gold." It was, of course, the priceless tomb and treasure of King Tutankhamen, the world's most exciting archaeological discovery. More than 3000 objects in all, taking Carter about ten years to remove, catalog, and restore. "Exquisite!" "Incredible!" "Elegant!" "Magnificent!" "Ahhh!" Words like this must have passed his lips dozens of times when he first whispered his way through that ancient Egyptian cocoon.

There are few joys like the joy of sudden discovery. Instantly forgotten is the pain and expense of the search, the inconveniences, the hours, the sacrifices. Bathed in the ecstasy of discovery, time stands still. Nothing else seems half so important. Lost in the thrill of the moment, we relish the inexpressible finding—like a little child watching a worm.

Such discoveries have many faces . . .

- ♦ the answer to a lengthy conflict
- ♦ insight into your own makeup
- ♦ understanding the "why" behind a fear
- ♦ just the right expression to describe a feeling
- ♦ the reason your stomach churns in certain situations
- ♦ getting to know your child's "bent"
- ♦ a technique that saves time and energy
- ♦ a simple way to communicate something complicated
- ♦ motivating those who work under your direction
- ♦ finding relief from needless guilt

Solomon talks about the greatest discovery of all. He puts it in words that describe the activity of a guy like Howard Carter—except in this case, he isn't searching for King Tut. Listen:

> My son, if you will receive my sayings,
> And treasure my commandments within you,
> Make your ear attentive to wisdom,
> Incline your heart to understanding;
> For if you cry for discernment,
> Lift your voice for understanding;
> If you seek her as silver,
> And search for her as for hidden treasures;
> Then you will discern the fear of the LORD,
> And discover the knowledge of God (Proverbs 2:1-5).

Talk about a discovery! Hidden in the Scriptures are priceless verbal vaults. Silent. Hard to find. Easy to miss if you're in a hurry. But they are there, awaiting discovery. God's Word, like a deep, deep mine, stands ready to yield its treasures.

Can you see anything?

COME ASIDE

Delve into the riches of Zechariah 8—or choose another passage you haven't been too familiar with—and write down all the new discoveries you make. Take your time—both to search and to savor what you find.

My dad

y dad died last night.

He left like he had lived. Quietly. Graciously. With dignity. Without demands or harsh words or even a frown, he surrendered himself—a tired, frail, humble gentleman—into the waiting arms of his Savior. Death, selfish and cursed enemy of man, won another battle.

As I stroked the hair from his forehead and kissed him goodbye, a hundred boyhood memories played around in my head.

♦ When I learned to ride a bike, he was there.

♦ When I wrestled with the multiplication table, his quick wit erased the hassle.

♦ When I discovered the adventure of driving a car, he was near, encouraging me.

♦ When I got my first job (delivering newspapers), he informed me how to increase my subscriptions and win the prize. It worked!

♦ When I mentioned a young woman I had fallen in love with, he pulled me aside and talked straight about being responsible for her welfare and happiness.

♦ When I did a hitch in the Marine Corps, the discipline I had learned from him made the transition easier.

From him I learned to seine for shrimp. How to gig flounder and catch trout and red fish. How to open oyster shells and fix crab gumbo . . . and chili . . . and popcorn . . . and make rafts out of old inner tubes and gunny sacks. I was continually amazed at his ability to do things like tie fragile mantles on the old Coleman lantern, keep a fire going in the rain, play the harmonica with his hands behind his back, and keep three strong-willed kids from tearing the house down.

Last night I realized I had him to thank for my deep love for America. And for knowing how to tenderly care for my wife. And for laughing at impossibilities. And for some of the habits I have picked up, like approaching people with a positive spirit rather than a negative one, staying with a task until it is finished, taking good care of my personal belongings, keeping my shoes shined, speaking up rather than mumbling, respecting authority, and standing alone (if necessary) in support of my personal convictions rather than giving in to more popular opinions. For these things I am deeply indebted to the man who raised me.

Certain smells and sounds now instantly remind me of my dad. Oyster stew. The ocean breeze. Smoke from an expensive cigar. The nostalgic whine of a harmonica. A camping lantern and white gas. Car polish. Fun songs from the 30s and 40s. Freshly mowed grass. A shrill whistle from a father to his kids around supper time. And Old Spice aftershave.

Because a father impacts his family so permanently, I think I understand better than ever what the Scripture means when Paul wrote:

> Having thus a fond affection for you, we were well-pleased to impart to you not only the gospel of God but also our own lives, because you had become very dear to us. . . . just as you know how we were exhorting and encouraging and imploring each one of you as a father would his own children, so that you may walk in a manner worthy of the God who calls you into His own kingdom and glory (1 Thessalonians 2:8, 11-12).

Admittedly, much of my dad's instruction was indirect—by model rather than by explicit statement. I do not recall his overt declarations of love as clearly as I do his demonstrations of it. His life revolved around my mother, the darling and delight of his life. Of that I am sure. When she left over nine years ago, something of him died as well. And so—to her he has been joined and they are, together, with our Lord. In the closest possible companionship one can imagine.

In this my sister, my brother, and I find our greatest comfort—they are now forever *with the Lord*—eternally freed from pain and aging and death. Secure in Jesus Christ our Lord. Absent from the body and at home with Him. And with each other.

Last night I said goodbye. I'm still trying to believe it. You'd think it would be easy, since his illness had persisted for more than three years. How well I remember the Sunday he suffered that first in a series of strokes as I was preaching. God granted him several more years to teach many of us to appreciate the things we tend to take for granted.

He leaves in his legacy a well-marked Bible I treasure, a series of feelings that I need to deepen my roots, and a thousand memories that comfort me as I replace denial with acceptance and praise.

I await heaven's gate opening in the not-too-distant future. So do other Christians, who anxiously await Christ's return. Most of them anticipate hearing the soft strum of a harp or the sharp, staccato blast of a trumpet.

Not me. I will hear the nostalgic whine of a harmonica . . . held in the hands of the man who died last night . . . *or did he?* The memories are as fresh as this morning's sunrise.

COME ASIDE

Consider John 5:19-20.

A MESSAGE FOR MISFITS

efore he ever came to the plate, Jephthah had three strikes against him.

- He was an illegitimate child. *Strike one.*
- He was the son of a barmaid and a brute. *Strike two.*
- He was raised in an atmosphere of hatred and hostility. *Strike three.*

Nurtured in an overcrowded cage of half-brothers, he was the constant target of verbal put-downs and violent profanity. Putting it mildly, Jephthah wasn't wanted. He compensated by becoming the meanest kid on the block.

Kicked out of home before he reached young manhood, he took up the lifestyle of a rebel among a tough bunch of thugs that hob-nobbed in a place called Tob. Earning a reputation as the hardest hard-guy, he was elected leader of a gang. They ripped and rammed their way through villages like a pack of wild hyenas. Had they ridden motorcycles, their black leather jackets could have read "The Tob Mob" as they raced over hills, outrunning the law of the land. Read Judges 11:1-3 for yourself. It's all there. A societal reject, Jephthah was Charles Manson, the Boston Strangler, and Clyde Barrow all wrapped in one explosive body. Having him and his apes drop into the Tob Pharmacy for Saturday night malts was about as comfortable as taking a swim with the Loch Ness monster.

Suddenly, a change occurred. The people of Israel encountered a barrage of hostilities from their not-so-friendly neighbors to the east—the Ammonites. The longer the battle raged against this hateful enemy tribe, the more obvious it became that Israel was against the ropes. Defeat was inevitable. The Jews needed a leader with guts to stand up against the fiery foes from Ammon. Guess who the Israelites thought of? Right! They figured that only a guy with his record would qualify for the job, so they called the man from Tob. Tremblingly, they said:

> Come and be our chief that we may fight against the sons of Ammon. . . . and [you may] become head over all the inhabitants of Gilead (Judges 11:6,8).

What a deal! Asking Jephthah if he could fight was like asking Al Hirt if he could blow some jazz or A. J. Foyt if he could drive you around the block. That was Jephthah's day in court. After a brief cat-and-mouse interchange, the mobster signed the dotted line. Predictably, he annihilated the Ammonites in short order and the Tob Evening News rolled off the presses with the headline:

HOODLUM BECOMES HERO—
EX-CON ELECTED JUDGE!

Jephthah the judge. Fellow gangsters had to call him "Your Honor." What a switch! He fit the throne about as appropriately as Fidel Castro would fit in the White House. Jephthah had no rightful claim to such a high calling.

That would have been true—except for one thing: God's grace. Remember now, God is the One who builds trophies from the scrap pile . . . who draws His clay from under the bridge . . . who makes clean instruments of beauty from the filthy failures of yesteryear.

To underscore this truth, consider Paul's stunning remark made to a group of unsophisticated Corinthian Christians:

> Do not be deceived: Neither the sexually immoral nor idolaters nor adulterers nor male prostitutes nor homosexual offenders nor thieves nor the greedy nor drunkards nor slanderers nor swindlers will inherit the kingdom of God. And that is what some of you were (1 Corinthians 6:9-11a NIV).

Don't rush over those last eight words:

> *And that is what some of you were . . .*

Our Father, in great grace, loved *us* when you and I were Jephthah— a rebel or a drunk or a gossip or a crook or a liar or a brawler or a Pharisee or a playboy or an adulteress or a hypocrite or a do-gooder or a drop-out or a drug addict. Looking for sinners, He found us in desperate straits. Lifting us to the level of His much-loved Son, He brought us in, washed our wounds, and changed our direction. All our church-going and hymn-singing and long-praying and committee-sitting and religious-talking will never ease the fact that we were dug from a deep, dark, deadly pit. And may we *never* forget it. Classic misfits . . . we.

But there is one major difference between Jephthah and us. God chose to *reveal* his past for everyone to read, while He chose to hide ours so none would ever know what colossal misfits we really are.

Talk about grace!

COME ASIDE

Get the full force of Jephthah's story by reading it all in Judges 11 and 12. What impresses you most about this rough fella?

GOING...NOT KNOWING

he statement recurs through Scripture like a repeating telegraph signal on a high frequency radio band. Sometimes faint, barely discernible—sometimes strong, clear. Over and over. Paul made the statement as he was saying goodbye to a group of friends standing with him on an Asian beach. Several of the men wept freely, realizing they would never see the missionary again. The aging apostle looked from man to man, holding each one's eyes for a brief moment. Then, looking out to sea with his weathered hand pointing south to the stormy skies above the Mediterranean, he voiced these words:

> And now, in obedience to the Holy Spirit I am going to Jerusalem, not knowing what will happen to me there (Acts 20:22 GNB).

What an honest admission!
I am going . . . not knowing what will happen . . .
That's what this thing called the Christian life is all about, isn't it? Going . . . yet not knowing. As followers of our Lord we believe He leads us in a certain direction . . . or in pursuit of a precise goal. That leading is unmistakably clear. Not necessarily logical or explainable, but clear. At least *to us.* So—out of sheer obedience—we go. We pack our bags, pull up stakes, bid our friends farewell, and strike out. We face a future as uncertain as our leading is sure. How strange . . . yet how typical!

There isn't a Christian reading my words who hasn't walked that path. And struggled with ways to convince others it was right. And endured the frowns and well-meaning counsel of those who tried to point out why the idea was a fluke . . . even downright foolish.

For sure Abraham faced it when he wrenched up roots from his hometown soil and struck out for—let's see, where *was* he going? He didn't know! There he was, almost seventy-five years old, loading up a camel caravan with his wife and family bound for . . . *somewhere.* Hebrews 11:8 puts it straight:

> By faith Abraham, when he was called, obeyed by going out . . . not knowing where he was going.

"Abraham, what are you doing?" asked a neighbor.
"I'm packing."
"Packing?"

235

"That's right. We're moving."

"Why? Why in the world would you want to leave Ur?"

"God has made it clear that I should go."

"God, huh? You've been talking to Him again?"

"Right. He told me to leave. I *must* go."

"Well, where are you going?"

"I don't know. He didn't tell me that."

"Wait a minute. Let me get this straight. You *know* you oughta go, but you don't know much beyond that, huh?"

"That says it pretty well."

"Wow . . . that's all I can say . . . wow. God sure gets blamed for a lot of stuff He doesn't have anything to do with. You know, man, some of us have been a little bit worried about the way you've been acting lately. Up to now, it's just been a little strange . . . but this, Abraham . . . this takes you off the end of the pier. It's like everyone's saying—you really *are* off the deep end!"

And so it goes. Who hasn't stepped off the end of the dock to stride on faith footing? It is no easy thing to leave a sure thing, walk away from an ace in the hole, and start down a long, dark tunnel with no end in sight. Absolutely frightening . . . yet filled with unimaginable excitement. Going . . . yet not knowing. Obeying . . . yet not understanding. Beginning a journey that is unpredictable, risky, untried, and appearing virtually insane—yet prompted by none other than the Lord Himself.

Like the competent Christian businessman I spoke to last week who recently left a secure $100,000-a-year position to enter a whole new career without training or expertise in the field. After he learns the ropes he may (repeat, *may*) gross $20,000 if things fall together. "Why?" I asked. With incredible assurance he answered, "One word—*God.*" I've seldom seen a person more confident, more fulfilled.

Are you on the verge of such a decision? Is the Lord loosening your tent pegs today, suggesting it's time for you to take a drastic leap of faith? Are you counting on Him to direct your steps through a future that offers no tangible map? Great! But before you jump, be sure of four things:

- ♦ Be sure it's the Lord who is speaking.
- ♦ Be sure the decision doesn't contradict Scripture.
- ♦ Be sure your motive is unselfish and pure.
- ♦ Be sure the "leap" won't injure others or your testimony.

Sometimes it helps to remember what God calls us during our short stint on Planet Earth: strangers and pilgrims. People on the move, living in tents, free and unencumbered, loose and available, ready to roll, willing to break the mold—whenever and wherever He leads. Regardless.

COME ASIDE

Read Exodus 15:13, and repeat with Moses his words of confident trust. Recall that Moses sang these words a full forty years before any of the people would dwell in the Promised Land. Does your faith in God's loving guidance match this?

A BETTER FOREMAN

person is a product of his own thoughts. Thoughts form the thermostat which regulates what we accomplish in life. My body responds and reacts to the input from my mind. If I feed it with doubt, worry, and discouragement, that is precisely the kind of day I will experience. If I adjust my thermostat forward—to thoughts filled with vision, hope, and victory—I can count on *that* kind of day. You and I become what we *think* about.

Take a minute to give your imagination a workout. Consider your mind a factory—a busy, bustling workshop of action and production. That's not far from the truth. Your mind is a *thought* factory. Every day on that internal assembly line it producers thousands, perhaps *hundreds* of thousands of thoughts. Production in your thought factory is under the charge of two foremen. The names on their hard hats are Mr. Gainground and Mr. Slideback. Mr. Gainground, as you'd imagine, oversees the production of positive thoughts. At the pull of a lever, wholesome, encouraging, reassuring plans and positive ideas roll down the belt and into the showroom.

That other foreman, Mr. Slideback, has responsibilities too. Over in a darker, damp wing of the plant, Gainground's counterpart manufactures negative, depreciating, worrisome thoughts. Both foremen are well qualified for their respective duties. Gainground specializes in producing reasons why you can face life triumphantly, why you can handle whatever comes your way, why you're more than a conqueror. Old Slideback earned his Master's at Inadequate U. He's full of reasons why you cannot succeed, why you're pitifully unable, why you should cave in, bow down, and surrender to the tangled thicket of inferiority, failure, and discouragement.

Both foremen, however, are instantly obedient. They await your signal to snap to attention. Provide yourself with a positive signal and Mr. Gainground throws himself into action. Pulling all the right switches, Gainground so gears production that one encouraging, edifying thought after another floods your mind and fills your life. As long as production is under his firm control, not even the slightest mist of misgiving may be observed hovering under the factory ceiling.

Foreman Slideback, however, awaits a negative signal (which he would prefer to call "reality" or "common sense") and he's off and running. At peak production, Slideback's assembly line cranks out discouraging, bad-news thoughts faster than the mind can process them. He will soon have you convinced that you *can't* or *won't* or *shouldn't*.

they'd have no trouble a'tall with that exam I started with:

MR PIGS . . . "em are pigs." MR NOT PIGS . . . "em are *not* pigs!" OSAR . . . "Oh, yes, 'ey are." CM PENZ . . . "See 'em pens?" LIB . . . "ul *I* be!" MR PIGS . . . "em *are* pigs!"

I had a guy tell me that that is part of the entrance exam into Auburn, Ole Miss, Alabama, Oklahoma, and Texas A & M. Why not? If ya cain't read plain ole American stuff, you ain't got no beniss goin' on to college! I better stop this nonsense or we'll *never* git through.

We can dress up, move away, run with another crowd, and try to keep our roots a secret, but our speech won't cooperate. There it is, plain as day for all to hear. Remember? That's what happened to Peter. Backsliding at breakneck speed, the once-loyal disciple tried to fake it by the fire that night they arrested Jesus. But a girl pointed him out. Picture the scene as Mark records it:

> While Peter was below in the courtyard, one of the servant girls of the high priest came by. When she saw Peter warming himself, she looked closely at him.
>
> "You also were with that Nazarene, Jesus," she said.
>
> But he denied it. "I don't know or understand what you're talking about," he said, and went out into the entryway.
>
> When the servant girl saw him there, she said again to those standing around, "This fellow is one of them." Again he denied it.
>
> After a little while, those standing near said to Peter, "Surely you are one of them, for you are a Galilean" (14:66-70 NIV).

He could hide his face, but not his speech. His Galilean "drawl" was clearly distinguishable, even in the wee hours of the morning. So what did he do to convince his accusers otherwise? The next verse answers that question:

> He began to call down curses on himself, and he swore to them, "I don't know this man you're talking about."

Galilean or Judean . . . now it didn't matter. He spoke words they all understood. Profanity blurted out publicly in *any* language or dialect makes it clear—even to total strangers—that the one swearing lives at a distance from the living God. Amazing . . . not another person in the crowd that night accused Peter any further. His street speech was sufficiently convincing.

Nobody ever said it better than the teacher from Tarsus:

Do not let any unwholesome talk come out of your mouths, but only what is helpful for building others up according to their needs, that it may benefit those who listen (Ephesians 4:29 NIV).

Let your speech always be with grace, seasoned, as it were, with salt, so that you may know how you should respond to each person (Colossians 4:6).

Looking for ways to make your witness more gracious, more winsome? Interested in communicating Christ's love and in building bridges that attract others to Him? Start with your speech . . . and don't worry if folks can guess what part of the country you're from.

It's when they would never guess you are a Christian that you've got something to worry about.

COME ASIDE

The turning point in the tense story recounted in the book of Esther is accomplished through a gracious but utterly fateful dialogue between Esther and her guardian-kinsman, Mordecai. Study the climax of this exchange in Esther 4:12-16, and appreciate well what their noble words led to in a life-and-death situation.

How can you also communicate serious matters with such grace?

242

BEING REAL

ave Cowens, one-time star basketball center for the Boston Celtics, disappeared. Without warning, he walked off the practice court, showered, dressed, and drove away. Alone.

He kept driving to . . . somewhere. His only explanation was the familiar comment, "I need to get my head together." He added that it could take as little as two weeks or as much as ten years. The sportscasters, management, team, spectators, and fans couldn't imagine what he was looking for.

I could.

The Carpenters used to do a number that helps explain the superstar's puzzling reaction. It's a peaceful soul-song that talks about needing a place to hide away . . . to be quiet . . . to think things through . . . to reflect.

Perhaps that's what the Boston superstar was trying to say. He had everything imaginable—fame, possessions, job security, a strong body, lots of bucks—but maybe at that moment in his life he lacked something far more important. Something like a sense of purpose and inner fulfillment. Something which basketball and all its benefits could never provide. An inner itch that can't be scratched by achievement or people or things or activities. To scratch it requires a great deal of internal searching, which the athlete felt he couldn't do and still keep pace with the maddening NBA schedule.

To "find yourself" requires that you take time to look. It's essential if you want to be a whole person, real to the core.

Now, I'm not advocating that one suddenly stop everything else so he can work the hide 'n seek process. That's rather unrealistic even if you aren't the starting center for an NBA franchise. It's a little like removing an anthill in your backyard with six sticks of TNT. Or like setting your car on fire because the engine knocks. Learning to be whole isn't prompted by copping out. But there are times in all our lives when we need to back away, slow down, stay quiet, think through, be still.

"I'd rather burn out than rust out!" shouts the zealot. Frankly, neither sounds very appealing to me. Either way you're *out*. People who are burning out may start a lot of fires and stir up a lot of noise and smoke. But who cares—if everything turns to ashes? People who are rusting out may move about as slowly as a sloth and live to a hundred and thirty. But so what—if all they accomplish in life is paying bills and staying out of jail?

There *has* to be more to life than just doing. There is! It's *being*. Becoming whole . . . believable . . . purposeful . . . lovable.

The word is *real*. It takes time and it usually hurts.

The Velveteen Rabbit is a classy book for children with a message for adults. In it is a revealing nursery dialogue between a new toy rabbit and an old skin horse. As they are lying side by side one day, Rabbit asks Horse:

> "What is REAL? Does it mean having things that buzz inside you and a stick-out handle?"
>
> "Real isn't how you are made," said the Skin Horse. "It's a thing that happens to you. When a child loves you for a long, long time, not just to play with, but REALLY loves you, then you become REAL."
>
> "Does it hurt?" asked the Rabbit.
>
> "Sometimes," said the Skin Horse, for he was always truthful. "When you are REAL you don't mind being hurt."
>
> "Does it happen all at once, like being wound up," he asked, "or bit by bit?"
>
> "It doesn't happen all at once," said the Skin Horse. "You become. It takes a long time. That's why it doesn't often happen to people who break easily, or have sharp edges, or have to be carefully kept. Generally, by the time you are Real, most of your hair has been loved off, and your eyes drop out and you get loose in the joints and very shabby. But these things don't matter at all because once you are Real you can't be ugly, except to people who don't understand."

Take a long look at *you*, suggests Skin Horse. Going through a lot of activities? Staying busy? In a hurry most of the time? Spinning around the squirrel cage? Seldom pausing to ask why? Still reluctant to be loved . . . to be real? Still keeping a distance between yourself and your family members? Still substituting *doing* for *being*?

It'll never satisfy. You cannot play cover-up forever. What does God suggest? Having a heart of compassion, being kind, tender, transparent, gentle, patient, forgiving, loving, and lovable. All those things spell R-E-A-L.

I'm certain that's what Cowens was looking for. He may not have found it in a few weeks, but it was certainly worth the effort. Losing your hair takes time, and it's pretty painful to have your eyes drop out and your joints get loose. But in the long run, that's the only way to be. REAL.

COME ASIDE

Read as much as you have time for in the short book of Ruth, and notice how closely this tender woman embraced life and love.

Ruth was real. What can you learn from her?

WHO'S DELINQUENT?

eenagers get a bum rap. Always have. For some reason, if you're between twelve and twenty, you're suspect. Cops stare and senior citizens glare. Why? Well . . .

You drive too fast, you think too slow, you aren't responsible, and you can't be trusted. The music you listen to is wild-n-wicked, the stuff you read is shallow or sleazy, the places you go are loud and low class. Your clothes are wrinkled, your room's a wreck, your car's a god, your friends are cheap, your ghetto blaster's too big, and your work is sloppy. And dare I mention manners? You talk with your mouth full, you slump and slurp, you don't look people in the eye, you treat your brother and sister like they have leprosy in the advanced stages, and you belch like there's no tomorrow. You're allergic to things like homework, dirty dishes, elevator music on KBIG, vacations with the family, hanging up the phone, saying "Thank you," the "off" switch on the TV, getting up in the morning, and going to bed at night.

If you've got a few bucks, you're probably dealing drugs. If you're interested in church, it's probably because there's some fox you're lookin' at. If you date a lot, you're probably messing around. If you don't come home when you said you would, you're probably where you shouldn't be. If you're not into the preppy Joe College scene, you probably have no ambition. And if you don't get a job, you're a slob. If you smile real big, you're up to something. If you frown at times, you've got a rotten attitude. If you cough a lot, you've been smoking pot, and if you weave out of your lane, you're obviously drunk.

Getting weary of all this? *So are they.* Having reared four of them (two flying high, two on the runway) and having talked with hundreds of others, I can tell you they frequently feel "I can't win." There are exceptions, I realize, but by and large, the teens of today are loaded with talent, have incredible potential, and whenever they get their rear in gear, can accomplish phenomenal feats.

I played a little ball in high school, but never in all those years did I ever meet, read about, or hear of another athlete who could come close to the raw skill of teenagers I see on tennis courts, basketball courts, and gridirons (not to mention the Olympics). I was involved for two years on the drama and debate teams, but the natural talent I see among teenaged actors, actresses, and public speakers today is enough to make me shake my head in amazement. These kids are unreal! And unless you are really into electronics, don't try to fool 'em with computer talk and don't try to beat 'em in video games. And if they get turned on spiritually . . . their level of zeal and joy is somewhere between maxi and mega.

Okay, okay, so they're not there when it comes to the finer things in life (were you?). Or finishing what they start (did you?). Or seeing the pitfalls ahead of them (could you?). Or being grateful, thoughtful, unselfish, and responsible. But what they may lack in those areas, they make up for in saying what they really think, giving themselves to what they really believe in, and surviving a jungle-like obstacle course of intense peer pressure, parental nagging, and teacher harassing.

Frankly, I'm crazy about teenagers. With all their imperfections, I appreciate their gut-level honesty. (Have you noticed? They can spot a religious phony a block away.) I also admire their resilience amidst the disillusionment of parents who split up, and I applaud their effort to stay morally pure while wading through the cesspool of magazine racks, lurid rock concerts, movies full of lust and profanity, and late-night cable TV. What surprises me is that more *aren't* delinquent.

And before you and I get smug, let's do a little remembering back when we were in *our* teens. I'm convinced that by the time I got out of high school, I'd gone through five, maybe six guardian angels. Scripture says that heaven rejoices when one sinner repents. For the longest time I've had this secret theory that Michael and Gabriel threw a series of celestial parties when some of us turned twenty. I mean, you and I weren't exactly Buffy and Jody at Happy Days High. Which reminds me of a piece that came from the oldest seafood place in Philadelphia. While you're waiting for your lobster, this provides food for thought.

WHO IS TO BLAME?

We read it in the papers and hear it on the air
   of killing and stealing and crime everywhere.
We sigh and we say as we notice the trend,
   "This young generation . . . where will it end?"
But can we be sure that it's their fault alone?
Are we less guilty, who place in their way
   too many things that lead them astray?

Too much money, too much idle time;
   Too many movies of passion and crime.
Too many books not fit to be read
   Too much evil in what they hear said.
Too many children encouraged to roam
   Too many parents who won't stay home.

Kids don't make the movies, they don't write the books
   They don't paint the pictures of gangsters and crooks.
They don't make the liquor, they don't run the bars,
   They don't change the laws, and they don't make the cars.

They don't peddle the drugs that muddle the brain;
   That's all done by older folks . . . eager for gain.
Delinquent teenagers; oh how we condemn
   The sins of the nation and blame it on them.

By the laws of the blameless, the Savior made known
   Who is there among us to cast the first stone?
For in so many cases—it's sad but it's true—
   The title "Delinquent" fits older folks too!

COME ASIDE

Take to heart Mark 9:42.

SOMEDAY

OMEDAY WHEN THE KIDS ARE GROWN, things are going to be a lot different. The garage won't be full of bikes, electric train tracks on plywood, sawhorses surrounded by chunks of two-by-fours, nails, a hammer and saw, unfinished "experimental projects," and the rabbit cage. I'll be able to park both cars neatly in just the right places, and never again stumble over skateboards, a pile of papers (saved for the school fund drive), or the bag of rabbit food—now split and spilled. Ugh!

SOMEDAY WHEN THE KIDS ARE GROWN, the kitchen will be incredibly neat. The sink will be free of sticky dishes, the garbage disposal won't get choked on rubber bands or paper cups, the refrigerator won't be clogged with nine bottles of milk, and we won't lose the tops to jelly jars, catsup bottles, the peanut butter, the margarine, or the mustard. The water jar won't be put back empty, the ice trays won't be left out overnight, the blender won't stand for six hours coated with the remains of a midnight malt, and the honey will stay *inside* the container.

SOMEDAY WHEN THE KIDS ARE GROWN, my lovely wife will actually have time to get dressed leisurely. A long, hot bath (without three panic interruptions), time to do her nails (even toenails if she pleases!) without answering a dozen questions and reviewing spelling words, having had her hair done that afternoon without trying to squeeze it in between racing a sick dog to the vet and a trip to the orthodontist with a kid in a bad mood because she lost her headgear.

SOMEDAY WHEN THE KIDS ARE GROWN, the instrument called a "telephone" will actually be available. It won't look like it's growing from a teenager's ear. It will simply hang there . . . silently and amazingly available! It will be free of lipstick, human saliva, mayonnaise, corn chip crumbs, and toothpicks stuck in those little holes.

SOMEDAY WHEN THE KIDS ARE GROWN, I'll be able to see *through* the car windows. Fingerprints, tongue licks, sneaker footprints, and dog tracks (nobody knows how) will be conspicuous by their absence. The back seat won't be a disaster area, we won't sit on jacks or crayons anymore, the tank will not always be somewhere between empty and fumes, and (glory to God!) I won't have to clean up dog messes another time.

SOMEDAY WHEN THE KIDS ARE GROWN, we will return to normal conversations. You know, just plain American talk. "Gross" won't punctuate every sentence seven times. "Yuk!" will not be heard. "Hurry up, I gotta go!" will not accompany the banging of fists on the bathroom door. "It's my turn" won't call for a referee. And a magazine article will be read in full without interruption, then discussed at length without mom and dad having to hide in the attic to finish the conversation.

SOMEDAY WHEN THE KIDS ARE GROWN, we won't run out of toilet tissue. My wife won't lose her keys. We won't forget to shut the refrigerator door. I won't have to dream up new ways of diverting attention from the gumball machine . . . or have to answer "Daddy, is it a sin that you're driving forty-seven in a thirty-mile-per-hour zone?" . . . or promise to kiss the rabbit goodnight . . . or wait up forever until they get home from dates . . . or have to take a number to get a word in at the supper table . . . or endure the pious pounding of one Keith Green just below the level of acute pain.

Yes, someday when the kids are grown, things are going to be a lot different. One by one they'll leave our nest, and the place will begin to resemble order and maybe even a touch of elegance. The clink of china and silver will be heard on occasion. The crackling of the fireplace will echo through the hallway. The phone will be strangely silent. The house will be quiet . . . and calm . . . and always clean . . . and empty . . . and filled with memories . . . and lonely . . . and we won't like that at all. And we'll spend our time not looking forward to *Someday* but looking back to *Yesterday.* And thinking, "Maybe we can baby-sit the grandkids and get some *life* back in this place for a change!"

Could it be that the apostle Paul had some of this in mind when he wrote:

> I have learned to be content in whatever circumstances I am (Philippians 4:11).

Maybe so. But then again, chances are good Paul never had to clean up many dog messes.

COME ASIDE

Catch all the implications for your life in Philippians 4:11-13. Have you "learned the secret"?

THE FINE ART OF BLOWING IT

I t happens to every one of us. Teachers as well as students. Cops as well as criminals. Bosses as well as secretaries. Parents as well as kids. The diligent as well as the lazy. Not even presidents are immune. Or corporation heads who earn six-figure salaries. The same is true of well-meaning architects and hard-working builders and clear-thinking engineers . . . not to mention pro ball players, politicians, and preachers.

What? Making mistakes, that's what. Doing the wrong thing, usually with the best of motives. And it happens with remarkable regularity.

Let's face it, success is overrated. All of us crave it despite daily proof that man's real genius lies in quite the opposite direction. It's really incompetence that we're all pros at. Which brings me to a basic question that has been burning inside me for months: How come we're so surprised when we see it in others and so devastated when it has occurred in ourselves?

Show me the guy who wrote the rules for perfectionism and I'll guarantee he's a nailbiter with a face full of tics . . . whose wife dreads to see him come home. Furthermore, he forfeits the right to be respected because he's either guilty of not admitting he blew it or he has become an expert at cover-up.

You can do that, you know. Stop and think of ways certain people can keep from coming out and confessing they blew it. Doctors can bury their mistakes. Lawyers' mistakes get shut up in prison—literally. Dentists' mistakes are pulled. Plumbers' mistakes are stopped. Carpenters turn theirs into sawdust. I like what I read in a magazine recently.

> Just in case you find any mistakes in this magazine, please remember they were put there for a purpose. We try to offer something for everyone. Some people are always looking for mistakes and we didn't want to disappoint you!

Hey, there have been some real winners! Back in 1957, Ford bragged about "the car of the decade." The Edsel. Unless you lucked out, the Edsel you bought had a door that wouldn't close, a hood that wouldn't open, a horn that kept getting stuck, paint that peeled, and a transmission that wouldn't fulfill its mission. One business writer likened the Edsel's sales graph to an extremely dangerous ski slope. He added that so far as he knew, there was only one case on record of an Edsel ever being stolen.

And how about that famous tower in Italy? The "leaning tower," almost twenty feet out of perpendicular. The guy that planned that foundation to be only ten feet deep (for a building 179 feet tall) didn't possess the world's largest brain. How would you like to have listed in *your* resumé, "Designed the Leaning Tower of Pisa"?

A friend of mine, realizing how adept I am in this business of blowing it, passed on to me an amazing book (accurate, but funny) entitled *The Incomplete Book of Failures*, by Stephen Pile. Appropriately, the book itself had two missing pages when it was printed, so the first thing you read is an apology for the omission—and an erratum slip that provides the two pages.

Among the many wild and crazy reports are such things as the least successful weather report, the worst computer, the most boring lecture, the worst aircraft, the slowest selling book, the smallest ever audience, the ugliest building ever constructed, the most chaotic wedding ceremony, and some of the worst statements . . . proven wrong by posterity. Some of those statements, for example, were:

> "Far too noisy, my dear Mozart. Far too many notes."
> —The Emperor Ferdinand after the first performance of *The Marriage of Figaro*.

> "If Beethoven's Seventh Symphony is not by some means abridged, it will soon fall into disuse."
> —Philip Hale, Boston music critic, 1837.

> "Rembrandt is not to be compared in the painting of character with our extraordinarily gifted English artist Mr. Rippingille."
> —John Hunt (1775-1848).

> "Flight by machines heavier than air is unpractical and insignificant . . . utterly impossible."
> —Simon Newcomb (1835-1909).

> "We don't like their sound. Groups of guitars are on their way out."
> —Decca Recording Company when turning down the Beatles in 1962.

> "You will never amount to very much."
> —A Munich schoolmaster to Albert Einstein, aged ten.

And on and on it goes. The only thing we can be thankful for when it comes to blowing it is that nobody keeps a record of ours. Or do they? Or do you with *others?*

when the "rapture" occurs, the Swindolls will be toward the rear on the way up. Unless, of course, He dispatches a dozen legion of winged station-wagon chariots to come to our rescue.

Oops, hold it! Suddenly I'm seized with the realization that—

> the day of the Lord will come like a thief, in which the heavens will pass away with a roar and the elements will be destroyed with intense heat, and the earth and *its works will be burned up*. Since *all these things are to be destroyed* in this way, what sort of people ought you to be . . . (2 Peter 3:10-11, emphasis mine).

There'll be no trunks or trailers, barges or garages in that day. Won't need 'em. All the stuff of three or more decades of marriage will go up with one great "whoosh." Everything. No, not everything. Relationships won't be destroyed, they'll continue on . . . transformed and renewed, eternal and simple once again.

Which reminds me . . . just as it is easy to travel too heavy and live too encumbered, it's also easy to let that happen between us and others, isn't it? Few people ever said it better than Ann Morrow Lindbergh:

> The pure relationship, how beautiful it is! How easily it is damaged, or weighed down with irrelevancies—not even irrelevancies, just life itself, the accumulations of life and of time. For the first part of every relationship is pure, whether it be with friend or lover, husband or child. It is pure, simple, unencumbered. . . .

> And then how swiftly, how inevitably the perfect unity is invaded; the relationship changes; it becomes complicated, encumbered by its contact with the world.

> The original relationship is very beautiful. Its self-enclosed perfection wears the freshness of a spring morning. . . . It moves to another phase of growth which one should not dread, but welcome as one welcomes summer after spring. But there is also a deadweight accumulation, a coating of false values, habits, and burdens which blights life. It is this smothering coat that needs constantly to be stripped off, in life as well as in relationships.

Packed-out garages, that's temporal stuff. No big deal if you stay unattached. It'll all burn up anyway. But people? That's *eternal* stuff. Let's keep the "deadweight accumulation" to a minimum. It'll take stripping off the "smothering coat" that blights life.

Want to know how to keep it simple, fresh as a spring morning? Tell the truth, the whole truth, and nothing but the truth.

COME ASIDE

What counsel for freed-up relationships do you find in Galatians 6:1-5?

THE CHURCH

So, what's the big deal about the church?

Good question. And it deserves a good answer. Something more than, "You gotta have one to get married in," or "It's the place kids oughta be on Sunday." Or how about, "There's not a better spot to make business contacts."

Really, now . . . haven't you wondered at times if the church is *that* significant in a day of high-level decisions and powerful international issues? I sure have. How could a congregation of folks carry much clout in our modern era of transcontinental missiles, mind-boggling scientific discoveries, space exploration, and impressive educational advancements? It's easy to be a tad cynical when you compare the importance of a brilliant body of keen-thinking minds wrestling over a decision that could impact a continent of humanity, with a few dozen people in some white clapboard building singing "In the Sweet Bye and Bye."

Yet, unless you've recently sliced Matthew 16:18 out of your Bible, it still says the same thing Jesus said. It still includes an unconditional promise that the church is His personal project ("I will build *my* church") and also that it will be perpetually invincible. No way will "the gates of hell" put it out of business. When you chew on that thought long enough, you begin to realize that the church is the impervious anvil, and all these other hot items, no matter how impressive and loud and intimidating, will ultimately cool off and be replaced.

I remember a message Dr. Jay Kesler gave at a family camp at Forest Home Conference Center. The title of his talk was unpretentious: "Why I Believe in the Local Church." Disarmed by simplicity, all of us in the audience walked away with our heads a little higher, our shoulders no longer slumped as though we had something to prove to a world that often doubts our reason for existence. Jay offered five splendid answers.

1. *The church is the only institution dealing with the ultimate issues*. Death. Judgment. Relationships. Purpose. Lasting priorities. Meaning in life. Identity. Heaven and Hell.

2. *The church provides perspective that gives dignity to mankind*. We live in a day in which man has become a means rather than an end. This creates a desperate sense of inner worthlessness. The church counteracts this insidious message.

3. *The church provides a moral and ethical compass in the midst of relativism*. Like a swamp of murky, slimy water, our society has either rethought, resisted, or completely rejected absolutes. Not the church! It still stands on the timeless bedrock of Scripture.

4. *The church is the only place to find true community, healing, compassion, and love*. It is here people care. Really care. Not because of status or

money. But because the Spirit of God is at work, weaving together the lives within the Body.

5. *The church (like no other institution) has provided motivation for the most lasting, unselfish, essential, courageous ministries on earth.* Schools. Hospitals. Halfway houses. Orphanages. Leprosariums. Missions.

Look back over the list. Think each one through. See if it doesn't thrill you to realize you are connected with such a significant arm of strength. No, it isn't perfect (you're a part of it, aren't you?) and it hasn't always modeled its message. But whatever is next in order of importance is a distant second—and I mean *way* down the line.

So, what's all the commotion about the church? Well, besides these things, I can think of only one other reason worth consideration. It is the church over which Jesus Christ says He rules as Head. He's in charge.

Not General Motors. Not American Airlines or the American Medical Association or the Academy of Arts and Sciences. Not the local fire station or theater or police department or library or courtroom. Although important and helpful, these cannot claim His headship. Only the church. With all its quirks and faults, it still ranks right up there at the top.

See you Sunday. That's when the Body and the Head meet to celebrate this mysterious union . . . when ordinary, garden-variety folks like us gather around the pre-eminent One. For worship. For encouragement. For instruction. For expression. For support. For the carrying out of a God-given role that will never be matched or surpassed on earth—even though it's the stuff the world around us considers weird and weak . . .

> Because the foolishness of God is wiser than men, and the weakness of God is stronger than men. For consider your calling, brethren, that there were not many wise according to the flesh, not many mighty, not many noble; but God has chosen the foolish things of the world to shame the wise, and God has chosen the weak things of the world to shame the things which are strong, and the base things of the world and the despised, God has chosen, the things that are not, that He might nullify the things that are (1 Corinthians 1:25-28).

No matter how it may appear to others, if the church is something God has chosen and God is pleased to use, it's a big deal.

COME ASIDE

Each of the following passages gives an exalted glimpse of the church's true nature. Explore them all—Acts 20:28, Ephesians 1:22-23, 1 Timothy 3:15, and Hebrews 12:23—and be glad.

COMPASSION

t was one of those backhanded compliments. The kind that makes one pause, think, *then* respond, rather than gush out a quick "Hey, thanks."

The guy had listened to me talk during several sessions at a pastor's conference. We had not met before, so all he knew about me was what he'd heard in days gone by: Ex-Marine . . . Texan by birth . . . schooled in an ultraconservative (dispensational!) seminary . . . committed to biblical exposition . . . noncharismatic . . . premil . . . pretrib . . . *pro* this . . . *anti* that. You know how all those scary labels go.

I really think he expected your basic, squeaky clean preacher: dark suit; white shirt (buttoned-down collar); tight-knot tie; scuffed, black, wing-tip cowboy boots; pocket stuffed full of tracts; a big Ryrie Study Bible (King James Version, of course); deep frown, thunderous shouts; and a rather large fist flailing away in midair.

Since that's not what he got, he was thrown a low curve over the inside corner of the pulpit. Finally, toward the end of the week, he decided to drink a cup of coffee with me and risk saying it straight.

It went something like this: "You don't fit. What's with you? You've got the roots of a fundamentalist, but you don't sound like it. Your theology is narrow, but you're not rigid. You take God seriously, but you laugh like there's no tomorrow. You have definite convictions, but you aren't legalistic and demanding."

Then he added:

"Even though you're a firm believer in the Bible, you're still having fun, still enjoying life. You've even got some compassion!"

That did it. By then both of us were laughing out loud. A few eyes from other tables flashed us those "Would-you-two-quiet-down!" looks. I often encounter such glares, especially when I'm having fun.

Well, what could I say? The man could've been more severe, but he had me pretty well pegged. It was that last statement, however, that really got me thinking. It woke up with me the next morning. *You've even got some compassion!* As though it was not supposed to be there. In other words, if you're committed to the truth of Scripture, you shouldn't sweat the needs of people. Don't get concerned about people stuff—heartaches; hunger; illness; fractured lives; struggles with insecurities, failures, and grief—because those are only temporal problems, mere horizontal hassles. Leave that to the liberals. Our main job is to give 'em the gospel. Get 'em saved! Don't get sidetracked by their pain and problems. It's conversion we're really interested in, not compassion. Once they're born again and get into the Word, all those other things will solve themselves.

Be honest now. Isn't that the way it usually is? Isn't it a fact that the more conservative one becomes, the less compassionate? I know there are some exceptions, but we're talking about the general rule, not a few exceptions, okay?

I want to know *why.* Why either-or? Why not both-and? I'd also like to know *when.* Not just Why can't we be theologically conservative and personally compassionate, but when . . . When did we depart from the biblical model? When did we begin to ignore Christ's care for the needy? When did we stop thinking of how valuable it is to be healing agents, wound wrappers like the good Samaritan? When did we opt for placing more emphasis on being proclaimers and defenders and less on becoming repairers and restorers? When did we decide to strengthen our focus on public condemnation and weaken our involvement in private restoration?

Maybe when we realized that one is much easier than the other. It's also faster, swift as the flash of a sword. When you don't concern yourself with being your brother's keeper, you don't have to get dirty any more or take risks or lose your objectivity or run up against the thorny side of an issue that lacks easy answers.

Let's go back to that repairer-restorer comment I just made. It's not an original idea. The prophet Isaiah mentioned it first, way back when. The nation to whom he wrote was going through the empty motions of a hollow religion. All the right words, all the right appearances, but zero results. They even fasted and prayed. Still nothing. I suppose we could say they looked and sounded orthodox, but missed God's favor. They observed the external Sabbath, but lacked the internal Shalom. Why? Don't hurry through the answer (Isaiah 58). It's worth reading aloud, perhaps more than once.

> "Is this not the fast which I chose, to loosen the bonds of wickedness, to undo the bands of the yoke, and to let the oppressed go free, and break every yoke? Is it not to divide your bread with the hungry, and bring the homeless poor into the house; when you see the naked, to cover him; and not to hide yourself from your own flesh? Then your light will break out like the dawn, and your recovery will speedily spring forth; and your righteousness will go before you; the glory of the LORD will be your rear guard. Then you will call, and the LORD will answer; you will cry, and He will say, 'Here I am.' If you remove the yoke from your midst . . . and satisfy the desire of the afflicted, then your light will rise in darkness, and your gloom will become like midday. And the LORD will

continually guide you, and satisfy your desire in scorched places, and give strength to your bones; and you will be like a watered garden, and like a spring of water whose waters do not fail. And those from among you will rebuild the ancient ruins; you will raise up the age-old foundations; and you will be called the repairer of the breach, the restorer of the streets in which to dwell" (Isaiah 58:6-12).

And what will happen when we traffic in such compassion? The Living Bible says, "then the Lord will be your delight, and I will see to it that you ride high, and get your full share of the blessings. . . . The Lord has spoken" (v. 14).

Yes, He has spoken, but have we heard?

The fact is that He has been talking like this ever since He asked Cain about the welfare of his brother Abel. When did we stop listening? How long will it be before we realize that others won't care how much we know until they know how much we care? If you really want to "ride high and get your full share of the blessings," prefer compassion to information. We need both, but in the right order.

Come on, let's break the mold and surprise 'em. Let's allow compassion to create a hunger for the truth. We'll be in good company. That's exactly what Jesus did with you and me and a whole bunch of other sinners who deserved and expected condemnation, but got compassion instead.

COME ASIDE

Turn to another prophet and hear the echoes of God's compassion for His people in Jeremiah 31:7-20. Who needs to see this kind of God through *your* life?

SAY IT WELL

aul was a misfit. When it came to a place like Athens, the crusty apostle clashed with the decor.

Made no sense at all. The classic oil-and-water combo. A monotheistic Jew smack dab in the middle of polytheistic Gentiles. Narrow-minded former Pharisee surrounded by broad-minded philosophers. One idol-hating Christian among many idol-worshiping pagans. Outnumbered. Outvoted. Outshouted. *But not outwitted.*

Those eggheads may have *felt* superior. They may have *looked* upon this little runt from Tarsus about like a grizzly views a dirt dauber, but when he opened his mouth and started preaching, they closed theirs and started listening. It wasn't very long before they realized this guy hadn't just fallen off some turnip truck. When it came to communicating, Paul had his stuff together. He was a class act.

The extemporaneous excellence of a message like the one in Acts 17:22-31 makes every preacher's and teacher's mouth water. Unintimidated by their brilliance, unimpressed with their position, and singularly unprovoked over their opinion of him, the apostle captured the attention of the Stoics and Epicureans by means of a genius game plan. With the confidence and deliberateness of a veteran returning to the heat of battle, the seasoned warrior tightened the belt on his toga and took charge. He covered every base necessary for quality communication.

Ever analyzed his Mars Hill message? Allow me:

♦ He started with an a jolting attention-getter.

"Men of Athens, I observe that you are very religious in all respects" (v. 22).

♦ He then used a relevant illustration to amplify his opening remark.

"For while I was passing through and examining the objects of your worship, I also found an altar with this inscription, 'TO AN UNKNOWN GOD'" (v. 23a).

♦ Next, he employed an interesting yet brief transition into the body of his speech.

"What therefore you worship in ignorance, this I proclaim to you" (v. 23b).

♦ At the heart of his speech, he presented sound theology in clear, easily understood terms.

"The God who made the world and all things in it, since He is Lord of heaven and earth, does not dwell in temples made with hands; neither is He served by human hands, as though He needed anything, since He Himself gives to all life and breath and all things; and He made from one, every nation of mankind to live on all the face of the earth, having determined their appointed times, and the boundaries of their habitation, that they should seek God, if perhaps they might grope for Him and find Him" (vv. 24-27a).

♦ He held their attention by making it personal . . . he even quoted from their own literature.

"though He is not far from each one of us; for in Him we live and move and exist, as even some of your own poets have said, 'For we also are His offspring'" (vv. 27b-28).

♦ He then challenged them with a theological truth woven neatly into Athenian culture.

"Being then the offspring of God, we ought not to think that the Divine Nature is like gold or silver or stone, an image formed by the art and thought of man" (v. 29).

♦ Finally, he "drove home" the application ("all everywhere should repent") by a declaration of two inescapable facts (God's judgment, Jesus' resurrection).

"Therefore having overlooked the times of ignorance, God is now declaring to men that all everywhere should repent, because He has fixed a day in which He will judge the world in righteousness through a Man whom He has appointed, having furnished proof to all men by raising Him from the dead" (vv. 30-31).

Put 'er down, friend. That's quality communication . . . all the ingredients necessary to guarantee edge-of-the-seat interest. The preacher could have gone longer (the speech didn't last two minutes), but the philosophers had gotten enough. Soon as they heard him mention the resurrection, end of Paul's speech. But *not* end of God's speaking. Some sneered. Others said they'd be back again. A few believed. Typical response. The song had ended, but the melody lingered on.

It's the same today. A mixed bag Sunday after Sunday. Change the particulars and you've got a similar setting in places the world over. One

263

speaks, many listen, some believe. How easy for the spokesman to be intimidated . . . to think, like Andrew, "But what are these among so many?" . . . to forget that empty philosophy doesn't stand a chance against biblical theology. It's the timeless David-and-Goliath principle—one plus God . . . aw, you know the equation.

But wait. A warning is in order. Before we rush to judgment and claim a pushover victory regardless, let's understand that the strategy calls for quality. It's not as simple as dumping a half-ton load of religious whine, a hodge-podge of verbs, nouns, and adjectives, but preparing the heart, sharpening the mind, delivering the goods with care, sensitivity, timing, and clarity. It's the difference between slopping hogs and feeding sheep.

Occasionally, it's good for communicators to go back to Athens. To blow the dust off those ancient idols in the street and hear again the voice of the preacher as it echoes across that historic wind-swept hill. To look into those dark eyes and to feel again his passion. Then to trace the incomparable heritage of God's mouthpieces down through the centuries.

What a band of magnificent misfits!

If you are one of them, study hard, pray like mad, think it through, tell the truth, then stand tall. But while you're on your feet, don't clothe the riches of Christ in rags. Say it well.

COME ASIDE

Look for more high-quality communication from Paul in Acts 13:16-41 where he addresses a mixed audience in a synagogue on his first missionary journey. How do the strengths of this message compare with those of Paul's speech in Athens?

UNDERSTATEMENTS

ou've heard of "too little and too late."

How about "too many and too much?" That's the way I'd describe our times. In a society overrun with overstatements, I find an occasional "not quite enough" a sheer delight.

Too much empty talk. Too much rich food. Too much emphasis on success, winning, being the biggest and the best. Too much comparison and commercialism. Too many meetings. Too many pages in the newspaper. Too many TV channels, neon signs, sports teams, schools, and opinions. Too many options on stuff like cars, sound systems, computers, and soft drinks.

We find ourselves making the extreme the standard. Periods are fast being replaced by exclamation points. "Nice" is no longer sufficient. Now it's got to be "fantastic" or "incredible."

Whatever happened to a quiet, barefoot walk along a beach? Or an evening of just listening to music? Or going on a bike ride, topped off with an ice cream cone, single dip? Or flying a kite, then lying on our backs and taking a snooze? When did we let candle-lit loveliness and holding hands with someone we love get bumped by the fluorescent and flashy?

How nice to be surprised by subtlety. To stumble across genuine beauty, true sincerity without overt attempts to impress. First-class *class* . . . understated elegance that leaves room to imagine, to think, to decide for ourselves, to appreciate. Films and other art forms that give us spaces of silence to feel, to sigh. Speeches, sermons, and writing that reflect true craftsmanship, convincing us that so much more was meant to be said.

My plea in a nutshell? More originals, fewer copies. More creativity, less technology. More implying, less explaining. More thought, less talk. Like the Wall Street Journal recently put it:

WHEN'S THE
BEST TIME TO
STOP TALKING?
Probably
now.
     A story is
     told about
     FDR when he
     was a young
     lawyer.

He heard his
opponent
summarize
a case before
the jury
in eloquent,
emotional,
but lengthy
appeal.
Sensing the
jury was
restless,
FDR is reported
to have said,
"You have heard
the evidence. You
have also listened
to a brilliant
orator. If you
believe him, and
disbelieve the
evidence, you
will decide
in his favor.
That's all I have to say."
He won.
Overstate
and bore.
Understate
and score.
When a baseball
umpire says,
"Strike three!"
he doesn't have
to add "Yer out."
That's what strike three
means.

"To state with restraint . . . for greater effect." That's what understate-
ment means. As in "I love you."

Next time you're tempted to say too much, just say that.

COME ASIDE

Read Psalm 12 (which exposes some ungodly overstatement) and notice especially the vivid picture in verse 6. What can you learn from this verse about the process that produces speech that is pure and free from overstatement? And how can you put that process to work today?

A ROUND TUIT

Whatever you do, *don't lose this.*

      I strongly suggest that you stop right now, cut it out, and save it. It is your own special "tuit." Because they are rare, you should lock yours up in a safe place. "Tuits" are not easy to obtain—especially the round ones. Wow . . . are they hard to find! You hear that people are looking for them all the time, but you seldom meet anyone who finds his. So—better hang on to this one. You'll need it!

Okay, now that we all have our very own (round) tuit, many of our problems should be over. No longer will there be the necessity of such remarks as:

> "I should take care of that—and I will as soon as I get a (round) tuit.

—or—

> "Just as soon as I get a (round) tuit, I'm going to finish that job."

No problem. Now you've got it! Fantastic, incredible, magnificent accomplishments can suddenly be achieved. Why, you might get that closet or garage cleaned out before the new year . . . you could fix the leaky faucet or hinge on the cabinet door . . . or you might even get your bills paid and start the year in the black (watch out for a self-induced coronary brought on by shock, by the way).

The possibilities are endless. You might be able to lose that extra weight . . . or stop that needless habit. Once you've done that, you could free yourself from such mental anchors that proper priorities in your life might start to emerge. Big chunks could actually start falling into place. Your own (round) tuit will help plug the undisciplined and careless leaks in your time dike. Because it is round, it will roll over and crush your fixation on procrastination. At last!

268

I'll bet Solomon had a (round) tuit. Maybe he got his from Moses, who once wrote:

> Teach us to number our days and recognize how few they
> are; help us to spend them as we should (Psalm 90:12 TLB).

Solomon hitchhikes on that idea vehicle and rides it down three realistic roads:

1. In Proverbs 16:1 he admits that "orderly thinking" (MLB) is unique to man. He tells us that being mentally organized is not an impossibility! Point: we are built with the ability to think and plan things out.

2. In Proverbs 13:4 (along with 21:5) he reminds us that the *desire* to carry out those plans is also built in . . . even "the sluggard" desires it. Stop and think about yourself. When you're late, you usually have had the desire to be on time. When you fail, you desired to succeed. When you have put something off, you often live with the desire to get it done. The internal equipment is fully furnished by our Heavenly Father.

3. In Proverbs 16:3 and 16:9 Solomon introduces a need dimension that works in conjunction with your (round) tuit . . . God's perfect will, His ability to "pull things off" in our lives. We must depend and count on Him!

So then—a final question must be answered: Why don't we accomplish our objectives? If we have the ability to think and plan, the inner desire to see it done, and the powerful will of God to pull it off, then why don't we reach our goals? I suggest three possible answers:

> We have set goals that are unwise and/or unrealistic.
> —or—
> We have made plans contradicting God's will.
> —or—
> We have failed to use our (round) tuit.

Take a thirty-minute look at your life this week. Go before God and give Him your list of objectives, asking Him for His green light . . . then with your desire in gear, tighten your belt and get on with it.

COME ASIDE

Make sure you get around to having that thirty-minute evaluation session with the Lord this week. Write it down on your calendar as if it were a doctor's appointment. Expect God to be there. Approach Him in the spirit of Psalm 90:17.

FROM A FATHER TO A BRIDE

y darling . . .

The familiar tune and lyrics from "Fiddler on the Roof" keep me company these days. I hum them to myself in the car and repeat the lines as I jog. Nostalgia nuzzles its way into my heart:

Is this the little girl I carried?
Is this the little boy at play?
I don't remember growing older. When did they?

When did she get to be a beauty?
When did he grow to be so tall?
Wasn't it yesterday when they were small?

Sunrise, sunset; sunrise, sunset;
Swiftly fly the days.

How often you have been the sunrise of refreshment in our home! It began with your birth shortly after your mom and I stepped into ministry together. Those were tough, lean, uncertain days for your daddy. Your brother was almost out of diapers and your parents were scratching around to find the place we would fit in God's family. In a couple of years, we were off to New England for a first taste of the pastorate on our own. Talk about scared! But there you were, Charissa, tiny little wisp of a girl, bringing color and beauty to dark gray days and cold, winter nights. I suppose we'll never forget how the winds of Boston swept you off your feet (literally)—you were about the weight of a feather and the size of a butterfly.

And wasn't camping in Vermont, New Hampshire, and Connecticut fun? We roamed the beaches of Cape Cod, you and I, digging clams with our toes. We sang crazy songs and played those silly car games, the four of us, as we laughed our way back to reality at the little home we occupied at 10 Bruce Road, remember?

Your mother and I learned so much there, much of which was painful . . . but there you were, day after day, so consistently full of life and sparkle, so innocently unaware of the things we were working through, so encouraging, so physically fragile yet emotionally affirming. I shall never forget how your tiny arms around my neck and your quiet words of reassurance, "I love you, Daddy," kept me going through the dimly lit tunnel of self-discovery. There were days, Sweetheart, when picking you up in that fuzzy gray coat with the hood and holding you close to my face made it possible for me to keep on truckin'. Thank you for being so easy to love, so undemanding. *Sunrise, sunset . . . sunrise, sunset.*

A few years and two more kids later our world had changed rather dramatically. From New England to Texas . . . from an old, established area to a bright, new suburb . . . from blizzards and snow shovels to long, hot summers, school days, and new horizons for your daddy. By now you were becoming quite sociable. A little sister was on the scene with whom you shared a bedroom—and a tiny brother you loved to hold like your own special doll. But even though our lives got busier and our pace increased, you never wavered in your affection. How I treasure the memories of your tiny hand in mine and watching you model those special "spin-around" dresses from Sunday to Sunday. Our six lives intertwined in that Finley Road dwelling, and we all continued to grow as God stretched us and molded us into a family unit. Growing up together was great! Without you, we would not have stopped to smell the flowers.

Just about the time we thought we had a handle on things—California, here we came. That was '71 . . . and you were only eight. *Sunrise, sunset . . . sunrise, sunset.* My little will-'o-the-wisp became a young lady. Junior high, senior high . . . cheerleading, dating, driving, growing into womanhood. Falling deeply in love with Jesus, thanks to good models, fine leaders, and a church full of folks who gave us the freedom to still be a family without having to be perfect. There was junior high "Rancho" at Forest Home, then high school winter camps, core groups, and Bible studies, but mainly, there were those talks we enjoyed at home, which solidified and affirmed so many of your decisions. Amidst all the involvements of a fast-moving, ever-enlarging, sometimes-hectic, come-on-let's-talk family, you seemed to remain a calming influence, a young woman of deep friendships and genuine love. You were never enamored of the superficial, forever committed to the truth. At that point, you are most like your mother. May that never change, Charissa.

And now? My, what can I say? A very discerning and capable young man has discovered you! And of all things, Byron has not only captured your attention, he has won your heart. Come Friday night, the man has you forever. *Sunrise, sunset . . . sunrise, sunset.* The little thing I held and loved, the butterfly of yesteryear, the lovely young woman who has graced our family and taught all of us the value of consistent love and hold-me-close affection moves from our arms to his . . . and rightly so. This little girl I carried is ready to become a wife. She is highly qualified, more than able to make another house into a home . . . to add her distinct dimensions and depth of character to a guy who deserves only the very best. With pardonable pride, I must add: Color him fortunate.

It is with the utmost delight that we applaud your marriage. We agree with your choice for a husband. We affirm your right to have freedom from our control and our leadership. And we anticipate a richness in your relationship with each other and strength in your commitment to Christ.

You will make a lovely bride, and much more important, a splendid wife, Charissa. Your mother and I will release you with unreserved confidence. But I am sure you understand that our memories will never be released. They are the stuff of which our lives consist after you say "I do."

> Sunrise, sunset . . . sunrise, sunset;
> Swiftly fly the years.
> One season following another
> Ladened with happiness and tears.

With all my love, Daddy.

———— 🍁 ————

COME ASIDE

Enjoy the good promise in Malachi 4:6.

GRANDPARENTING

It's bad enough that Webster omits "parenting" in his dictionary ... but disregarding "*grand*parenting" is somewhere between incompetent and inexcusable! Okay, okay, so it isn't an official word. So it lacks sufficient roots in Anglo-Saxon linguistic lore to merit a position in the ranks of Webster's major reference work. So who cares about all that stuffy pedigree through which terms must pass to earn recognition in the verbiage of our American culture? I sure don't ... and neither do thousands of other conscientious folks who are doing the very thing Webster chooses to ignore.

Webster—the old codger—would've been a good stand-in for Scrooge. Or maybe he was like the late W. C. Fields and just didn't like kids. On the other hand, he probably played everything by the rulebook and didn't let his emotions get in the way of his literary contribution.

Too bad. Guys like that may make great scholars, but little people who are looking for laps to sit on and hands to hold and somebody to sing with or help 'em learn how to skate don't give a rip about advanced degrees earned at snooty schools or grammatical trivia. So what if the gray-haired gentleman or gracious lady splits an infinitive or leaves a preposition dangling? What's really important is that the wee ones know that here's somebody they can lean on, talk to, laugh with, learn from, walk beside, and, mainly, hug. And chances are good those same grown-ups won't ask a lot of pin-you-to-the-wall questions, like "Did you make your bed?" or "Have you finished your homework," or "Isn't it your turn to do the dishes?"

Grandparents' favorite gesture is open arms and their favorite question is, "What do you wanna do?" and their favorite words are "I love you, honey." They don't look for mistakes and failures; they forgive them. They don't remember that you spent your last dollar foolishly; they forget it. And they don't skip pages when they read to you ... nor do they say "Hurry up" when you want to see how far you can make the rock skip across the lake. They'll even stop and lick an ice cream cone with ya.

But best of all, when you want to talk, they want to listen. Long, loud lectures are out ... so are comments like "You ought to be ashamed of yourself" and "That's stupid!" It's funny, but you somehow get the impression that things like money and possessions and clothes aren't nearly as important as *you*. And getting somewhere on time isn't half as significant as enjoying the trip.

Isn't God good? Generation after generation He provides a fresh set of grandparents . . . an ever-present counterculture in our busy world. Lest everyone else get so involved they no longer stop to smell the flowers or watch tiny ants hard at work, these special adults are deposited into our life-style account. They've made enough errors to understand that perfectionism is a harsh taskmaster and that self-imposed guilt is a hardened killer. They could be superb instructors, but their best lessons are caught, not taught. Their Christianity is seasoned, filtered through the tight weave of realism, heartache, loss, and compromise. Jesus is not only their Lord, He's their Friend and long-time Counselor. Like a massive tree, they provide needed shade, they add beauty to the landscape, and they don't mind being used. They're there. Even if not much is happening, they are there.

Why all this surge of what some would call sentimentality? Well, my life took on a new dimension not long ago. Another hat was added to those I'm already wearing. It's one that will become increasingly more significant as time passes, I realize. Ryan Thomas was born to our older son and daughter-in-law. A six-pound, eight-ounce grandson who will provide my wife and me a chance to try again . . . only this time with a lot more to give and a lot less to prove. Stretching out in front of us are an uncertain number of years in which we'll be able to reinvest our time and energy, our treasure and love. And even though Webster won't acknowledge the word, grandparenting is now ours to enjoy . . . thoroughly and continually.

It was back in 1961 that God first allowed us to call ourselves parents. How gracious of Him to give us a new title—grandparents. I remember reading back then the words of General Douglas MacArthur, entitled, "A Father's Prayer," a beautiful piece in which the aging leader asks God to build him a son of strong character, humble spirit, a person of compassion, determination, simplicity, greatness. His closing words almost brought tears to my eyes. After claiming all these things by faith, he adds: "Then I, his father, will dare to whisper, 'I have not lived in vain.'"

Today, the same prayer is on my lips and actual tears are on my face. The prayer is for you, little Ryan, as it once was for your daddy. And the tears? Well, you'll have to get used to them, little guy.

That's how it is with granddaddies.

COME ASIDE

In prayer, commit yourself—for now and for the rest of your days on earth—to the pattern taught in Psalm 78:4-7.

BATTLEFIELD MEMORIES

O
n the once bloody battlefield at Saratoga there stands a towering obelisk. A one-hundred-and-fifty-five-foot-high monument commemorative of that decisive struggle where the British made their last stand over two centuries ago. It is a solemn and sober moment as visitors stand on that windswept hill, savoring that slice of national history. In the distance are the stately Adirondacks and the Taconics. The monument gives mute testimony to those heroes of yesteryear who refused to bow the knee to England.

About its base are four deep niches, and in each niche appears the name of one of the American generals who commanded there. Above the names stand giant bronze figures on horseback . . . as famous today as in the day they shouted their commands. You can almost hear their voices. In the first stands Horatio Gates; in the second, Philip John Schuyler; and in the third, Daniel Morgan.

But the niche on the fourth side is strangely vacant. The name appears, but the soldier is absent. Conspicuously absent. As one reads the name, the mind rushes on to the foggy banks of the Hudson where the man sold his soul and forfeited the right to be remembered. How the mighty are fallen! The brigadier general who once commanded West Point, the major general who distinguished himself at battles along Lake Champlain, Mohawk Valley, Quebec, and Saratoga, committed treason and died a synonym of disgrace—the infamous Benedict Arnold. As Clarence Macartney once put it so eloquently, "The empty niche in that monument shall ever stand for fallen manhood, power prostituted, for genius soiled, for faithlessness to a sacred trust." The man who turned traitor despised the Puritan morality of his mother and died in greater disgrace and poverty than his drunken father.

There is another empty niche, far more famous and in sharp contrast to that monument in the state of New York. It, too, stands in memory of a battle, but not the kind fought with guns and bayonets. This niche is actually a tomb . . . a place that once held a body, in fact, the most significant body that ever housed a human soul. The tomb was borrowed, appropriately, and "used" for only a few hours. But in perfect fulfillment of Scripture, it enveloped the dead Messiah.

The battle against sin had been bloody and treacherous. Anyone who had the courage to visit that tomb shortly after it was sealed would certainly have wept bitterly. The battlefield, strewn with the litter of an awful fight, was only too vivid in everyone's memory—a small pile of clothing, a spear, a matted network of thorns in the shape of a head, a bloody cross. And those words, those final words the victim uttered, especially that awful scream—

Eloi, Eloi, lama sabachthani!

But what appeared to be defeat was actually the preface of victory. That ugly, rugged cross took its toll, but it failed to have the final voice.

Deep in the silence of night, against all odds and in mockery of strong-armed soldiers, that victim became the Victor. "Up from the grave He arose, with a mighty triumph o'r His foes." Or, as Charles Wesley wrote of that Easter-morning miracle:

> Love's redeeming work is done, Alleluia!
> Fought the fight, the battle won, Alleluia!
> Death in vain forbids Him rise, Alleluia!
> Christ has opened Paradise, Alleluia!

The bloody battlefield paled into a misty memory as the tomb opened its jaws for all to enter. Death could not keep its prey . . . He tore the bars away . . . He came back from beyond.

Every year the empty niche makes its own bold proclamation. Etched into the stone is a Name that is above every name, the gentle Conqueror, the King of Kings, the sovereign Lord.

On Easter Sunday we shall again visit that historic battleground near another hill. We won't find Him there on a cross or standing tall as a bronzed statue. For "He is not here . . . He has risen, just as He said."

Let's meet at the monument and let's think about Him. And reflect on His victory. And remember His Name as we worship near that windswept hill . . . called Calvary.

COME ASIDE

Through Isaiah 53:10-12, think about Him, reflect on His victory, remember His Name as you worship.

THE TURNING POINT

I remember it well. Almost as clearly as if it happened last month. But it didn't. It happened deep in the summer of '58.

I was a Marine. Almost eight thousand miles of ocean between me and my wife. One-word descriptions of my condition? Disillusioned. Stretched. Learning. Lonely. Determined. Sincere. Uncertain. Afraid.

The Quonset hut I called home housed forty-seven other Marines, and row after row after row of the identical round-top dwellings wrapped around hundreds of other young fighting men—men who had been trained to kill. No need to contaminate your mind with the stuff that went on inside those barracks. If you have trouble imagining, just think of a pack of hungry junk-yard dogs that have been teased until they're snarling and foaming at the mouth. Add an endless stream of profanity, subtract all moral restraint, multiply by tropical heat and humidity, divide it by 365 days a year, and you have some idea of life on *The Rock*, Okinawa. Thanks to those eighteen months, I have never felt the urge to tour Alcatraz.

But it took that experience to convince me of one of the most basic of theological facts: Man is totally depraved. Within the span of my first six months in that ungodly environment, believe me, I became convinced. God used that inescapable, oppressive atmosphere to draw me to Himself, to find refuge and refreshment in His Book, and to break my stubborn will. It was there I decided to change careers, go back to school, and pursue the gospel ministry.

Quietly, almost imperceptibly, my heart began to soften to the idea. Rather than offending me, all the verbal filth made me pity the guys who were trapped like rats in a sewer pipe. Their inability to gain control over their lust, in spite of the epidemic level of venereal disease, caused me to feel compassion rather than criticize and alienate myself from my outfit. Instead of remaining aloof and monkish, I risked getting up close, being a friend, rubbing shoulders with men whose lifestyle was, to me, nauseating and empty. But God honored that approach. Before I said *sayonara*, seven had come to Christ. Now seven out of forty-eight may not seem like much to shout about, but in a Marine Corps Quonset hut, friend—it's a *revival!*

Looking back, I distinctly remember the turning point. No heavenly vision caused my attitude to change. My resentment toward God didn't decrease because of some audible voice in the night. I can trace the acceptance of my circumstance and the shift of my focus to a single verse of Scripture. When I happened upon it, it seemed to leap from the page. I found myself like author Annie Dillard, who, upon realizing a vast number of things in the flash of a moment, exclaimed, "I had been my whole life a bell, and never knew it until at that moment I was lifted and struck."

It was late on a Sunday evening. I was on one of those rickety old Oriental buses as it weaved and bobbed its way back to the base. Everyone else around me was in a drunken stupor or snoring in an exhausted sleep. I was sitting in the back seat, thumbing through my new copy of the Amplified New Testament with the aid of a flashlight, and there it was, waiting to be discovered . . . to be believed . . . to be put into action. Philippians 3:10 said all I needed to hear:

> [For my determined purpose is] that I may know Him—that
> I may progressively become more deeply and intimately ac-
> quainted with Him, perceiving and recognizing and under-
> standing [the wonders of His Person] more strongly and
> more clearly. And that I may in that same way come to know
> the power outflowing from His resurrection [which it exerts
> over believers]; and that I may so share His sufferings as to
> be continually transformed [in spirit into His likeness even]
> to His death . . ."

I thought, "That's it . . . that is *everything* in one grand statement.
"I want to know Him. I also want to model the power outflowing from His resurrection. And I certainly want to be continually transformed into His likeness . . . which requires accepting my share of suffering."

From the moment my bell was "lifted up and struck," oh, the difference it has made! I remember it well, like it happened last month.

Now, why would I take your time to serve up this slice of life? Three reasons. First, because our Lord never wastes times of testing. The pain and struggles and confusion connected with my circumstances only *seemed* futile and unfair. Second, because His Word holds out hope when all seems hopeless. There are hundreds of other Philippians-three-ten truths awaiting discovery. Third, because turning points aren't limited to Marine barracks on *The Rock.*

All three of those principles could come together for you . . . this very year . . . perhaps this very month. I hope so. Then it'll be *your* turn to tell it, so remember it well.

COME ASIDE

Out of the damp darkness, hear in Jonah 2:1-9 the words of a man at a most unique turning point.

How would you describe Jonah's new awareness?

THE PROBLEM WITH PROGRESS

rogress seems like a two-headed giant, doesn't it?

Looking back on it, it is admirable, almost heroic. We salute visionaries of yesteryear. They emerge from the pages of our history books as men and women of gallant faith. We shake our heads in amazement as we imagine the herculean courage it took to stand so confidently when the majority frowned so sternly. Yesterday's progress earns for itself today's monuments of stone.

Looking back, we laud those who refused to take no for an answer. We quote them with gusto. We even name our children after them.

But today? What do we do with such creatures today? We brand them as irritating malcontents, reckless idealists who simply won't sit down and be quiet. Today's progressive dreamers are seen as permissive, wild-eyed extremists.

Not showing much corporate promise (since they hate the status quo mold), most of them have a tough time going along with the system. They in fact *loathe* the system. But what they lack in diplomacy they make up for in persistence. Cooperative they're not. Resilient they are. Give most of them a couple hundred years and they'll be virtually knighted. But at the present moment, they seem nuts.

I can scarcely think of a half dozen churches today, for example, that would so much as consider having Martin Luther candidate for the pulpit. It's doubtful that very many of you in business would hire Thomas Edison or Leonardo da Vinci into your company. And which evangelical seminary would chance turning over its students majoring in systematic theology to a firebrand like John Knox? Or tell me, how would an emotionally charged free spirit like Ludwig van Beethoven fit the stuffy chair of any university's department of music? And who today would choose to go into battle with a blood-n-guts, straight-shooting commanding officer like George Patton or "Howlin' Mad" Smith? For that matter, how many votes would a crusty, outspoken, overweight visionary like Winston Churchill . . . or the rugged Andrew Jackson get in our day of slick government and touch-me-not bureaucrats and politicians? You think we'd respect their progressiveness and value their vision? Don't bet on it. People didn't in *their* day.

I came across a rather remarkable letter purportedly written over one hundred and fifty years ago by Martin Van Buren to President Jackson. The contents? A strong, critical warning that the "evil" new railroads would disrupt business, boost unemployment, and weaken our nation's defense. Historians may debate the authenticity of this little epistle, but see if the underlying tone doesn't sound vaguely familiar.

> January 31, 1829
>
> To: President Jackson:
>
> The canal system of this country is being threatened by the spread of a new form of transportation known as "railroads." The federal government must preserve the canals for the following reasons:
>
> One. If canal boats are supplanted by "railroads," serious unemployment will result. Captains, cooks, drivers, hostlers, repairmen and lock tenders will be left without means of livelihood, not to mention the numerous farmers now employed in growing hay for horses.
>
> Two. Boat builders would suffer and towline, whip and harness makers would be left destitute.
>
> Three. Canal boats are absolutely essential to the defense of the United States. In the event of the expected trouble with England, the Erie Canal would be the only means by which we could ever move the supplies so vital to waging modern war.
>
> As you may well know, Mr. President, "railroad" carriages are pulled at the enormous speed of fifteen miles per hour by "engines" which, in addition to endangering life and limb of passengers, roar and snort their way through the countryside, setting fire to crops, scaring the livestock and frightening our women and children. The Almighty certainly never intended that people should travel at such breakneck speed.
>
> Martin Van Buren
> Governor of New York

How wildly progressive can you get? Just imagine the shock of the Almighty(!) as those iron horses began to rumble by at such "breakneck speed." It may be amusing in our day of moonshots, Concorde jet flights to London, and intercontinental ballistic missiles, but when the late Governor Van Buren dispatched that epistle in the winter of 1829, he was sober and serious as a judge. The very idea of a President even *tolerating* such a thought smacked of temporary insanity. Maybe the heat from Old Hickory's "kitchen cabinet" was getting to him.

Are you an eagle-type, soaring to heights beyond your peers? Do you find yourself bored with the maintenance of the machinery . . . yawning through the review of the rules . . . restless to cut a new swath . . . excited rather than intimidated by the risks? Don't expect pats on the back or great waves of applause. Not today. Chances are good you'll lose a few jobs, fail a few courses, ruffle tons of feathers, and be the subject of the town gossip. Mavericks who don't color within the lines are also notorious for not staying within the fences. And that makes folks terribly uncomfortable.

There's something about that old progressive giant that currently casts a shadow on your genius. But take heart! Many an alleged heretic today will be a hero tomorrow. Which is another way of saying, "first the cross, then the crown."

COME ASIDE

One biblical hero who was especially upsetting to the national status quo—and whose life spanned agony and ecstasy—was Elijah. Follow the rise of his prophetic career in 1 Kings 17-19. What is his legacy for you?

HOUDINI'S SECRET

rich Weiss was a remarkable man.

By the time of his death he was famous around the world.

Never heard of him, huh?

Maybe this will help. He was born of Hungarian-Jewish parentage at Appleton, Wisconsin, in 1874. He became the highest-paid entertainer of his day.

That still doesn't help much, does it? This will.

When he finally got his act together, Weiss adopted a stage name: Harry Houdini . . . the master showman, a distinguished flyer, a mystifying magician, and—most of all—an unsurpassed escapologist.

On March 10, 1904, the London *Daily Illustrated Mirror* challenged Houdini to escape from a special pair of handcuffs they had prepared. Are you ready? There were six locks on each cuff and nine tumblers on each lock. Seven days later, 4,000 spectators gathered in the London Hippodrome to witness the outcome of the audacious challenge which Houdini had accepted.

At precisely 3:15 P.M., the manacled showman stepped into an empty cabinet which came up to his waist. Kneeling down, he was out of sight for a full twenty minutes. He stood up smiling as the crowd applauded, thinking he was free. But he was not. He asked for more light. They came on brighter as he knelt down out of sight. Fifteen minutes later he stood to his feet. Applause broke out—again, premature. He was still handcuffed. Said he just needed to flex his knees.

Down into the cabinet again went the magician. Twenty minutes passed slowly for the murmuring crowd before Houdini stood to his feet with a broad smile. Loud applause quickly stopped as the audience saw he was not yet free. Because the bright lights made the heat so intense, he leaped from the cabinet and twisted his manacled hands in front of him until he could reach a pocket knife in his vest. Opening the knife with his teeth, he held its handle in his mouth and bent forward to such a degree that the tail of his coat fell over his head. He grasped the coat, pulled it over his head, then proceeded to slash it to ribbons with the knife between his teeth. Throwing aside the strips of his heavy coat, he jumped back into the box as the audience roared its approval and cheered him on.

Down went Houdini, but this time for only ten minutes. With a dramatic flourish, he jumped from the box—wrists free—waving the bulky handcuffs over his head in triumph. Pandemonium exploded in London. Once again the showman had achieved the incredible—almost the *impossible*.

Afterwards, Houdini was interviewed. Everyone wanted to know why he had to interrupt the process of his escape as often as he did. With a twinkle in his eyes, the magician freely admitted that he really didn't *have* to interrupt the process. He repeatedly explained that his ability to escape was based on knowledge.

"My brain is the key that sets me free!" he often declared. Then why did he keep standing up before he was loose? He confessed it was because he wanted the audience's applause to keep up his enthusiasm!

Two things, then, set Houdini free: (1) his *knowledge* of what he knew to be true and (2) the cultivation of his own *enthusiasm*.

What an essential role enthusiasm plays in our lives! In many ways, it is the key ingredient that frees us from the cramping, dark, overheated confinement of a task. When the odds are against us, the hours are long, and the end is not yet in view, enthusiasm rescues us from the temptation to quit—or run away—or complain. It takes the grit and grind out of boredom. It calls in fresh troops when the battle gets long and the body gets weary.

Athletes feed on it. Salesmen are motivated by it. Teachers count on it. Students fail without it. Leadership demands it. Projects are completed because of it. Emerson's motto is as true today as the day he wrote it:

Nothing great was ever achieved without enthusiasm.

Few characteristics are more contagious, more magnetic. I'm convinced that one of the reasons God gives us so many personal promises in His Word is to stir up our enthusiasm—to build a bonfire in the steamroom of our souls.

Houdini had it right: Knowledge is essential—but knowledge without enthusiasm is like a tire without air . . . like a pool without water . . . like a bed without sheets . . . like a "thank you" without a smile. Remove enthusiasm from a church service on Sunday and you have the makings of a memorial service at a mortuary on a Monday. Remove enthusiasm from the daily whirl of family activities and you've made a grinding mill out of a merry-go-round. Enthusiasm acts as the oil on Saturdays in our home when it's clean-up day and the family machine needs a boost.

Two men were in a military prison. One was sad and depressed. The other was quite happy. The sad soldier lamented that he had gone AWOL and was in for thirty days. His smiling companion replied that he had murdered a general and was in for three days. Astonished, the gloomy GI complained, "That isn't fair! Your crime was far more serious. Why am I in for thirty days—and you for only three?" Still smiling, the other answered, "They're going to hang me on Wednesday."

The difference? Enthusiasm.

COME ASIDE

Hear again the words of a Winner in Matthew 28:18-20—and get excited!

THE FAMILY:
NO SUBSTITUTE WILL DO

ry all you like, you simply cannot find a substitute for the family. God planned it that way. In spite of all we're reading and seeing these days designed to make us think we've entered the family-phase-out era, don't you believe it! There is nothing on earth that comes close to the benefits derived from relationships revolving around our roots. Nothing.

Edith Schaeffer's *What Is a Family?* offers some wise and meaningful answers:

- ◆ the birthplace of creativity
- ◆ a shelter in the time of storm
- ◆ a perpetual relay of truth
- ◆ a door that has hinges and a lock
- ◆ an educational control
- ◆ a museum of memories

Sometimes those family memories are absolutely hilarious. I think back to an incident around the Swindoll supper table that I related in an earlier book, *You and Your Child*.

Before supper began I suggested to Curtis (who was six) that he should serve Charissa (she was four) before he served himself. Naturally, he wondered why, since the platter of chicken sat directly in front of him . . . and he was hungry as a lion. I explained it is polite for fellas to serve girls before they served themselves. The rule sounded weird, but he was willing . . . as long as she didn't take too long.

Well, you'd never believe what occurred. After prayer, he picked up the huge platter, held it for his sister, and asked which piece of chicken she wanted.

She relished all that attention. Being quite young, however, she had no idea which piece was which. So, very seriously, she replied, "I'd like the foot."

He glanced in my direction, frowned as the hunger pains shot through his stomach, then looked back at her and said, "Uh . . . Charissa, Mother doesn't cook the foot!"

To which she replied, "Where is it?"

With increased anxiety he answered (a bit louder), "I don't know! The foot is somewhere else, not on this platter. Look, choose a piece. Hurry up."

She studied the platter and said, "Okay, just give me the hand."

By now their mother and father were biting their lips to refrain from laughing out loud. We would have intervened, but decided to let them work it out alone. That's part of the training process.

"A chicken doesn't have a hand, it has a wing, Charissa."

"I hate the wing, Curtis . . . Oh, go ahead and give me the head."

By then I was headed for the bathroom. I couldn't hold my laughter any longer. Curtis was totally beside himself. His sister was totally frustrated, not being able to get the piece she wanted.

Realizing his irritation with her and the absence of a foot or hand or head, she finally said in an exasperated tone, "Oh, all right! I'll take the belly button!"

That did it. He reached in, grabbed a piece, and said, "That's the best I can do!" He gave her the breast, which was about as close to the belly button as he could get.

Fun. Just plain ol' nutty times when hearty laughs and silly remarks dull the edge of life's razor-sharp demands and intensity. Families and fun go together like whipped cream on a hot fudge sundae.

Other times those family memories are deeply profound and stabilizing. Who can ever forget the impact of a father's strong arms around the shoulders of his kids following the loss of someone they all loved? Or the comfort communicated by a mother's embrace? Or the hope generated through a family discussion when stress had reached an all-time high? Or how about those occasions when you needed to talk . . . to let it all out . . . and a brother or sister was willing just to listen without preaching or even frowning? Families and encouragement mix well together.

Occasionally, God gives a family memory that becomes so deep a crease in the brain time can never erase it. Pause a moment and meditate on Solomon's psalm:

> Unless the LORD builds the house,
> They labor in vain who build it. . . .
> Behold, children are a gift of the LORD;
> The fruit of the womb is a reward. . . .
> How blessed is the man whose quiver is full of them (127:1,3,5).

Three questions emerge from this discussion:

1. Is the Lord really building your home? Stop and think.

2. Do you view the kiddos as His gift, His reward? Gifts and rewards in life are usually treated with special care, you know.

3. Are you genuinely happy with your full quiver? Is it pleasant for the family to be with you?

Face it, friend. When we allow the tyranny of the urgent—the ever-increasing demands—to siphon our tank of energy and interest so that the family is left with nothing but the fumes of broken promises and empty dreams, we are laboring in vain! We are substituting the artificial for the authentic. And that includes Christians who are so busy in "the Lord's work" (?) they haven't time for the home. What a sad contradiction!

It isn't a question of "Am I building memories?" but "What kind?"

Start this week. Right away, in fact. How about *tonight*? Get reacquainted with those folks who live under your roof and eat at your table and bear your name . . . and prefer you to *any* substitute. God planned it that way, remember.

COME ASIDE

Treat yourself to Psalm 128, as well as a special time with your family tonight.

BEYOND TODAY

f you can look into the seeds of time,
and say which grain will grow,
and which will not,
Speak then to me . . ."
Macbeth, act I, scene 1, line 58

Who wouldn't want to hear from someone like that? Who hasn't felt himself standing on tiptoe, straining to see what lies ahead? I. F. Clarke, a British professor, has written a book entitled *The Pattern of Expectation*. In it he claims to trace "the search for the true shape of things to come." And then there's Alvin Toffler's *Third Wave*, along with Herman Kahn's *The Year 2000*, plus John McHale's *Future of the Future* to keep us guessing. And thinking—stretching us far beyond the mental boundaries we once drew.

Some of their stuff is downright scary. Like the growth of fetuses in artificial wombs. And household robots. And such an enormous explosion of involvement in certain population centers that cities will have 50 to 100 million inhabitants, which Kahn calls "megalopolises." He humorously tags the future city stretching between Boston and Washington D.C. *Boswash* ; From San Francisco to San Diego, *San San*; and from Chicago to Pittsburgh, *Chickipitts!* And can you imagine the traffic jam from Houston to Corpus Christie? I'd suggest that death trap be called *Whose Corpse?*

Even the writers of a recent weekly news magazine tried to look beyond today. They didn't try many predictions but they did ask some tough, sweeping questions. Among them:

- ◆ Is America in retreat?
- ◆ Will our nation regain its trust?
- ◆ Is public education doomed?
- ◆ Can the world be fed?
- ◆ Can we find more oil?
- ◆ Is peace with Russia possible?
- ◆ Can we keep hoping?

That last one is really the root issue, isn't it? To borrow from Buckminster Fuller's title, unless *Spaceship Earth* has hope, it could mean some pretty dismal years in front of us. Shakespeare's "seeds of time" might very well be scattered and dangerously thinned out by the 1990s.

But let's limit our thoughts to something we can handle. Most of us must admit those news magazine questions are too vast for us. And the idea of living in a megalopolis is too remote to interest us. We need a bite-size chunk to chew on.

Okay then, how about that unit called your family . . . now there's something worth thinking about beyond today. Where are you going? What's your game plan for the next ten years? Given any thought to specific objectives you want to reach—or at least shoot for? How about selecting some priorities? You say there's no hurry? I challenge that. These ten years will literally fly by. A decade from now you'll rip the December sheet off your calendar wondering, "How did ten years go by so fast?"

Ten years. The Swindoll "kids" will all be out of the nest . . . possibly finished with schooling, married, perhaps living long distances away. It takes no crystal ball to see those kinds of facts in our future. *You* try it. Right now. Stop and add ten years to your life and (if you have a family) do the same with each of your children.

Suddenly we're all a bit more sober. The clapper of urgency has struck the bell of reality, and some of us sense a summons back to our inescapable responsibility. God commands us to "number our days, that we may present to [Him] a heart of wisdom" (Psalm 90:12).

Forgive me for pressing the issue near the point of offense, but unless some of you who read these words *stop* and *think* and start to *execute* essential goals for the next ten years, indifference, passivity, and procrastination will win another victory. And instead of making a few hard decisions that will initiate beneficial changes, your family ties will loosen, your children will drift, and you'll dread the memory of the way you were.

How much better to invite the living, all-knowing Lord to show you ways to make the coming years much better than the years before! To allow you to become *better*, as well as older.

How about offering this prayer—in faith:

> Lord, since You can look into the seeds of time,
>   and say which grain will grow,
>   and which will not,
> Speak then to me . . .

——————⟨🍂⟩——————

COME ASIDE

To help you get started on the hard decisions you need to make, give careful thought to the lesson in Haggai 1:2-11. Have you neglected some aspect of your responsibility to the Lord? Is now the time to find timber in the mountains and start building?

THE TONGUE OF THE WISE

 isely labeled "the saving virtue," tact graces a life like fragrance graces a rose. One whiff of those red petals erases any memory of the thorns.

Tact is like that.

It's remarkable how peaceful and pleasant it can make us. Its major goal is avoiding unnecessary offense . . . and that alone ought to make us *crave* it. Its basic function is a keen sense of what to say or do in order to maintain the truth *and* good relationships . . . and that alone ought to make us *cultivate* it. Tact is *savoir faire* on the horizontal plane. It is incessantly appropriate, invariably attractive, incurably appealing, but rare . . . oh, so rare!

Remember the teacher you had who lacked tact? Learning was sacrificed daily on the altar of fear. You wondered each session if *that* was the day you'd be singled out and embarrassed through some public putdown.

Remember the salesman you encountered who lacked tact? Once you found out (and it usually doesn't take sixty seconds), you wanted only one thing—to get *away*.

Remember the boss you worked for who lacked tact? You never knew if he *ever* understood you or considered you to be a valuable person.

And who could forget that tactless physician? You weren't a human being, you were Case 36—a body with a blood pressure of 120/70 . . . height 5'7" . . . weight 160 . . . a history of chronic diarrhea . . . stones in your gall bladder—"*and you need radical surgery immediately!*" All this was spoken in perfect monotone as he glared grimly at a folder stuffed with x-rays, charts, and long sheets of paper covered with advanced hieroglyphics. Brilliant, capable, experienced, dignified, respected . . . but no tact.

Perhaps you heard about the husband who lacked tact. Early one morning his wife left for a trip abroad . . . and that very day their poodle died. When she called home that evening, she asked how everything was—and he bluntly blurted out, "Well, the dog died!" Shocked, she chided him through tears for being so tactless, so strong.

"What should I have said?" he asked.

"You should have broken the news gently, perhaps in stages. When I called you from here in New York, you could have said, 'The dog is on the roof.' And the next day when I called you from London, 'He fell off the roof.' The following day from Paris, you could have told me, 'He is at the vet's . . . in the hospital.' And finally, from Rome, I could have then been informed, 'He died.'"

The husband paused and thought about the advice. His wife then asked, "By the way, how is mother?"

He responded, "She's on the roof!"

Ah, that's bad. But it isn't the worst. The classic example of tactless humanity, I'm disappointed to declare, is the abrasive Christian (so-called) who feels it is his or her calling to fight for the truth with little or no regard for the other fella's feelings. Of course, this is supposedly done in the name of the Lord. "To do anything less," this tactless individual intones with a pious expression, "would be compromise and counterfeit." So on he goes, plowing through people's feelings like a clumsy John Deere tractor, leaving everyone he encounters buried in the dirt, and worst of all, deeply offended. For all his rapid-fire Scripture quotations, you will rarely find Proverbs 18:19 on the lips of this armored crusader:

> A brother offended is harder to be won than a strong city,
> and contentions are like the bars of a castle.

His favorite plan of attack is either to overlook or strongly demand, and the backwash is a back alley strewn with the litter of broken hearts and bitter souls. Unfortunately, the preacher himself is often the greatest offender, who seems to delight in developing a devastating pulpit that scourges rather than encourages, that blasts rather than builds. His murder weapon is that blunt instrument hidden behind his teeth.

"The heart of the righteous ponders how to answer," wrote Solomon. "That which turns away wrath is *a gentle answer."*

The wise person uses his tongue to *"make knowledge acceptable,"* the king added. And who could ever forget the impact of the proverb that says: *"The tongue of the wise brings healing"* . . . or *"a man has joy in an apt answer and how delightful is a timely word!"*

There's a TV ad for a first-aid ointment that says, "Stop hurting . . . start healing." Another offers a bandage that takes the "ouch" away. That's good counsel. Let's be gentle and sensitive when we are touching the tender feelings of others. Moms and dads, it's hard to exaggerate the value of tact within the walls of your home. Soften the blows a little! You'll preserve some very valuable self-esteem while gaining respect, believe me.

By the way, no facts need be subtracted when tact is added. I used to sell shoes years ago. With a twinkle in his eye, my seasoned employer instructed me not to say, "Lady, your foot is too big for this shoe!" Instead, I was taught to say, "I'm sorry, ma'am, but this shoe is just a little too small for your foot." Both statements expressed the facts, but one was an insult and the other a tactful compliment. Same facts, different words.

It didn't shrink her foot, but it did save her face.
And that's what tact is all about.

COME ASIDE

Paul's brief letter to Philemon—regarding the return of a runaway slave—is a model of tact and wisdom in a potentially divisive situation. Read through it and mentally give Paul a compliment each time he shows good judgment in his choice of words.

LIE BACK AND LOOK UP

kay, are you ready to have your mind boggled? If not, better shove this aside until you can handle it. It's too stretching to pass over with a yawn.

The germ thought struck me when I was deep in the redwoods some time ago. I laid back and looked up. I mean really up. It was one of those clear summer nights when you could see forever. So starry it was scary. The vastness of the heavens eloquently told the glory of God. The expanse silently declared the work of His hands.

No words would adequately frame the awesomeness of that moment. I remembered a statement one of my mentors used to say: "Wonder is involuntary praise." That night, it happened to me. I loved it!

What struck me deepest as I curled up in my sleeping bag was this: Everything I have seen belongs to this one galaxy. There are hundreds more beyond our own. Maybe thousands . . . some much larger than ours. Astronomers are now convinced there are twenty galaxies within two and a half million light years; there may be a billion galaxies within photographic range of the 200-inch Mount Palomar telescope.

Let's limit our thinking, for a moment, just to this one solar system . . . a tiny fraction of the universe above us. Because it is impossible to grasp the astounding distance about us, we need analogies, simple comparisons, to assist us. Hold on as we take a quick trip to the regions beyond.

If it were possible to travel the speed of light, you could arrive at the moon in one and a third seconds. But continuing that same speed, do you know how long it would take you to reach the closest star? Four years. Incredible thought!

If you've ever visited New York City's Hayden Planetarium, you've seen that miniature replica of our solar system showing the speeds and sizes of our planets. What is interesting is that the three outer planets are not included. There wasn't room for Uranus, Neptune, and Pluto. Uranus would be in the planetarium's outer corridor, Neptune would be around Eighth Avenue. And Pluto? Another three long avenues away—Fifth Avenue. By the way, no stars are included, for obvious reasons. Can you imagine (on the same scale) where the nearest star would be located? Cleveland, Ohio. Vast! And that's just our own local galaxy, remember.

A scientist once suggested another interesting analogy. To grasp the scene, imagine a perfectly smooth glass pavement on which the finest speck can be seen. Then shrink our sun from 865,000 miles in diameter to only two feet . . . and place the ball on the pavement to represent the sun. Step off 82 paces (about two feet per pace), and to represent proportionately the first planet, Mercury, put down a tiny mustard seed.

Take 60 steps more, and for Venus put an ordinary BB.

Mark 78 more steps . . . put down a green pea representing earth.

Step off 108 paces from there, and for Mars put down a pinhead.

Sprinkle around some fine dust for the asteroids, then take 788 steps more. For Jupiter, place an orange on the glass at that spot.

After 934 more steps, put down a golf ball for Saturn.

Now it gets really involved. Mark 2,086 steps more, and for Uranus . . . a marble.

Another 2,322 steps from there you arrive at Neptune. Let a cherry represent Neptune.

This will take two and a half miles, and we haven't even discussed Pluto! If we swing completely around, we have a smooth glass surface five miles in diameter, yet just a tiny fraction of the heavens—excluding Pluto. On this surface, five miles across, we have only a seed, BB, pea, pinhead, some dust, an orange, golf ball, a marble, and a cherry. Guess how far we'd have to go on the same scale before we could put down another two-foot ball to represent to represent the nearest star. Come on, guess. Seven hundred paces? Two thousand steps more? Four thousand four hundred feet? No, you're way off.

We'd have to go 6,720 miles before we could arrive at that star. Miles, not feet. And that's just the first star among millions. In one galaxy among perhaps thousands, maybe billions. And all of it in perpetual motion . . . perfectly synchronized . . . the most accurate timepiece known to man.

Phenomenal isn't the word for it.

No God? All by chance? Whom are you kidding? I honestly cannot think of a more erroneous thought than that. Listen carefully to the truth:

> For the truth about God is known to them [men who don't acknowledge God's truth] instinctively; God has put this knowledge in their hearts. Since earliest times men have seen the earth and sky and all God made, and have known of his existence and great eternal power. So they will have no excuse . . . (Romans 1:19-20 TLB).

The boggled mind leads to a bended knee.

COME ASIDE

The next chance you have, go outside on a clear night and gaze up in wonder. Take with you, in mind and heart, the endtime prophecy in Daniel 12:3. Study it now.

READING

he three Rs have stood the test of time as reliable criteria for a dependable education. They are poised like disciplined sentinels against one of man's greatest enemies: ignorance. The original blocks of granite, unimpressed by educational styles, unmoved by change, these three solid friends are trustworthy to the end. Like salve on an open sore, they reduce the fever of panic, giving stability when so many voices demand obedience.

But there is a fly in the ointment . . . one chunk of granite is beginning to crack . . . the sentinel is getting sleepy. The enemy has found the chink in our armor. He has discovered that the first "R" is up for grabs in the twentieth century. *And he is smiling*.

"Send me a man who reads" is no longer the clarion call of industry or management . . . or sales, for that matter. Nor is the professional person necessarily known today, as he once was, for his breadth of knowledge . . . and that includes (much to my disappointment) the clergy.

Few current tragedies pain me more. It is now a fact that one half of the students who graduate from college never read another book. Even though a Ph.D. is virtually obsolete in five years unless he or she continues to read, many of them opt for an easier out. It would shock us all if we knew how little the person reads who defends us in court or does surgery on our bodies or gives us financial counsel. Aside from daily doses of *TV Guide* (America's top-selling magazine), a chuckle at "Peanuts" on Sunday, and a quick skim over the sports section, many a man never cracks another magazine or book.

It's amazing! Before kids are in school, they can give you the day, hour, and channel for a dozen different TV programs, but have trouble struggling through *Dick and Jane Play with Spot* into the second and third grades. Little Leaguers can spit out the batting averages, RBIs, and stolen base totals for each of their favorite baseball pros . . . but stick a copy of *Tom Sawyer* in front of them (or their dads!) and boredom strikes like summer lightning. A growing number of California high school grads have trouble comprehending basic application forms for employment.

Enough about the problem; let's consider the benefits. I can think of four.

1. *Reading sweeps the cobwebs away.*

It enhances thinking. It stretches and strains our mental muscles. It clobbers our brittle, narrow, intolerant opinions with new ideas and strong facts. It stimulates growing up instead of growing old.

Bacon's famous rule is so true, so good:

Read not to contradict or confute, nor to believe and take for granted, nor to find talk and discourse, but to weigh and consider. Some books are to be tasted, others to be swallowed, and some few to be chewed and digested.

Reading expands us. It scratches those itches down deep inside. It navigates us through virgin territory we would not otherwise explore.

2. *Reading increases our power of concentration.*

Through this discipline, the mind is programed to observe and absorb. It replaces the "Entertain Me" mentality with "Challenge Me." The eye of a reader is keen, alert, probing, questioning.

I will never forget being aboard a huge troop ship en route from Formosa to America. A lazy afternoon led me to a book of poetry, which I began to devour with delight. I was suddenly struck with the realization that someone was staring at me. Looking up, I saw a fellow Marine who outranked me by a few stripes. I expected him to order me into some duty, but to my surprise he asked: "Hey, Marine, you got any books with *pictures* in 'em?" Knowing him, he probably would have colored outside the lines!

3. *Reading makes us more interesting to be around.*

Small wonder the boredom factor in social gatherings is so great! After you've run through the weather, the kids, the job, and your recent surgery, what else is there? Being a reader adds oil to the friction in conversation. Furthermore, it opens to the Christian new avenues of approach in evangelism. It helps to meet the lost on their own ground and have them realize that becoming a Christian isn't like committing intellectual suicide. We need to read widely, including some periodicals as well as the classics.

4. *Reading strengthens our ability to glean truth from God's Word.*

As I mentioned in my introduction to this book, when the old warrior Paul was in the dungeon awaiting death, he asked his friend to—

> bring the cloak which I left at Troas . . . and the books, especially the parchments (2 Timothy 4:13).

The "parchments" referred to the sacred manuscripts, copies of Scripture. But what about "the books"? What books? Obviously, those volumes he was reading prior to his imprisonment. Right up to death, that capable spokesman for God—that master of logic—was reading. He certainly would have agreed with John Wesley:

> Either read or get out of the ministry!

Can't find the time? Come on, now . . . not even fifteen minutes? Don't know where to start? How about the library? Most every town has one. So do many churches. Why not surprise the librarian and drop by on Sunday.

They probably even have books with pictures in 'em. (For your kids, right?)

COME ASIDE

Just to stretch and strain and strengthen you today, let your Bible reading be in Leviticus 16—a rich enough passage, but probably not one you would normally choose to digest.

Get thoroughly acquainted with it, even with verses you don't fully understand.

THE SHORES OF LAKE CONTENTMENT

elieve it or not, the average American is exposed to about three hundred advertisements a day. Personally, I believe it! The magazine in which I read that fact yesterday has more pages dedicated to advertisements than articles of interest to the reader. Shiny, slick, appealing print and pictures designed to hijack your concentration and kidnap your attention. Before you realize it, the Madison Avenue Pied Piper has led you into a world of exaggerated make-believe, convincing you that you simply cannot *live* without . . .

♦ a new Polaroid camera stuffed with SX-70 film (that develops *twice* as fast!)
♦ an elegant diamond solitaire (a diamond is *forever!*)
♦ a Dodge Sportsman Wagon to pull your new outboard
♦ a set of Firestone's finest
♦ Carter's Little Pills "specially coated to pass right through your stomach releasing their action only in your lower tract"

Or two dozen other double-page, full-color missiles that explode in your mind with the messages, "Try me, you'll see" and "You deserve the very best."

Such bombardments do a number on us. Some of the results are obvious. They stimulate our curiosity, they urge us to buy goods or services, they make us aware of what is available, they announce new products, and—of course—they shape our tastes, habits, and customs. That's all well and good, since it's "the American way" and intricately interwoven into our economy. After all, it's a mega-billion-a-year business.

But there is a subliminal message that detonates deep down inside our heads—silently yet forcefully. Like shrapnel, thoughts are embedded in the brain, conveying a damaging message if we're not careful.

And what is that message?

In a word, it is *discontentment*. Dissatisfaction. It creates (if we let it) a restless drive for more . . . or better . . . or bigger. Three hundred times a day it chips away at the dam that supports one of the last reservoirs of inner peace known to man—*contentment*. What a beautiful scene in the soul is Lake Contentment! Undisturbed by outside noises brought on by the jackhammers of exaggeration, those who enjoy the lake know what relaxation is all about. They know nothing of any winter of discontent—or spring or fall or summer, for that matter. Such an existence breeds security and happiness.

Paul lived on that lake once he got his life squared away. He's the one, remember, who wrote:

> And if we have food and covering, with these we shall be content (1 Timothy 6:8).

That's a pretty simple list, isn't it? Something to eat and a place to live. Period. Just before he said that, he mentioned:

> We have brought nothing into the world, so we cannot take anything out of it either (v. 7).

Funny how our lives often contradict that statement. We find ourselves clawing, grabbing, hoarding, saving . . . seldom releasing, seldom giving. The wealthy John D. Rockefeller was once asked, "How much does it take to satisfy a man?" With rare wisdom he answered, "A little bit more than he has."

Does contentment mean I need to sell all my possessions and never buy anything new? Does it mean I cannot have nice things? No—it just means those nice things don't possess you. If all this seems suddenly appealing to you, a warning is in order. Becoming a contented person is a process, never an instant decision. The same man who mentioned being satisfied with food and covering earlier in his life admitted:

> I have learned to be content in whatever circumstances I am. I know how to get along with humble means, and I also know how to live in prosperity; in any and every circumstance I have learned the secret of being filled and going hungry, both of having abundance and suffering need (Philippians 4:11-12).

Go back and reread those first three words. Now look at the extremes of his life: "humble means . . . prosperity . . . filled . . . hungry . . . having abundance . . . suffering need." On the yo-yo of life, he had *learned* to relax and enjoy whatever circumstances came his way. Somehow he had taught himself the discipline of saying, "I don't need that," and "That isn't really essential."

And then when things opened up, the apostle had no anxiety encountering "the good life." Balanced as he was, Paul equally enjoyed hot dogs or a filet mignon . . . a vacation on the Riviera or under the bridge . . . a gold-covered, diamond-studded, velvet-cushioned chariot Seville or a dirty burro with a limp. How? His focus was right on target. He held every earthly "thing" loosely. He refused to leave Lake Contentment in search of some shallow stream that was sure to dry up.

You can do that too. But it will take the grace of God and all the discipline you can muster.

Three hundred times a day.

COME ASIDE

Escape from the prison walls of reinforced materialism, and breathe the Lord's free air in Psalm 104. Slowly. Please.

CONTRADICTORY TRUTHS

oach Tom Landry of the Dallas Cowboys was recently quoted as saying something like:

"I have a job to do that is not very complicated, but it is often difficult: to get a group of men to do what they don't want to do so they can achieve the one thing they have wanted all their lives."

Coach Landry, in that seemingly contradictory statement, described what discipline is all about . . . doing what we don't want to do so we can accomplish what we've always wanted.

So much of what results in a fulfilled life is really the product of a contradiction. Those who wish to be the best leaders must demonstrate true servanthood. Those who ultimately are given the oversight of vast regions and broad responsibilities have initially proven themselves faithful in the little things. The most effective form of retaliation is an *absence* of retaliation . . . leaving all vengeance to God. In doing so, to quote the Scriptures, we "heap burning coals upon the head" of an adversary, which is nothing more than overcoming evil with good—another contradictory truth.

Want a few more?

The way to show yourself wise is not so much by speech but by silence.

The way to stop a loud argument is by a soft-spoken word. The most powerful rebuke is not a loud, negative blast, but a quiet, positive model.

The secret of helping others mature is not more rules and stricter laws but greater trust.

Those who are most respected for their knowledge and the skill of drawing others into it are not those who have all the right answers but rather those who ask the right questions.

Those who give generously have much more than those who hoard.

One lovely flower, personally picked from the garden by tiny hands, can mean much more than two dozen long-stemmed roses ordered from the florist.

A handwritten note of love and affection lingers longer in one's memory than a $3.50 embossed card from Hallmark.

Forgiveness is the key to handling our enemies, not revenge.

A brief, warm, tender embrace with very few words says more to the grieving than an evening's visit full of sympathy talk and long prayers.

Funny, isn't it? God often delivers His best gifts to us through the back door of our lives. In unexpected ways . . . with surprises inside the wrappings. Somewhat like the therapy He used when Elijah was so low, so terribly disillusioned. How did the Lord minister to him? By an earth-quake? In a whirlwind? Through a scorching fire? You'd expect all the above since Elijah was such a passionate, hard-charging prophet. But no. The story from 1 Kings 19 makes it clear that Jehovah was not in the earthquake or the wind or the fire. Too obvious. Too predictable. That's not the Sovereign's style.

After all the hullabaloo died down, there came "a gentle blowing" and shortly thereafter, ever so softly, "a voice" came to him (vv. 12-13) with words of reassurance and affirmation. Not, "You oughta be ashamed of yourself!" Or "What's a man of your stature doing in a crummy place like this?" None of that. No blame, no shame, no sermon, no name-calling, no blistering rebuke. In contradiction to the popular idea of confrontation (and surely surprising to Elijah himself), the Lord encouraged His friend to go on from there. He gave him a plan to fol-low, a promise to remember, and a traveling companion to help him make it through the night.

Another mysterious back-door delivery . . . another victim of despair rescued from the pit. No wonder Paul burst forth in praise of God's wis-dom and knowledge by exclaiming:

> How unsearchable are His judgments . . . [how] unfathom-able His ways! (Romans 11:33b).

About the time we think we've got the whole picture in finite focus, an infinite hand quickly grabs the camera, changes lenses on us, points in another direction, and has us take an entirely different picture. Yet to our amazement, when everything is developed, we get the one thing we wanted all our lives through a process we would never have chosen.

It's like the anonymous poet's profound admission:

> I asked God for strength, that I might achieve;
> I was made weak, that I might learn to humbly obey.
>   I asked for health, that I might do greater things;
>   I was given infirmity, that I might do better things.
> I asked for riches, that I might be happy;
> I was given poverty, that I might be wise.
>   I asked for power, that I might have the praise of men;
>   I was given weakness, that I might feel the need of God.
> I asked for all things, that I might enjoy life;
> I was given life, that I might enjoy all things.
>   I got nothing that I asked for,
>   But everything I had hoped for.
> I am, among all men, most richly blessed.

COME ASIDE

Be in awe of the ways of God as you read again in Philippians 2:5-11 about the greatest contradiction in eternal history.

HEALING

ave you heard of the Four Spiritual Laws?"

That question, found in a small booklet, has been asked and answered thousands—perhaps *millions*—of times in our generation. These "laws" have been used by God to introduce His plan of love and forgiveness to countless numbers of people who had no idea how to have a meaningful relationship with Him.

I have a similar question. It is designed to introduce some foundational facts to those who are confused over the painful circumstance they are enduring . . . and how the whole issue of healing applies to them.

"Have you heard of the Five *Suffering* Laws?"

That question appears in no booklet—but it should! These "laws" will do more to help the hurting and erase their confusion than perhaps anything else they could read. All five are well supported in Scripture.

Law One: There are two classifications of sin.

1. Original sin . . . the inherited sin nature traceable to Adam, original "head" of the human race (Romans 5:12a).

2. Personal sins . . . individual acts of wrong we regularly commit (Romans 3:23).

Because we all have an inherited sin nature (the root), we commit sins (the fruit).

Law Two: Original sin introduced suffering, illness, and death to the human race (Romans 5:12b).

Had there never been the presence of original sin in the Garden of Eden, mankind would never have known sickness or death. In the broadest sense of the word, all sickness and suffering today are the result of *original sin*. Literally, the Lord told Adam "in the day that you eat from it, *dying you will die*" (Genesis 2:17).

Law Three: Sometimes there is a direct relationship between personal sins and sickness.

David testified of such in Psalm 32:3-5 and 38:3-5. Paul warned that some of the Corinthian believers were "weak and sick" and a number of them were *dead* (1 Corinthians 11:27-30) because they were sinning.

Law Four: Sometimes there is no relationship between personal sins and sickness.

Some are *born* with afflictions—suffering before they ever reach the age of committing sins (John 9:1-3; Acts 3:1-2). Others, like Job (1:1-5), are living upright lives when suffering occurs. Jesus Himself "sympathizes with our weaknesses" (Hebrews 4:15) rather than rebuking us because we have sinned. Remember, "although He was a Son, He learned obedience from the things which He suffered" (Hebrews 5:8). Jesus never committed sins, yet He suffered.

Law Five: It is not God's will that everyone be healed in this life.

Those who believe it *is*, invariably support their convictions with the words of Isaiah:

> By His scourging we are healed (53:5b).

"There is healing in Christ's atonement!" they shout. Of course there is! But what kind? Check the context, O shouter. By His scourging we are *spiritually* healed. The whole flow of thought in the fifty-third chapter has to do with the inner, spiritual needs of man and Christ's priceless provision. That is why He was wounded and bruised. That is why He died . . . not to heal sick people but to give life to dead ones.

Take Paul. Three times he asked God to remove the thorn. Three times he got a "no" answer (2 Corinthians 12:7-9). Following that traumatic experience he stated he was "well content with weaknesses . . . difficulties" because even without healing, the Lord proved Himself sufficient and strong in the apostle's life (2 Corinthians 12:10).

There they are. The Five Suffering Laws regarding sin, sickness, health, and healing. Read each one again. Write them in the back of your Bible. Sure as the world you are going to run into folks who will wonder why they (or their loved ones) are not being healed. Maybe God will use your words to quiet their hearts and remove their confusion.

Just for the record, let me clarify two matters.

Am I suggesting God does not perform healing? Am I discounting divine healing?

Absolutely not.

Every time healing happens, God has done it. It occurs daily. Occasionally it is miraculous. More often, it is aided by proper diagnosis, expert medical care, essential medicinal assistance, plus common sense. No hocus pocus. No mumbo jumbo. No hot-shot carnal circus. When God heals there is *no way* man can grab the glory.

Am I declaring God does not need healers? Am I discounting divine healers?

Absolutely.

That's the obvious conclusion to the Five Suffering Laws. Maybe you'd better read them again. Healers prey on those who don't know the facts. And by the way, they never visit hospitals and make "healing calls" with physicians. Nor do they announce the "fallout problem"—the vast number of those whose healing didn't "take."

307

Seems to me we may have the malpractice gun pointed in the wrong direction.

COME ASIDE

Study Romans 5:12-17.

Then, if you haven't already, write down the "Five Suffering Laws" (along with the corresponding scriptural references) in the back of your Bible.

THE HOME

od has ordained and established three great institutions:

1) the *home* (Genesis 1:27-28; Ephesians 5:22-31),
2) the *church* (Matthew 16:18; Acts 2:41-47), and
3) *government* (Romans 13:1-7).

There is no question regarding our belief that the church and state (government) should be separate and distinct. Each is a unique entity, not to be consolidated. Our Lord Jesus Christ stated as much in Mark 12:17 when He said: "Render to Caesar the things that are Caesar's, and to God the things that are God's."

But what about the church and the home? Is there cooperation . . . or competition? To be specific: Has your home lost its identity? Has the role or responsibility of your home been lost in the "religious shuffle" of the church?

How very many churches you and I could name that plan a calendar of events so involved for its members that a meaningful home life is virtually impossible! "Something for everyone, every night" is a slogan that must be considered as an enemy to our homes.

If you are involved in church or religious activities to the point that your home life is hurting, you're too involved—and you're heading for trouble. The law of diminishing returns is soon to catch up with you. Somewhere down the busy religious road you're traveling, a dead-end sign will appear, forcing you to stop, turn around, and return to the place of balance and restful blessing . . . at home . . . if it's not too late.

One sage put it this way: "Too much of our religious activity today is nothing more than a cheap anesthetic to deaden the pain of an empty life." Does that describe you? If so—if your involvement is an escape from home—*stop* where you are. *Look* at what you're doing in the light of eternity. *Listen* to what God says about activity that is done simply in the energy of the flesh:

> Now if any man builds upon the foundation with gold, silver, precious stones, wood, hay, straw, each man's work will become evident; for the day will show it, because it is to be revealed with fire; and the fire itself will test the quality [*not quantity*] of each man's work. . . . If any man's work is burned up, he shall suffer loss [loss of eternal rewards]; but he himself shall be saved" (1 Corinthians 3:12-13, 15).

God, you see, is primarily interested in the *quality* of our fruit. He looks behind our hurry and hustle . . . He probes and penetrates down to our motive, our inner purpose . . . and on the basis of that discovery, He plans our eternal rewards. What if He examined your home life today? What would He find about your relationship with your wife, my friend? Are you loving her "as Christ loved the church?" Are you showing honor to her and building up her character? Wives—how's the inner beauty of a "gentle and quiet spirit" progressing? Does the man of your home know you're really behind him? Does he sense your undivided loyalty?

And dare I speak to the children? Do you promote harmony and happiness . . . or have you created a pressure-packed atmosphere? If you are among the younger ones in the home, are you showing respect . . . are you giving your folks the assurance that you're submissive and willing? Look over Ephesians 6:1-4 as a family tonight. Discuss it together.

One final reminder. The church can seldom resurrect what the home puts to death. The very best proof of the genuineness of your Christianity occurs within the framework of your home. If you must become overinvolved—become overinvolved in your role as a character builder in the home. Believe me—the church will stay healthy and strong as long as its homes are healthy and strong. God's priority system seems to begin at the grassroots level—at home. Cultivate that soil with care.

COME ASIDE

Review Ephesians 5:21 through 6:4, and ask God to show you *one* way in which you can better obey one of these commands before this day is over.

VISION

t's a cartoon I've smiled at again and again.

There are two Eskimos sitting on chairs, fishing through holes in the ice. The fella on the right has draped his line through your typical disk-like opening . . . about the size of a small manhole.

The Eskimo on the left has his line in the water, too. He also waits calmly for a nibble. His hole, however, is more like a crater, a Rose Bowl-sized opening that reaches to the horizon—in the shape of a whale.

Now that's what I call *vision*.

Smile all you please, but you gotta hand it to that Eskimo on the left. He's ready! You can be sure that his fellow fisherman thinks he's a nut. He might even be mumbling words of criticism, like:

"How greedy can you get?"

Or "Man, talk about a showoff!"

But there's one thing he must admit about his buddy, he's thinking big! The time he spent preparing for the catch was both extensive and tiring—he probably wore out three saws hacking and chewing through all that frozen stuff. But there is nothing that tugs on his line—and I mean nothing—that he won't be able to handle. From the very start of the project, the man has been visionary.

Vision becomes contagious. You can't sit very long beside a fisherman like that without enlarging your own hole in the ice. Something down inside us admires a person who stretches our faith by doing things that are filled with vision. Initially such actions might appear to be foolish. That occurs when we don't know the facts behind the action.

For example, I heard some time ago about a couple of nuns who worked as nurses in a hospital. They ran out of gas while driving to work one morning. A service station was nearby but had no container in which to put the needed gasoline. One of the women remembered she had a bedpan in the trunk of the car. The gas was put into the pan and they carried it very carefully back to the car. As the nuns were pouring the gasoline from the bedpan into the gas tank, two men were driving by. They stared in disbelief. Finally, one said to the other,

"Now Fred, that's what I call faith!"

It appeared to be foolish. Trouble was, those doubters just didn't have the facts. And were they ever surprised when those nuns went ripping by them on the freeway!

So much of what we undertake lacks vision. We cut our tiny holes in the ice and make plans to go home cold and hungry. And then if we're not careful, we'll find ourselves criticizing and scoffing at those who, as

Luis Palau puts it, dream great dreams and plan great plans. "Sensationalists," we call them. Or worse—"Foolish."

Jesus, however, when he called Andrew and Simon, promised:

> "Follow Me, and I will make you become fishers of men" (Mark 1:17).

The two fishermen probably thought too small. I gather this idea because Dr. Luke records their reaction the time they caught two boatloads of fish. They were dumbfounded! But Jesus replied with insight:

> "Do not fear, from now on you will be catching men" (Luke 5:10).

It seems as though Jesus realized their inborn "fear" of something sizable. He challenged them, "Don't be uneasy. With My help, you'll catch people just like you caught these fish."

How long has it been since you've punched a hole in the ice and thrown out a line? Sure, it may mean "breaking the ice" with "pre-Christian" neighbors or colleagues at work—getting beyond the slick surface stuff like the weather and sports and the condition of your lawn. It may mean investing some time, taking some risks, and putting out some effort in practical acts of loving compassion. Fishing for men and women is no casual thing.

Are you expecting success? Listen to Joe Aldrich:

> For many, the first step in neighborhood evangelism is attitudinal. If they think they will be successful or unsuccessful, they're right. What we anticipate in life is usually what we get. If you say, "I can't do it," you're probably right, especially if you firmly believe you can't. God says you can. Who do you intend to believe? . . . It's true, where there is no vision, people (your neighbors) perish.

Take another mental glimpse at those two Eskimos. Be honest now. Which hole are you fishing in?

COME ASIDE

Look back at the visionary promise Christ gave the church in Acts 1:8.

Can you do it?

WRITING WITH THORNS

In pain, grief, affliction, and loss, it often helps to write our feelings . . . not just feel them. Putting words on paper seems to free our feelings from the lonely prison of our souls.

It was C. S. Lewis who wrote:

Her absence is like the sky, spread over everything. . . . No one ever told me that grief felt so like fear. I am not afraid, but the sensation is like being afraid. The same fluttering in the stomach, the same restlessness, the yawning. I keep on swallowing.

It was William Armstrong who wrote:

Back in the house I moved on leaden feet from chore to chore.

It was Ada Campbell Rose who wrote:

The mantle of grief falls on every hour of the day and covers me while I sleep. Will it ever go away?

It was King David who wrote:

Even when walking through the dark valley of death I will not be afraid, for you are close beside me, guarding, guiding all the way (Psalm 23:4 TLB).

It was the apostle Paul who wrote:

I will say this: because these experiences I had were so tremendous, God was afraid I might be puffed up by them; so I was given a physical condition which has been a thorn in my flesh, a messenger from Satan to hurt and bother me, and prick my pride. Three different times I begged God to make me well again.

Each time he said, "No. But I am with you; that is all you need. My power shows up best in weak people." Now I am glad to boast about how weak I am; I am glad to be a living demonstration of Christ's power, instead of showing off my own power and abilities. Since I know it is all for Christ's good, I am quite happy about "the thorn," and about insults and hardships, persecutions and difficulties; for when I am weak, then I am strong—the less I have, the more I depend on him (2 Corinthians 12:7-10 TLB).

It was George Matheson who wrote:

> My God, I have never thanked Thee for my thorns. I have thanked Thee a thousand times for my *roses*, but not once for my *thorns*. I have been looking forward to a world where I shall get compensation for my cross: but I have never thought of my cross as itself a present glory. Teach me the glory of my cross: teach me the value of my thorn. Shew me that I have climbed to Thee by the path of pain. Shew me that my tears have made my rainbow.

As you feel the stinging thorns of pain today, what do *you* write? *Nothing*? Healing stands with folded arms waiting to read your words.

Small wonder you're still bleeding.

COME ASIDE

Write down on a sheet of paper the words of Nahum 1:7. Then use your own words to fill as much of the rest of the page as you can.

"WON'T SOMEONE PLEASE STOP ME?"

I recently laughed my way through Judith Viorst's *How Did I Get to Be Forty and Other Atrocities*. Since I've passed the half-century mark, it seemed reasonable that I should at least face the music of being forty. Even though I must admit I feel more like thirty . . . until I think about my schedule of involvements. Then I wish I were eighty and had an excuse for hiding away in a cabin, writing my memoirs . . . as if anybody would ever care to read them.

It's bad enough just meeting the daily and weekly deadlines along with fulfilling some people's expectations—ugh!—but when I include a bunch of other self-assigned projects, the stress level can approach borderline madness. Which explains why, in my reading, I toss in Bombeck along with Steinbeck and Schulz along with Schaft and Pirsig along with Paul. Gotta have that balance! Otherwise, the screws get cinched down so tightly that I revert to nail-biting and fist-slamming and choking down too much food without tasting it.

I've got enough people in my life who frown authoritatively and admonish me to get serious. I need a few who smile relaxingly and encourage me to kick back, loosen up, and laugh a little more. I've got more than my share of "get-with-it" ghosts haunting me already, don't you? Maybe that's why I'll pull Viorst from the shelf on a Saturday afternoon or a Monday morning. She helps Sunday make better sense. Extreme and uptight, she ain't. But she is clever, witty, sometimes subtle, and always real.

Take this piece called "Self-improvement Program." If you're the type who tends to turn a simple plan into a federal case, you'll smile at her admission.

> I've finished six pillows in Needlepoint,
> And I'm reading Jane Austen and Kant,
> And I'm up to the pork with black beans in Advanced
>   Chinese Cooking.
> I don't have to struggle to find myself
> For I already know what I want.
> I want to be healthy and wise and extremely good-looking.
>
> I'm learning new glazes in Pottery Class,
> And I'm playing new chords in Guitar,
> And in Yoga I'm starting to master the lotus position.

I don't have to ponder priorities
For I already know what they are:
To be good-looking, healthy, and wise.
And adored in addition.

I'm improving my serve with a tennis pro,
And I'm practicing verb forms in Greek,
And in Primal Scream Therapy all my frustrations are
    vented.
I don't have to ask what I'm searching for
Since I already know that I seek
To be good-looking, healthy, and wise.
And adored.
And contented.

I've bloomed in Organic Gardening,
And in Dance I have tightened my thighs,
And in Consciousness Raising there's no one around who
    can top me.
And I'm working all day and I'm working all night
To be good-looking, healthy, and wise.
And adored.
And contented.
And brave.
And well-read.
And a marvelous hostess,
And bilingual,
Athletic,
Artistic . . .
Won't someone please stop me?

Strange, isn't it, how we tend toward extremes? What begins as self-improvement becomes self-enslavement . . . what starts as merely a mellow change of pace leads to a marathon of fanaticism. We're nuts! Left to ourselves, we'll opt for extremes most every time. Which explains why God's Book so often stresses moderation, self-control, softening our sharp-cornered lives with more curves that necessitate a slower speed.

The psalmist calmly counsels us to "Be still" so we can know that God is God. Jesus Himself found it essential to escape the press of people to get His bearings. On several occasions He arose quite early just to be alone. Immediately after His twelve returned hot and sweaty from ministry, it was His idea that they retreat and repair. And who can ever forget His gracious invitation? I often return to it just to let the words wash over me.

> Come to Me, all who are weary and heavy laden, and I will
> give you rest. Take my yoke upon you, and learn from Me,
> for I am gentle and humble in heart; and you shall find rest
> for your souls. For My yoke is easy, and My load is light
> (Matthew 11:28-30).

In a high-tech day of high-level pressures, He offers us *rest*. Twice in one statement. While so many others are demanding, He's gentle. While competition is rugged and being in partnership with hard-charging, bullish leaders is tough, being yoked with Him is easy. Yes, *easy*. And instead of increasing our load of anxiety, He promises to make it lighter. Is it any wonder Jesus' style and message created such a stir? While so many were piling on more guilt, more "shoulds" and "musts," He quietly offered relief.

Question: Where do you go to find enough stillness to rediscover that God is God? Where do you turn when your days and nights start running together? What spot becomes your hide-away so that a little perspective is gleaned as a little sanity returns? Where do you get relief from the fever-pitch extremes?

"Won't someone please stop me?"

Someone will, if you'll let Him. As in days of old, He's waiting in that little boat, ready to sail with you to a quieter shore. But *getting in* first requires some *letting go*. You can't haul along all of that personal luggage.

There's only room for two.

COME ASIDE

Let it be just you and the Lord, and let your mind be only on Him, as you hear each word of love for you in John 14:1-4.

TRUST

hose guys who put together *Campus Life* magazine get my vote. Talk about relevant! With an incredible regularity they put the cookies on the lower shelf so that any high-schooler in America can thumb through the thing without getting turned off. One of their secrets is frequent humor, lots of jokes. You know, all kinds of stuff to laugh at . . . some a little gross, but all designed to scratch a teenager where he's itching. And most kids I know at that age are never very far from fun.

I'm sure they got as big a laugh out of Stephen Erickson's article as I did. It's called:

HOW TO CHOOSE A DENTIST

Never trust a dentist . . .

    . . . who wears dentures.
    . . . who has hairy knuckles.
    . . . whose drill is driven by a system of pulleys connected to three mice on a treadmill.
    . . . who sends you a Christmas card and charges you for it.
    . . . who chews tobacco and spits the juice into the sink.
    . . . who uses the suction hose to empty your pockets.
    . . . who is also a barber.
    . . . who sprays his equipment with Lysol to sterilize it.
    . . . who uses lead for fillings.

You can always trust a dentist . . .

    . . . who has never chewed gum.
    . . . who looks like Jack Nicholson.
    . . . who doesn't ask you questions when your mouth's full.
    . . . who puts you to sleep two weeks before your appointment.
    . . . who uses a laser instead of a drill.
    . . . who cancels your appointment to play tennis.
    . . . who has mellow rock piped into his office instead of elevator music.
    . . . who doesn't strap you in the chair.

STOP THE REVOLVING DOOR

he history of great civilizations reminds me of a giant revolving door. It turns on the axis of human depravity as its movement is marked by the perimeter of time. With monotonous repetition each civilization has completed the same cycle, having passed through a similar sequence of events. It could be visualized like this:

From bondage to spiritual faith
From spiritual faith to great courage
From great courage to strength
From strength to liberty
From liberty to abundance
From abundance to leisure
From leisure to selfishness
From selfishness to complacency
From complacency to apathy
From apathy to dependency
From dependency to weakness
From weakness *back to bondage*

Whether Roman or Athenian empires . . . Egyptian or European cultures, the chronicle tells its own baleful tale. Regardless of geography, origin, achievements, or level of prosperity, each one has sunk deeply into the vortex of ruin.

Consider Babylon. It can hardly be found today. It is nothing more than a lonely whistle stop along the Baghdad railroad. Its beauty and significance now lie buried beneath tons of dirt, rocks, and debris in a forlorn and forgotten land. *How she has fallen!*

321

Israel can also teach us the same lesson. Inquire at the gate called *Judges*. That place reaffirms the truth of man's cyclical habit. Time after time—for over three hundred years—the Jews went through the succession of events mentioned above. Like pawns on a chessboard, they lived under the bondage of superior powers until God gave them a deliverer, who fired the furnace of spiritual fervor . . . which inflamed their courage . . . which kindled military strength . . . then liberty . . . then abundance . . . then leisure—and then right back down the tube again into bondage. The age-old path of that same revolving door has etched itself upon the tablet of Israel's antiquity.

It was about two hundred years ago, while the thirteen colonies were still part of Great Britain, that Professor Alexander Tyler addressed himself to the fall of the Athenian Republic. He declared:

> A democracy cannot exist as a permanent form of government. It can only exist until the voters discover they can vote themselves excessive gratuities from the public treasury. From that moment on the majority always votes for the candidates promising the most benefits from the treasury, with the result that a democracy collapses over loose fiscal policy, always followed by a dictatorship.

It's a stunning fact of history that the average age of the world's great civilizations has been approximately two hundred years. According to that reckoning, America may be living on borrowed time. The age-old revolving door is turning and we are —as I see it—somewhere between apathy and dependency on the historical cycle. It doesn't take a meteorologist to predict rain if the sky is black and drops are starting to fall. Neither does it take a prophet to predict future bondage if we are now a majority of apathetic and dependent people!

Hope for our great nation rests upon independent thinking and individual effort. The revival of discipline, integrity, work, determination, and healthy pride is not a national matter but a *personal* one. Inward change and godliness are not legislated by congress—they are spawned in the heart and cultivated in the home before they are bred in the land. Frankly—it boils down to one person, *you*.

A revolving door has to be pushed by those within it. When we stop pushing, it will stop turning . . . but not until.

COME ASIDE

Pray the words of Psalm 119:33-40 and commit yourself to God's program of personal renewal in your life.

THE STING OF THE THORN

ive the Reverend Dullard Drydust enough time and he will manage to confuse most sections of the Bible. Because we preachers are notorious for getting hung up on Greek tenses and purpose clauses and theological trivia, we often shy away from those passages that appear non-technical and plain.

Like the parables, to be specific. Like Mark 4, to be exact. Not only is that particular parable simple and straightforward, it's even interpreted for us by Jesus, the One who thought up the story in the first place. And since it has to do with a farmer-type who pitches some seed on different kinds of soil, it doesn't seem to have the sophisticated ingredients needed for homiletical hash. After all, there's not a lot you can say about the story of a farmer who drops little seeds here and there in haphazard fashion—*or is there?*

At first glance, maybe not, but after some thought, I'm convinced there's more here than any of us ever dreamed. And since the Son of God explains its essential meaning, the story cannot be twisted or forced to fit the fancy of some hungry-eyed pulpiteer looking for three points and a poem.

This is a profound story about life—real life—your life and mine. It boils life down to the four basic responses people have toward spiritual things.

The "seed," according to the speaker, is "the word." I believe we're safe in saying that "the word" refers to truth. God's truth. Truth for living. Life-giving words provided for us by the Lord our God. The Scriptures, yes, but also the insights, the perspective, and the wisdom that grow in us when the seed takes root.

The four different "soils" represent people of all ages and interests and backgrounds who respond to the things of the Lord in various ways. *Some* listen, then immediately reject—instantly they turn it off. *Others* hear and seem to enjoy it and even respond well on the surface, but soon spin off when their bubble bursts and the going gets rough. Still others grab hold and initially embrace what they hear, but by and by they get sidetracked as their growth is throttled by life's "thorns." *Then,* as always, there are those who hear, believe, grow, hang in there, and before long begin to reproduce as healthy plants in God's vineyard.

It's obvious that the first two groups are those who are *not* born again. They are rootless, lifeless, and fruitless. It's obvious that the last group *is* born-again: submissive, active, and productive. But frankly, I'm bothered by the third group.

They are Christians, because they grow and get right on the verge of bearing fruit, but their growth becomes retarded. These people hear everything the fourth group hears. But those insights and needed truths are never really accepted, never allowed to take root and grow. Why? Because thorns have come in—thorns which suffocate the normal healthy growth of each plant.

It is interesting that the thorns were already present at the time the seed entered, and that the thorns were never completely out of the picture even though the seeds began to take root (Mark 4:7).

And what do the thorns represent? Again, we have Jesus' own words to answer that question. They represent "the worries of the world," "the deceitfulness of riches," and "the desires for other things" (4:19). When these thorns enter, spiritual growth and production slip out the rear exit. Our Lord doesn't say they *might* cause trouble, nor does He suggest they *have been known* to hinder us. He says that they . . . *enter in and choke the word, and it becomes unfruitful* (v. 19).

Period. No ifs, ands, or maybes. The thorns are dictators. They know nothing of peaceful coexistence with the life of freedom and victory. Shunning a brash frontal attack, these enemies of our soul employ a more subtle strategy. Slipping under the back door, their long tentacles advance so slowly, so silently, the victim hardly realizes he's being strangled. Demanding first place, they ultimately siphon off every ounce of spiritual interest and emotional energy.

Are you a compulsive worrier? The term *worry* is derived from the old German word *wurgen*, which means "to choke." Somehow, by extension, the word came to denote "mental strangulation," and finally to describe the condition of being harrassed with anxiety. All of that and more are in Jesus' mind as He presents this parable.

It's the thorns that bug us. Always growing, forever aggressive and ready to "choke the word" right out of our minds. Like worry—a thin stream of fear trickles through our minds. If entertained, it cuts a deeper channel into which other thoughts are drained—often good thoughts, God-given thoughts gleaned directly from His Book.

The same is true of "the deceitfulness of riches." What a consuming passion . . . yet how empty, how unsatisfying! We rationalize, of course, by saying it doesn't mean that much to us. Like the late heavyweight champ, Joe Louis, who smiled and said, "I don't like money actually, but it quiets my nerves." Yeah, sure, Joe.

But this third species of thorns is the killer—"the desires for other things." Better think that one through. It's the picture of discontent, the plague of pursuit: pushing, straining, stretching, relentlessly reaching while our minds become strangled with the lie, "enough just isn't enough."

Do you find it next to impossible to be satisfied with your present situation? If so, these words are nothing new to you—you've been stuck by those thorns since your soil first received God's seed . . . and if the truth were known, you inwardly enjoy their presence. After all, it's risky to abandon your entire life to God *by faith*. You'd rather worry, possess, and complain, than rest, release, and rejoice. Thorns inject a powerful anesthesia.

Why do so many Christians live among thorns like these? Because we have a quiet, respectable, secret *love* for them. I know. I've got the ugly scars to prove it. Each one is a mute reminder of years trapped in the thicket. And periodically, I still have to yank a few.

I've never heard of such, but I'd like to proclaim today as Thorn Pulling Day. We may bleed and it may hurt . . . but, oh, the beauty of a thornless day!

COME ASIDE

Are there any lovely little thorn plants that need weeding out of your life?

Use 1 John 2:15-17 to help you identify and abhor them.

PERSPECTIVE

hat *is* perspective?

Well, it's obviously related to the way we view something. The term literally suggests "looking through . . . seeing clearly." One who views life through perspective lenses has the capacity to see things in their true relations or relative importance. He sees the big picture. He is able to distinguish the incidental from the essential . . . the temporary from the eternal . . . the partial from the whole . . . the trees from the forest.

The artist without perspective is, in Shakespeare's words, "weary, stale, flat, and unprofitable." The leader without it is visionless, intimidated, vulnerable, and overly concerned with public opinion.

Perspective, you see, adds a breath of fresh air to the otherwise suffocating demands of life. It opens new dimensions that enable us to cope with the predictable . . . it eases the tyranny of the urgent. Perspective provides needed space.

Perspective encourages the new mother: "Life is more than changing diapers, warming bottles, and rocking babies to sleep." It helps convince the young medical intern "these long months of training and sleepless nights are worth it all. Stay alert. Your whole future is at stake."

To the struggling businessman who has a tough series of weeks, perspective brings hope and the promise of a brighter day tomorrow.

And who needs perspective more than teachers? Day in and day out, the endless grind of the classroom can drain the river of determination and creativity until it becomes a mere trickle of frustration and discouragement. But let that educator catch a renewed glimpse of the impact his life is having upon students and the ultimate difference it will make in their future . . . and the flow of new ideas will likely return in torrents.

Many things help prompt perspective. Quietness. A walk in a forest. Time spent along the roaring surf. A view from a mountain. Poetry. Travel. A stroll through an old graveyard. An evening beside a fireplace. Camping out under the stars. A visit to historical landmarks. Protracted times of prayer. Deep, profound strains of music. Meaningful worship. Meditation upon scriptures. A leisurely drive at sunset.

On such occasions time stands still. The chips of insignificance fall away as the broad images of truth emerge in the monuments of our minds. We begin to see more clearly as the fog lifts . . . and we are running no longer. Or confused. Or angry. Or overwhelmed. Or afraid.

Could such places of perspective be considered "shelters of the Most High"? When we are there, could we be "abiding in the shadow of the Almighty" which David mentions in Psalm 91?

If so, isn't it about time you found a shelter of perspective in His shadow?

COME ASIDE

Stand aside from the rush of life and meditate for a while on Hebrews 12:1-3.

SORROW AND HOPE

f tears were indelible ink instead of clear fluid, all of us would be stained for life. The heartbreaking circumstances, the painful encounters with calamities, the brutal verbal blows we receive from the surgeon or an angry mate, the sudden loss of someone we simply adored, riding out the consequences of a stupid decision—ah! Such is the groan and grind of life.

As I write these words, there are families less than one hour away from me with no home to return to tonight. A freakish landslide swept them away like a sand castle at high tide. Not a fire. Not an earthquake. Not even a warning tremor. Just an unheard-of sudden slippage of soil and fifteen million dollars of damage . . . and unerasable memories. I dare you to ponder their plight for two minutes without being ripped apart inside.

A letter arrived today from Portland. Nicely typed. Carefully worded. But behind the print, bone-deep grief:

> My life has been turned upside down in the last two years and God has not left me much time to catch my breath!
>
> My husband was killed in a military plane crash in Greenland a year ago, and I have two young sons, 7 and 9, who are my responsibility alone now.

My phone rang in the middle of the night a few weeks ago. With a quivering voice the young man who chose not to identify himself began:

> I have a gun. It is loaded. I plan to use it on myself tonight. Somebody told me you could help me. I don't see any reason to keep on living and failing. Tell me why I shouldn't kill myself. [He began to sob.] Talk to me, *fast* . . .

Dear old Joseph Parker, a fervid pulpit orator and fine pastor and author for several decades, said it well three years before he died:

> There's a broken heart in every pew. Preach to the sorrowing and you will never lack for a congregation.

Shelley was right. He personified Sorrow as a mother "with her family of sighs." And so she is. Stooped and weary of the monotony, yet ever bearing more children only to sigh and cry and die.

Without God—*end of message*. Finis. Termination of misery. Curtains. It is here humanism puts its final period. It is here philosophy takes its last bow. The only encore, to borrow from Robert Ingersoll's dying words of horror, is:

"the echo of a wailing cry."

But that *need* not be the end. Life, with all its pressures and inequities, tears and tragedies, can be lived on a level above its miseries. If it could not, Christianity has little to offer. Jesus is reduced to nothing more than an apologetic beggar at the back door with His hat in His hands and a hard-luck story you can take or leave.

No—don't you believe it! It is upon the platform of pressure that our Lord does His best work . . . those times when tragedy joins hands with calamity . . . when Satan and a host of demons prompt us to doubt God's goodness and deny His justice. At such times Christ unsheathes His sword of truth, silencing the doubts and offering grace to accept, hope to continue.

Hear Him well:

> For whatever is born of God overcomes the world; and this is
> the victory that has overcome the world—our faith.

Not a reluctant hunch. Not some fairy-tale dream . . . but an accomplished fact as solid as granite and twice as sure—overcoming victory claimed by faith!

Is it for everyone? No. The majority? No. Read it again. It's only for those who are "born of God" . . . only God's born-ones are the overcomers.

Does it mean, then, that we won't have sorrow? No. It means we'll be able to *overcome* it . . . live in His victory in spite of it. How? *By faith*, just as He promised. By staking my hope on the absolute assurance that He is aware of my situation. He is in charge of it . . . and He will give all the grace I need to sail through it, rough seas and all, one stormy day at a time.

Sorrow and her grim family of sighs may drop by for a visit, but they won't stay long when they realize faith got there first . . . and doesn't plan to leave.

COME ASIDE

Lift up your heart to the hope offered in 1 John 3:1-3.

330

The tailor's name is change

W hen you boil life down to the nubbies, the name of the game is *change*. Those who flex with the times, refuse to be rigid, resist the mold, and reject the rut—ah, *those* are the souls distinctively used by God. To them, change is a challenge, a fresh breeze that flows through the room of routine and blows away the stale air of sameness.

Stimulating and invigorating as change may be—it is never easy. Changes are especially tough when it comes to certain habits that haunt and harm us. That kind of change is excruciating—but it isn't impossible.

Jeremiah pointed out the difficulty of breaking into an established life pattern when he quipped:

> Can the Ethiopian change his skin
>   or the leopard its spots?
> Neither can you do good
>   who are accustomed to doing evil (13:23 NIV).

Notice the last few words, "accustomed to doing evil." The Hebrew says, literally, "learned in evil." Now, that's quite an admission! We who are "learned in evil" cannot do good; evil habits that remain unchanged prohibit it. Evil is a habit that is learned; it is contracted and cultivated by long hours of practice. In another place, Jeremiah confirms this fact:

> I warned you when you felt secure,
>   but you said, "I will not listen!"
> This has been your way from your youth;
>   you have not obeyed me (22:21 NIV).

All of us have practiced certain areas of wrong from our youth. It is a pattern of life that comes "second nature" to us. We gloss over our resistance, however, with the varnish of excuse:

"Well, nobody's perfect."

"I'll never be any different; that's just the way I am."

"I was born this way—nothing can be done about it."

"You can't teach an old dog new tricks."

Jeremiah tells us why such excuses come so easily. We have become "learned in evil" . . . it has been our way from our youth. In one sense, we have learned to act and react in sinful, unbiblical ways with *ease* and (dare we admit it?) with a measure of *pleasure*. Admittedly, there are many times we do it unconsciously; and on those occasions, the depth of our habit is more revealing.

It is vital—*it is essential*—that we see ourselves as we really are in the light of God's written Word . . . then be open to change where change is needed. I warn you, the number one enemy of change is the hard-core, self-satisfied sin nature within you. Like a spoiled child, it has been gratified and indulged for years, so it will not give up without a violent temper tantrum. Change is its *greatest* threat, and a confrontation between the two is inevitable. Change must be allowed to face and conquer the intimidations of inward habit—and I repeat the warning that a nose-to-nose meeting will never be an easy one.

The flesh dies a slow, bitter, bloody death—kicking and struggling all the way down. "Putting off" the clothes of the old man (the old, habitual lifestyle) will not be complete until you are determined to "put on" the garment of the new man (the new, fresh, Christian lifestyle). The tailor's name is Change, and he is a master at fitting your frame. But the process will be painful . . . and costly.

Change—real change—takes place slowly. In first gear, not overdrive. Far too many Christians get discouraged and give up. Like ice skating or mastering a musical instrument or learning to water ski, certain techniques have to be discovered and developed in the daily discipline of living. Breaking habit patterns you established during the passing of years cannot occur in a few brief days. Remember that. "Instant" change is as rare as it is phony.

God did not give us His Word to satisfy our curiosity; He gave it to change our lives. Can you name a couple of specific changes God has implemented in your life during the past six or eight months? Has He been allowed, for example, to change your attitude toward someone . . . or an area of stubbornness . . . or a deep-seated habit that has hurt your home and hindered your relationship with others for a long, long time . . . or a pattern of discourtesy in your driving . . . or a profane tongue . . . or cheating . . . or laziness?

Perhaps a better question would be, "Exactly what changes do you have on your personal drawing board?"—or—"What are you asking the Lord to alter and adjust in your life that needs immediate attention?"

The tailor's real name is the Holy Spirit. You can count on Him to dispose of your old threadbare wardrobe as quickly as He outfits you with the new. By the way, He's also on call twenty-four hours a day when you have the urge to slip into the old duds "just one more time." If you ask Him, He'll help you remember what you looked like on the day you first walked into His shop. He has a mirror with memories—the Bible.

'Nuff said.

COME ASIDE

Turn to the mirror in Mark 12:28-31. What needs changing in your life?

TENSION IN THE TANK

ver felt sorry for certain Scriptures? I sure have. I'm talking about passages like John 3:17, Hebrews 4:13, 1 John 1:10, and Philippians 4:14. Great verses, all . . . yet the popularity of their next-door neighbors has resulted in their being virtually ignored.

Everybody who spends even a little while in the Family can quote Proverbs 3:5-6, but unfortunately, an equally significant verse 7 goes begging. And take Galatians 2:20. It is so powerful, so magnificent, it's often viewed as the final climactic verse of the chapter, yet it's actually the next-to-last verse. But who in the world knows Galatians 2:21 by heart? The twenty-third Psalm is the most famous of all in the ancient hymnal, but it's sandwiched between two other psalms that, when studied, yield fruit that is succulent to the soul and actually far more vital, theologically, than the popular and picturesque "shepherd psalm."

Perhaps the most obvious case in point is found in one of the greatest chapters Paul ever penned, Romans 8. From our mother's knee we have been nourished by the twenty-eighth verse. It brings comfort when our world crushes in. It softens the blows of calamity. It calms us when panic would otherwise steal our peace. It reassures us when wrong temporarily triumphs . . . when the fever doesn't break . . . when the brook dries up . . . when death strikes. I hardly need to write it out.

> And we know that God causes all things to work together for good to those who love God, to those who are called according to His purpose.

Great words! But left alone, they're incomplete. Anyone who has taken the time to look discovers that this verse starts a chain reaction that doesn't end before the magnificent statement found in the final two verses of Romans 8, which assure us of our inseparable love-relationship with the living God.

Woven into the fabric of this elegant garment of truth is an often-forgotten, easily overlooked thread that adds richness and color. Because it lacks the eloquence of verse 28, because it doesn't roll off the tongue quite as easily, it tends to get lost amidst other more obvious and more attractive phrases. I'm referring to the verse that follows verse 28, the one that explains *why* "all things work together for good to those who love God." Why?

For whom He foreknew, He also predestined to become con-
formed to the image of His Son, that He might be the first-
born among many brethren.

Put simply, we are God's personal project. He is committed to the task
of working in us, developing us, rearranging, firming up, and deepen-
ing us so that the character traits of His Son—called here "the image"—
begin to take shape. The emerging of the Son's image in us is of primary
importance to the Father. In fact, it is impossible to thwart His commitment to the project. His work goes on even though we scream and
squirm, doubt and debate, run and shun. There's no denying it, the
tools He uses hurt, but it all "works together for good." It takes tension
to develop the right texture. Without it, forget it.

In the northeastern United States, codfish are not only delectable,
they are a big commercial business. There's a market for eastern cod all
over, especially in sections farthest removed from the northeast
coastline. But the public demand posed a problem to the shippers. At
first they froze the cod, then shipped them elsewhere, but the freeze
took away much of the flavor. So they experimented with shipping them
alive, in tanks of seawater, but that proved even worse. Not only was it
more expensive, the cod still lost its flavor, and in addition, became soft
and mushy. The texture was seriously affected.

Finally, some creative soul solved the problem in a most innovative
manner. The codfish were placed in the tank of water along with their
natural enemy—the catfish. From the time the cod left the East Coast
until it arrived in its westernmost destination, those ornery catfish
chased the cod all over the tank! And you guessed it, when the cod arrived at the market, they were as fresh as when they were first caught.
There was no loss of flavor nor was the texture affected. If anything, it
was better than before.

A couple of questions seem worth asking. First, can you name some
catfish swimming in your tank? Maybe you live with one of them. Or it's
somebody at work whose irritating presence drives you to your knees
several times a week. Every church has a few catfish as well! They're
there to keep all the cod from getting soft, mushy, and tasteless. Second,
have you given thanks for them lately? Just think, it's that tension in the
tank that helps "the image" emerge. With the right attitude, we can
learn how to keep from resenting them as intruders as the chase continues.

To do so we'll need to put an end to pity parties and whine clubs and
gripe gatherings in the tank. When we do, it is nothing short of remarkable how closely the chase begins to resemble "the race" mentioned in

Hebrews 12 . . . but whoever heard of Hebrews 12 since Hebrews 11 is so much more popular?

If you haven't, it's *you* I feel sorry for.

COME ASIDE

Beginning in 2 Kings 18:13 and continuing through chapter 19, read about a catfish named Sennacherib who helped keep King Hezekiah and the prophet Isaiah in good spiritual condition.

Are you responding to life's tension producers in the same way they did?

Hidden heroes

p-front heroes are often seen as being larger than life. Overstated. That's unfortunate.

Because they are public figures, folks think of them as broad-shouldered giants who can leap tall buildings in a single bound. They are thought of as superpeople possessing endless strength, limitless vision, relentless determination, effortless skills, and matchless charisma. Their courage is legendary. Their words drip with eloquence. Their endorsements carry weight. Their presence, well, it's like a touch o' magic. It's an exaggeration, you understand, but . . .

So it goes with certain callings . . . strong-voiced, often multitalented leaders, whose names become quotable points of reference. Their opinions and their decisions stand out, almost as if they possess an inside track to pristine truth. Agree with it or not, we still need some who can take the lead and set the pace. Big shoes must be filled.

And that is certainly the way it was with Martin Luther.

You and I cannot think of the Reformation without mentioning that name. What Henry Ford was to the auto industry, what Ben Franklin was to electricity, what George Halas was to professional football, what Albert Einstein was to nuclear physics, Martin Luther was to the Protestant Reformation. What a man. What a model! What a *maverick!* The classic shaker and mover.

> I am born to fight against innumerable monsters and devils.
> I must remove stumps and stones, cut away thistles and thorns, and clear the wild forest.

Vintage Luther. Prophetlike hero talk. With sweeping statements to match his gestures, the mighty monk of Wittenberg set fire to slumbering saints all across Germany as he vigorously fanned the flame, shouting, "Heresy . . . heresy!" While prelates frowned and popes condemned, the hero kept them buzzing and forever off balance. Brushfires from his abusive language, his private debates and public disputes resulted finally in Luther's excommunication. But his exit was like his entrance, alone . . . independent . . . invincible. He needed no one but God to lean on.

Or did he?

Is that true of any "hero"?

No, indeed not. Back in the shadows, hidden from public view behind the massive personality of Martin Luther, was the real hero . . . the authentic intellectual of the Reformation. Yet to this day, most Christians would be unable to state his name—let alone spell it correctly.

"Below middle size, diffident, hesitating, of frail body . . ." describes one of Philip Melancthon's biographers. With a "stammering tongue, he carried one shoulder higher than the other."

Not enough public relations "uumph" to make a single head turn, yet it was he who exerted the most powerful influence over Luther when the spokesman carried the torch and shook it in the face of the Church.

It was he who pioneered the first Protestant edition of systematic theology. He was the genius of the educational systems of Europe . . . indeed, "the father of modern scholarship." In his generation, his knowledge of the New Testament Greek was unsurpassed by any scholar in all of Europe. How greatly Luther needed such a friend! Martin consulted Philip on difficult passages of Scripture so often, Luther's translation was really a combined effort rather than a solitary achievement.

Luther had warmth, vigor, and explosive strength; Melancthon, however, had clarity of thought, discretion, and mildness. Luther energized his quiet friend; Melancthon tempered his. The stump-moving, thorn-pulling Luther realized the treasure he had in his brilliant compatriot. "Master Philip," he wrote, "comes along gently and softly, sowing and watering with joy, according to the gifts which God has abundantly bestowed upon him."

What a one-two punch! It took Luther to commend the Reformation to the common people. But by his gracious moderation, his quiet love of order, his profound and indisputable scholarship, Melancthon won for it the support of the learned.

When Luther died, it was Melancthon, of course, who pronounced the oration over his tomb. A few short years later, the scholar's body was lowered into the same grave alongside the more famous hero of the Reformation. Appropriately, they now rest side by side in the Old Castle Church at Wittenberg. Death, not life, the equalizer.

Are you the bigger-than-life "hero" . . . the public figure folks want to see and meet and quote? If so, are you big enough to acknowledge the wind beneath your wings? Perhaps you are more like Melancthon—in the shadows, faithfully and humbly at work, making someone else successful, providing better fuel for an ever greater fire. Be encouraged! It's for you that songs like this are written:

YOU ARE THE WIND BENEATH MY WINGS

It must have been cold there in my shadow,
To never have the sunlight on your face.
You've been content to see me shine.
You always walked a step behind.

I was the one with all the glory
While you were the one with all strain.
Only a face without a name.
I never once heard you complain.

Did you ever know that you're my hero?
And everything I'd like to be?
I can fly higher than an eagle,
But you are the wind beneath my wings.

—Roger Whittaker

Hidden heroes are often seen as being *smaller* than life. Underrated. That's most unfortunate.

COME ASIDE

Think about Mark 10:35-45. What service can you provide today to help make someone successful?

MY LORD AND HIS RETURN

he other evening my wife and I were enjoying a quiet conversation together. We were sipping some fresh-perked coffee, the house was unusually still, and there were no plans to go anywhere that evening. You know, one of those priceless moments you wish you could wrap up and reserve for later use when it's really needed again.

For some strange reason our discussion turned to the subject of Christ's return. Almost out of the blue, I found myself tracking that thought further than I have for months. Cynthia and I chuckled at some comments each one made about letting the folks in the tribulation worry about the hassles that we have to handle now—like cleaning out our garage or landscaping the backyard! We also smiled together, contemplating the joys that will be ours to share our lives throughout eternity with family and friends in the Body of Christ.

As the evening slipped away, I kept returning to the thought, "He *is* coming back. What a difference it will make!" It is remarkable, when you stop and get specific about it, how many things we take for granted will suddenly be removed or changed drastically. Think about that.

Is it a waste to focus on the Lord's descent? Quite the contrary. It's biblical; it's the very thing Titus 2:13 says we ought to do:

> Looking for the blessed hope and the appearing of the glory
> of our great God and Savior, Christ Jesus.

When's the last time you—on your own—meditated on that fact? If you're like me, it's been too long. People who are more practical than mystical, who are realistic rather than idealistic, tend to shove that stuff to times like funerals or near-death experiences. Most of us are more oriented to the here-and-now than the then-and-there. But Scripture says we are to "comfort one another" (1 Thessalonians 4:13-18) with information about Jesus' return for us. It says these truths form the very foundation of a "steadfast, immovable, always abounding" lifestyle (1 Corinthians 15:50-58).

Listen, this Bible of ours is full and running over with promises and encouragements directly related to the return of our Lord Christ. I just checked. The Second Coming isn't just hinted at, it's *highlighted*—it's an obvious theme of New Testament truth. You can't read very far without stumbling upon it no matter which book you choose. In the New Testament alone the events related to Christ's coming are mentioned over three hundred times. It's like white on rice.

Critics have denied it. Cynics have laughed at it. Scholars have ignored it. Liberal theologians have explained it away (they call that "rethinking" it), and fanatics have perverted it. "Where is the promise of His coming?" (2 Peter 3:4) many still shout sarcastically. The return of the Savior will continue to be attacked and misused and denied. But there it stands, solid as a stone, soon to be fulfilled, ready to offer us hope and encouragement amidst despair and unbelief.

"Okay, swell. But what do I do in the meantime?" I can hear a dozen or more pragmatists asking that question. First, it might be best for you to understand what you *don't* do. You don't whip up a white robe and buy a helium-filled balloon with angels painted all over it. And, if you're a Californian, you don't quit work and move to Oregon for fear you'll miss Him because of the smog. And for goodness' sake, don't try to set the date because of the "signs of the times!"

You *do* get your act together. You *do* live every day (as if it's your last) for His glory. You *do* work diligently on your job and in your home (as if He isn't coming for another ten years) for His Name's sake. You *do* shake salt out every chance you get . . . and *do* shine the light . . . and remain balanced, cheerful, winsome, and stable, anticipating His return day by day. Other than that, I don't know what to tell you.

Except, maybe, if you're not absolutely ready to fly, get your ticket *fast*. As long as they are available, they're free. But don't wait. About the time you finally make up your mind, the whole thing could have happened, leaving you looking back instead of up.

What good is a ticket if the event is over?

COME ASIDE

Review 1 Corinthians 15:50-58, soaking up the glory and encouragement.

Commit yourself afresh to the goals in verse 58, and ask the Lord to make clear to you any slackness in your faith or obedience.

CONCLUSION

here once lived a farmer who became jaded in his faith. Skeptical, he chose to isolate himself from others and live out his days without the hassles connected with people involvements. It took a never-to-be-forgotten experience in the dead of winter to jar the man free from his self-imposed cynicism and draw him back to the One from whom he had distanced himself for so many years.

Author Philip Yancey relates the unforgettable story, which he first heard from Paul Harvey:

> One raw winter night the man heard an irregular thumping sound against the kitchen storm door. He went to a window and watched as tiny, shivering sparrows, attracted to the evident warmth inside, beat in vain against the glass.
>
> Touched, the farmer bundled up and trudged through fresh snow to open the barn for the struggling birds. He turned on the lights, tossed some hay in a corner, and sprinkled a trail of saltine crackers to direct them to the barn. But the sparrows, which had scattered in all directions when he emerged from the house, still hid in the darkness, afraid of him.
>
> He tried various tactics: circling behind the birds to drive them toward the barn, tossing cracker crumbs in the air toward them, retreating to his house to see if they'd flutter into the barn on their own. Nothing worked. He, a huge alien creature, had terrified them; the birds could not understand that he actually desired to help.
>
> He withdrew to his house and watched the doomed sparrows through a window. As he stared, a thought hit him like lightning from a clear blue sky: If only I could become a bird—one of them—just for a moment. Then I wouldn't frighten them so. I could show them the way to warmth and safety. At the same moment, another thought dawned on him. He had grasped the whole principle of the Incarnation.
>
> A man's becoming a bird is nothing compared to God's becoming a man. The concept of a sovereign being as big as the universe He created, confining Himself to a human body was—and is—too much for some people to believe.

343

This has been a book for frightened sparrows. Its raw, wintry scenes with their naked branches on barren trees have portrayed life as it is for many who attempt to exist out in the cold. My thoughts and phrases have been my attempts to show you the way to warmth. Perhaps they have been as ineffective as flipping on a light in a barn or sprinkling crackers on fallen snow. Because we don't know and understand each other, you've not realized that I have genuinely desired to help. How could you? Here I sit at my desk like "a huge alien creature," smearing words across pages, distant and removed . . . light years from your world. How could I possibly understand?

Admittedly, all my efforts to lure you within would be in vain were it not for the fact that God did indeed become a man. Because of Him—Jesus—because He died for your sins and because He rose from the grave, my words have substance. My offer is authentic, trustworthy. He promises you not merely a temporary barn for overnight shelter but a permanent home with Him, eternal in the heavens . . . if you will only come.

The leaves of your life will again turn to gold, red, and yellow. They will be ripped from their branches by autumn's winds of adversity. Heavy snow clouds are sure to return as dungeon-like days again become dark and dreary. This fall may be your finale. Death may step into your dungeon before spring emerges. As Paul once needed Timothy, you need Jesus. Don't delay.

Please come. Come before winter.

SCRIPTURE INDEX

SUBJECT INDEX

SUBJECT INDEX